Women and the Gallows
1797–1837

Dedication

Dedicated to all people under sentence of death and
to the memory of those who have suffered.

* * *

My aching heart with pity bled,
When poor Eliza! Cloth'd in white;
At Newgate drop't her lovely head,
And clos'd her eyes in endless night.

From a broadside published
on the execution of Eliza Fenning (1815)

'Women, as they are naturally much more amiable, tender and compassionate than the other sex, become, when they pervert the dictates of nature, more remorseless and cruel, and can conceive and execute the most diabolical of crimes.'

From *Extraordinary Life and Character of Mary Bateman, the Yorkshire Witch* (1811)

Women and the Gallows 1797–1837

Unfortunate Wretches

Naomi Clifford

First published in Great Britain in 2017 by
PEN AND SWORD HISTORY
an imprint of
Pen and Sword Books Ltd
47 Church Street
Barnsley
South Yorkshire S70 2AS

Copyright © Naomi Clifford, 2017

ISBN 978 1 47386 334 7

The right of Naomi Clifford to be identified
as the author of this work has been asserted by her in accordance
with the Copyright, Designs and Patents Act 1988.

A CIP record for this book is available from the British Library
All rights reserved. No part of this book may be reproduced or
transmitted in any form or by any means, electronic or
mechanical including photocopying, recording or
by any information storage and retrieval system, without
permission from the Publisher in writing.

Printed and bound in England
by TJ International Ltd, Padstow, Cornwall

Typeset in Times New Roman by
CHIC GRAPHICS

Pen & Sword Books Ltd incorporates the imprints of Pen & Sword
Archaeology, Atlas, Aviation, Battleground, Discovery,
Family History, History, Maritime, Military, Naval, Politics, Railways,
Select, Social History, Transport, True Crime, Claymore Press,
Frontline Books, Leo Cooper, Praetorian Press, Remember When,
Seaforth Publishing and Wharncliffe.

For a complete list of Pen and Sword titles please contact
Pen and Sword Books Limited
47 Church Street, Barnsley, South Yorkshire, S70 2AS, England
E-mail: enquiries@pen-and-sword.co.uk
Website: www.pen-and-sword.co.uk

Contents

Preface	vi
List of Illustrations	vii
Introduction	x
Timeline of Capital Punishment	xviii

Part 1 – PERSON   1
1	Eliza Fenning: Attempted Murder	3
2	Ann Heytrey: Murder and Petty Treason	31
3	Esther Hibner: Murder of a Child	44
4	Mary Morgan, Mary Voce, Mary Thorpe: Infanticide	54
5	Mary Bateman: Murder	73
6	Eliza Ross: Murder	84
7	Catherine Frarey and Frances Billing, Sophia Edney: Husband Murders	91

Part 2 – PROPERTY   103
8	Sarah Lloyd, Melinda Mapson, Elizabeth Fricker: Theft	104
9	Ann Hurle and Mary Ann James: Fraud	119
10	Sarah Bailey, Charlotte Newman, Harriet Skelton: Uttering Forged Bank Notes	130
11	Charlotte Long: Arson	144
12	The End of the Bloody Code	150

Part 3 – CHRONOLOGY   153
13	Women Executed 1797-1837	

Acknowledgements	210
Bibliography	211
Notes	220
Index	231

Preface

This book is not intended as a broad history of capital punishment. Rather, it is a collection of stories about women who were hanged in England and Wales between 1797, the year of the Bank Restriction Act which led to the deaths of scores of people, and 1837, shortly after major changes to the penal code were made. Victoria acceded to the throne in 1837, thereby ending the Georgian era.

The book is divided into three parts, starting with selected stories of women who were hanged for crimes against the person and followed by the same for crimes against property. These are broad categories of my own devising and are offered for ease of understanding rather than as definitions in law. The book ends with a chronological list of all the women who are known to have suffered the death penalty in England and Wales in the period covered here, and some details of their fates.

List of Illustrations

'The manner of burning a woman convicted of treason' from Jackson. W. (1795), *The New and Complete Newgate Calendar* (1). London: Alexander Hogg. Courtesy of Wellcome Library, London.

'Dr. Syntax Attends the Execution' by Thomas Rowlandson (1820). Courtesy of Yale Center for British Art, Paul Mellon Collection.

'The Idle Apprentice Executed at Tyburn' after William Hogarth (1768). Courtesy of Yale Center for British Art, Paul Mellon Collection.

The temporary gallows in the Old Bailey, north of Newgate. Courtesy of Wellcome Library, London.

'A public execution at Newgate in February 1807, when many people in the crowd were killed' reproduced in *The Graphic* (5 March 1910). Author's collection.

'Newgate Chapel' by Thomas Rowlandson, from Rowlandson, T., Pugin, A. A. (1809). *The Microcosm of London*. London: R. Ackerman. Author's collection.

The condemned cell at Newgate. Unknown provenance. Author's collection.

'Elizabeth Fry' from a painting by C. K. Leslie. Courtesy of *The National Library of Medicine*, Digital Collections, Bethesda, Maryland, USA.

'Eliza Fenning' after George Cruikshank, from Hackwood, F. W. (1912), *William Hone: His Life and Times*. London: T. F. Unwin. Courtesy of University of California Libraries.

'William Hone' from Hackwood, F. W. (1912), *William Hone: His Life and Times*. London: T. F. Unwin. Courtesy of University of California Libraries.

Playbill for Pavilion Theatre, Whitechapel Road, London (1854). Courtesy of the JISC East London Theatre Archive project.

WOMEN AND THE GALLOWS 1797–1837

'George Hardinge' from Nichols, J. (1818). *Illustrations of the Literary History of the Eighteenth Century* (3). London: Nichols. Courtesy of University of Toronto Library.

Mary Morgan's gravestones at Presteigne, courtesy of Bill Shakespeare (flickr.com/photos/35721191@N08/).

'The Coroner's Jury viewing the murdered body of Margaret Hawse' from John Fairburn's chapbook of 1829. Courtesy of the Bishopsgate Institute, London.

'The Horrid Cruelties Inflicted by Elizabeth Brownrigg upon her Apprentices' from *God's revenge against murder! Or, the tragical histories and horrid cruelties of Elizabeth Brownrigg, midwife, to Mary Mitchell, Mary Jones, & Mary Clifford, her three apprentices* (c.1767). London: R. Macdonald, T. Broom, J. Llewellen, and J. Herbert. Courtesy of Francis A. Countway Library of Medicine.

Execution of Esther Hibner for the murder of a parish apprentice girl, 1828 © Look and Learn / Peter Jackson Collection.

'William Hey' by E. Scriven after Allen. Courtesy of Wellcome Library, London.

The skeleton of Elizabeth Brownrigg, displayed in a niche at the Royal College of Surgeons. Courtesy of Wellcome Library, London.

Sketch of Elizabeth Ross, from Sketches of the heads of murderers by William Clift, MS0007/1/6/1/3, The Archives at the Royal College of Surgeons England.

'Eliza Ross – murderess' from *The history of the London Burkers; containing a faithful and authentic account of the horrid acts of the noted Resurrectionists, Bishop, Williams, May etc.* ...(1832). London: T. Kelly. Courtesy of Wellcome Library, London.

'The Rotunda in the Bank of England' by Edward Pugh, from *Modern London; being the history and present state of the British Metropolis* (1804). London: Richard Phillips. Courtesy of Wikimedia Commons.

Ann Hurle and Methuselah Spalding, from Jackson, W. (1818). *The New and Complete Newgate Calendar* (Volume 8). © The British Library Board.

LIST OF ILLUSTRATIONS

Banknotes © The Governor and Company of the Bank of England.

'Bank Restriction Note' by George Cruikshank and William Hone, from Hackwood, F. W. (1912), *William Hone: His Life and Times*. London: T. F. Unwin. Courtesy of University of California Libraries.

'Panorama of the Times' (c.1821). Courtesy of British Cartoon Prints Collection (Library of Congress).

'Robert Peel' from Guy Carleton, L. (1899). *The World's Orators*. New York: G. P. Putnam's Sons. Courtesy of University of Connecticut Libraries.

'Millbank Penitentiary' by J. Tingle after T. H. Shepherd (1829). London: Jones & Co. Courtesy of Wellcome Library, London.

Introduction

Between 1797 and 1837, 131 women were executed in England and Wales. Apart from a handful of causes célèbres, psychopathic sadists and notorious husband poisoners, most of them have disappeared from history. Who were they? What kind of lives did they lead? And why were these individuals chosen to die while others who had committed felony crimes were punished with imprisonment or transportation?

Most, but not all, came from a background of poverty, members of the masses sometimes referred to as the labouring poor or, lower still on the social ladder, the criminal classes. Some were caught after giving in to temptation and appropriating other people's property; others were simply trapped in abusive marriages and saw a dose of arsenic as their only path to escape; a large proportion had recently given birth and were facing destitution. A few of the women had what we might now call personality disorders. Others were mentally ill.

What had they done to deserve death? While ninety-one of them were charged with murder or attempted murder, a third of these were infanticides, some of which were carried out under severe mental pressure. Twenty-three women were hanged for deception (forging documents, counterfeiting currency or passing off bank notes), ten for stealing, five for arson and two for sheep killing or rustling. A handful were convicted of rare crimes (for women anyway) such as highway robbery. A few were, in all likelihood, innocent of the crime laid at their door.

By the middle of the eighteenth century there were 160 capital crimes. In 1815 there were 288. Collectively these crimes were known as the 'Bloody Code' – a phrase first coined in the early decades of the nineteenth century by the supporters of reform. Many of the crimes now strike us as absurd, and nearly all of them were connected to the Georgian establishment's abiding obsession with the protection

INTRODUCTION

of property. Of course, the law was made by and for the ruling class who were, almost without exception, landowners, whose priorities were never clearer than in the legislation they passed. You could be hanged for stealing goods worth five shillings (25p), stealing from a shipwreck, pilfering from a naval dockyard or impersonating a Chelsea Pensioner. The Waltham Black Act of 1723, designed to combat game poaching, made hanging offences of going on a hunt in disguise, poaching deer, rabbit or fish and damaging orchards, gardens or cattle.

Huge numbers of people were sentenced to death, and although most were reprieved from the gallows, it was not unknown to execute large numbers of felons together in gruesome displays of state power. On 2 February 1785, twenty men were hanged at Newgate, none of them for murder. Their crimes were stealing, burglary, highway robbery and forgery. As we enter our timeframe these occasions became less common, although to hang ten at a time was not unusual.

Far fewer women than men were charged with felonies and therefore far fewer were condemned to death. There was also a clear gender difference in the offences with which they were charged. Men were frequently charged with murder and manslaughter but women could not easily lay their hands on lethal weapons and were less likely to be involved in brawls and sudden fights involving firearms, swords and daggers which would be charged as manslaughter. Women only rarely committed crimes such as highway robbery and animal rustling, or indeed the crimes covered in the Waltham Black Act. They could not be charged with rape.

Did misogyny contribute to guilty verdicts against women? Undoubtedly, in some cases. Violent women were unusual and attracted severe disapproval from society; they were disparaged as 'masculine' in behaviour. Their appearance was scrutinized for signs of criminality, in the belief that the evil within showed without. In cases where women had illicit sexual intercourse, judges berated them more for sexual incontinence than for the crime for which they had been convicted. Husband killing was considered particularly heinous and attracted special punishment.

WOMEN AND THE GALLOWS 1797–1837

However much judges were biased against felons, male or female, until the Judgement of Death Act in 1823, they had no powers of discretion in sentencing them after they were found guilty. The penalty for felony crimes was always death. What we would think of as mitigating factors, such as an abusive marriage or destitution, could not alter this. The most a judge could do in instances of murder, for example, was waive the postmortem dissection. However, at the end of an assize or session he could recommend individuals for reprieve by the king (friends of the convict could also petition for mercy). The lucky ones might have their sentences commuted to transportation to Australia or to imprisonment; a very few were let off entirely. There were some crimes, principally treason, murder and forgery, that were rarely commuted, although, as we shall see, on occasion forgery charges could be plea bargained before the trial.

Were women less likely than men to be reprieved? Generally, no. There is evidence to show that, once condemned, women avoided the gallows more successfully than men. Between 1797 and 1837 an average of just over seven per cent of women were executed after a guilty verdict; the figure for men was nine per cent. This protection can be attributed to chivalric paternalism, anxiety about the destruction of bodies designed by God for procreation, and fastidiousness about the public exposure of female corpses. Some years the rate of female execution was on a par with male, for instance at the height of the explosion in bank note forgery, when the Bank of England pursued an aggressive policy of prosecution. In 1817 and 1818, of the 144 women who were condemned (for all crimes) twelve were executed, while of 2,422 men 200 were executed. There were also years when women were executed at higher rates than men. This was true in six of the nine years from 1829 to 1837 and can be explained by the crimes for which they were convicted. Apart from two cases of arson, the women were guilty of murder whereas the men faced a variety of offences, some of which attracted lower rates of execution.

There was certainly gender discrimination in the form of capital punishment given out. This was a matter of law rather than the whim

INTRODUCTION

of the judge. There was a special premortem punishment for women guilty of petty treason, a charge applied to the murderers of employers or husbands (and of ecclesiastical superiors, although no woman was charged with that). A man could not be guilty of petty treason against his wife because in the natural order of life she was his subordinate. A woman guilty of petty treason was punished by being dragged to the place of execution on a sledge or hurdle and then burnt at the stake. The burning of women ended in 1793 but dragging remained until 1828, when the crime was removed from the statute book. Murderers were usually also subjected to postmortem public dissection which, given feelings about the indecency of exposing naked female body parts (even when dead), could be regarded as a special punishment for women.

The journeys of the 131 hanged women all ended in one place: the gallows. Outside London, the condemned were executed within two days of the trial, except if one of those days was a Sunday, in which case she would be hanged on Monday. Those convicted in London could wait anything from two weeks to four months to be executed, their fate decided at the so-called 'Hanging Cabinet' meeting when the king and Privy Council reviewed the recommendations made by the Recorder of London.

A condemned prisoner's diet would be reduced to bread and water. She would be comforted by the prison chaplain or allowed Roman Catholic or Dissenting ministers. She would attend the condemned sermon in the prison chapel. There would be a final meeting with family members in the condemned cell. When the appointed hour arrived, officials and clergy accompanied her to the 'press room' – so called because it had once been used to squash prisoners to death – where she was pinioned at the elbow, a precaution to prevent last-minute resistance while allowing her to put her hands together to pray. From here, in a slow and solemn procession, she would walk or be taken by cart to the gallows for her final – and public – humiliation. In rare cases, a woman might make the journey to the gallows carrying a suckling child, as Elizabeth Warriner, condemned for the murder of her stepson, did in 1817 at Lincoln. The hangman removed her child while her cries of 'Oh my child! My child!' were heard 'at a great distance'. As a penny broadside published after her death put it, they were 'shocking to the multitude!'

Sometimes vast numbers would watch a hanging. The triple hanging at Newgate of Elizabeth Godfrey, John Holloway and Owen Haggerty in 1807 attracted a crowd so dense that a surge caused over thirty people to be crushed to death. The 1835 execution in Bristol of Mary Ann Burdock for poisoning Clara Ann Smith was said to have attracted 50,000.

Why would they come to such a sad, macabre event? The reasons were various and complex. To some it was a day away from home or work, an opportunity to buy pies and beer, to let off steam and to enjoy a bout of heightened emotion. Execution day was an entertainment, a break from the drudgery of routine, with a frisson of bloody drama and perhaps a feeling that 'there but for the grace of God go I.' For pickpockets and thieves it was a chance to take advantage of the inattention of the crowd to their valuables. For parents and schoolteachers, it was an opportunity to teach a simple lesson of action and consequence.

In London's Old Bailey, the lane outside Newgate, the best vantage points were available at a premium. Just before the drop, a shout of 'Hats off!' went up, not out of respect for the wretches on the platform but so that people at the back could get a good view. The less genteel among the crowd might shout out their disapproval of the felon with boos and crude epithets. Females were by no means immune to this. Women who had killed children, such as Esther Hibner, whose cruelty led to the death of her apprentice, and Elizabeth Smith, who starved her young stepdaughter, were especially reviled.

Not all hangings were raucous affairs. Some invoked feelings of sympathy for the hanged and revulsion at their fate. Occasionally very large crowds might witness a hanging, even for murder, in near silence. Kezia Westcombe and her lover Richard Quaintance were hanged in Exeter in 1829 in front of a subdued crowd. Sometimes, observers voiced their objections to what they saw as injustice. In 1820 when

INTRODUCTION

43-year-old Sarah Price, found guilty of uttering a forged one pound note, climbed the Newgate scaffold, the crowd shouted, 'No Bank!' and later 'Murder, murder!' and 'Down with the Bank!' Five years earlier, the mob reacted to the hanging of Eliza Fenning by rioting outside the house of her accuser.

Anecdotally, hangings could result in erotic arousal. On a rainy day in August 1856 (two years before the end of public hanging), 16-year-old Thomas Hardy positioned himself close to the Dorchester gallows in order to watch Martha Brown hang for the murder of her husband. After she dropped, he was entranced by the sight of her features showing through the wet hood over her face and by the rustle of the thin black gown that had been wrapped tightly around her (ironically, to preserve her modesty). The memory of that day never left him: thirty-five years later he used Martha's fate, and her allure, as inspiration for his novel *Tess of the D'Urbervilles* and frequently referred to Martha's death in his old age.

For the establishment, the moving tableau of an execution was an opportunity to influence the poor into turning away from transgression and to impress on them the dangers of departing from the straight and narrow. Crime inevitably led to justice, shame and suffering – to an 'ignominious end'. For this reason, they sought to suppress anything that might provoke sympathy, whether it be a declaration of innocence delivered from the scaffold or an attempt to play the crowd with 'gallows humour'. Confession and remorse were crucial. For everyone involved in the legal process, from the legal clerks, through the coroners, magistrates, lawyers, judges, prison chaplains, up to the king himself, the prisoner's contrition ended niggling doubts, if they existed. It also confirmed that the executed felon would be going to a place that was better for her (or him) and for society as a whole. It affirmed the rightness of the punishment.

Before 1783, London executions were carried out at Tyburn in the west of London. The three-mile journey with the convict on the back of a cart, accompanied by a coffin, was a notoriously rowdy, often drunken, affair, which some of the condemned managed to 'own' with displays of bravado and levity. Consequently, a new regime was required to bring hangings back to the control of the authorities. Now hangings took place in the lane known as Old Bailey, just outside Newgate. They were shorter, more controlled and more brutal affairs designed to instill fear.

A 'machine' on wheels was used at Newgate, a black box surmounted by two supports and a beam, which could be stored when not in use and brought out for execution days by a team of horses. It replaced the old 'horse and cart' method during which the condemned stood with the noose around his or her neck, the rope slung over a tree or gallows, and was strangled when the cart was moved away. In the old method, there was no drop and the hanged died slowly. Friends and family were known to leap forward and pull on their legs to hasten death. This new method, named the 'New Drop', required prisoners to stand on the elevated platform, which gave way when a lever or pin acting on a drawbar underneath was pulled. A double beam, capable of hanging twenty people at once, was used until the 1820s when it was replaced by a single beam accommodating six. The drop was not long (around 45cm or 18ins) and formulae for the optimum distance for different bodyweights had not yet been developed (although it was known that too long a drop might cause a decapitation). However, the spectators would not see the worst of the grisly effects of strangulation. The victims wore hoods and black drapes or hoardings might be positioned around the platform shielding the lower half of the body from view. Its use gradually spread across the country. In 1822 *The Derby Mercury* reported that one of the advantages of the city's new gallows was 'the facility with which it can be put up, the consequent diminution of expense on every execution, and the decreased annoyance to the neighbourhood'. It could be erected and dismantled in ten minutes.

What was it like, to be brought from a prison cell to the gallows? That is an unanswerable question but Sarah Jones's death on Wednesday, 11 April 1827 in Monmouth illustrates something of the typical terror, pomp and pathos of the event. She emerged from the gates of Monmouth Gaol accompanied by under sheriffs, javelin men and clergymen and was walked towards the scaffold that had been

INTRODUCTION

erected just outside its walls. A large crowd had gathered, most of them women. Sarah climbed the ladder to the platform with difficulty as her arms were pinioned at the elbow, but her step was firm. Unlike some in her situation, she did not need to be physically supported on her 'final journey'. After prayers were said, she stood on the trap door and announced that she was ready. She asked the hangman to put the white hood over her head and to make sure the knot was in the right place. She was especially concerned that he tie her skirts around her ankles as she did not want spectators to see her underwear. At the prearranged signal – the release of the handkerchief in her hand – the hangman pulled the lever, the platform opened and Sarah Jones was 'launched into eternity'.

It is interesting that a report published in *The Morning Post* presented Sarah not as a monster but as an 'unhappy woman' and an 'unfortunate victim'; the paper noted that 'her fate excited much commiseration.' This was probably because the murder of her illegitimate baby after she was abandoned by her lover, who married another woman, was seen in some ways as understandable. It was certainly not a general threat to society in the way that the poisoning of a husband might be. Sarah was praised for her acceptance of the punishment and her sincere contrition.

While *The Morning Post*'s description of Sarah's death and of her brave 'suffering' verges on the romantic, the reality was ghastly. Her writhings would have lasted for three or four minutes, maybe longer, during which her face became engorged and her eyes protruded. The purpose of the hood was not to protect her from the gaze of the crowd but to hide from them her shocking and hideous deformity. As she twisted, she expelled the contents of her bladder and bowels – the bread and water diet given to the condemned after sentencing was an attempt to mitigate this – and spontaneously bled as her womb ruptured.

The final moments of these 131 women, and their more numerous male counterparts, surely earn them the epithet 'unfortunate wretches'. Whatever their crimes, the facts of their deaths and the manner of their dispatch – in haste, in pain, in public – should be remembered.

Timeline

1797	Bank Restriction Act, allowing the issuing of low denomination notes.
1799	Number of capital offences reaches 220.
1803	Lord Ellenborough's Offences Against the Person Act: the murders of illegitimate newborn children to be subject to the same rules of evidence as other murder cases.
1808	Private stealing from the person no longer a capital crime.
1811	End of death penalty for stealing from bleaching grounds.
1812	End of capital sentences for soldiers and sailors found vagrant without their passes.
1817	End of public whipping of women.
1820	December: Sarah Price, the last woman executed for forgery offences, hanged at Newgate.
1821	Bank Restriction Act rescinded.
1822	Robert Peel becomes Home Secretary.
1823	Judgement of Death Act: death penalty discretionary for all capital crimes except treason and murder. End of capital punishment for stealing in shops and stealing goods on a navigable river.
1827	Consolidation of capital laws relating to theft, including raising from forty shillings (£2) to £5 the value of stolen goods that determined whether an offence was capital.
1828	Abolition of petty treason as an offence distinct from murder.
1829	Robert Peel's Metropolitan Police Act establishes a professional civilian police force in London. Thomas Maynard is the last person hanged for forgery.
1830	One hundred and twenty forgery statutes consolidated into one Act.

TIMELINE

1832 Anatomy Act: the end of dissection of bodies after execution. Punishment of Death Act reduces number of capital offences to about sixty. Shoplifting, stealing horses, cattle and sheep, and forgery (except the forgery of wills and of powers of attorney for the transfer of stock) were removed from the capital list.

1834-5 Death penalty abolished for remaining forgery crimes, coining, sacrilege, letter stealing and returning from transportation.

1836 End of immediate execution: Prisoners' Counsel Act allows defendants in felony cases the right to a barrister who could directly address the jury.

1837 Death penalty abolished for arson, burglary and theft from a dwelling house. Abolition of the Recorder's Report: Old Bailey judges allowed to mitigate the sentence of death on non-murderers.

Part 1

Crimes Against the Person

In the nineteenth century, females accounted for about twenty per cent of summary convictions, mainly for drunkenness and common assault. Because disorderly behaviour was seen as essentially unfeminine, women were perhaps more likely to be arrested for these offences than men. Women were indicted in forty per cent of murder cases, but a large proportion of those were for infant murder; if these are disregarded, the figure reduces to twenty-five per cent.

Criminal women used less violence, less often, and they less frequently used weapons such as swords and guns to attack victims. Although they took part in brawls with neighbours and family members, they rarely came to blows with strangers. Their killings were less 'accidental' and less often the result of a sudden escalation of tension. For this reason, they were less frequently than men charged with manslaughter, a misdemeanour usually punished by imprisonment or fine, and sometimes not at all, and proportionally they less often had a murder charge downgraded to manslaughter. Cases such as that of Susannah Mottershall and Elizabeth Lamb, who robbed farmer Samuel Glew of £40 (a huge amount), murdered him with an axe and threw his body in a ditch, were highly unusual. With Maria Phipoe and Mary Cain they are among the few women who offered deadly violence to people who were not family members, and even here Phipoe's victim was known to her and Cain's had tried to intervene in her quarrel with her husband. Most of the murder victims were husbands or children or occasionally a parent.

Insanity was a valid defence. The accused would then be acquitted of murder and consigned to a mental asylum. As we shall see, there were specific requirements for insanity to be accepted, including previous behaviour. In infanticide cases, a woman might be diagnosed with 'milk fever' but she would have had to display clear and prolonged symptoms of psychosis before the killing.

CHAPTER 1

Eliza Fenning
London, 26 July 1815

*

Attempted Murder

In 1806 Henry Wyatt, a 15-year-old apprentice watch wheel finisher, appeared at the Old Bailey accused of trying to poison his employer and his family by lacing their coffee with arsenic. The prosecution failed and Henry was acquitted: no motive had been established and Henry drank the coffee himself, falling ill afterwards and, although a witness claimed Henry knew where the arsenic was kept, no one saw him administer it. Henry's defence lawyer was Peter Alley.

Nine years later Alley defended Eliza Fenning, a young cook accused of trying to kill her employer and his family by sprinkling dumplings with arsenic. The case had remarkable similarities to Henry Wyatt's: Eliza herself had been poisoned, she was said to have known where the arsenic was stored, and no one saw her use it on the dumplings.

In July 1815 Eliza, dressed in white and vehemently protesting her innocence, went to her death in the street outside Newgate. Why, given the weakness of the case against her, was she not acquitted?

On 30 January 1815 Eliza Fenning arrived in the Turner household at 68 Chancery Lane, London to begin work as a cook-maid. She had been hired by the elder Mrs Turner, Margaret, but she would be working for Margaret's daughter-in-law, Charlotte, who was married to Robert. Margaret Turner's husband Orlibar owned a law stationery business, which operated out of the Chancery Lane address, but they had since moved to Vauxhall, on the other side of the Thames, while

Robert and Charlotte, who were expecting their first child, lived at Chancery Lane. The household included a maid, Sarah Peer, and Roger Gadsden and Thomas King, teenage law stationery apprentices.

At 21 Eliza was young, although not much younger than Charlotte herself, but had an excellent character and good experience: she had been in service from the age of 14 and had already had eight jobs. She was also bright and amusing and could read and write. Her first two weeks went well, when the senior Mr and Mrs Turner stayed at Chancery Lane to help her settle in, but then they returned to Vauxhall, leaving Eliza to be managed by Charlotte.

For Eliza, this position was an opportunity to prove her skills in a solidly middle-class household, but it quickly became apparent that it was not without its problems. Charlotte had been married only eight months and was still finding her feet as a mistress. Eliza noticed that she had a habit of closely supervising her, questioning what she was doing and finding fault, and she much preferred working for Margaret. There were other tensions too. Sarah Peer was cool towards her but seemed to be close with Charlotte. Before long, the two servants fell out when Eliza used one of Sarah's shifts as a duster but, never one to brood, Eliza assumed they had managed to smooth things over. She focused on managing the kitchen efficiently and saving her employers money.

Feelings between the inhabitants of 68 Chancery Lane came to a head one night in early March. On her journey up to bed Eliza's candle went out, so she knocked at the apprentices' bedroom door to beg a light. Eliza later described what happened: '[They] began taking liberties I did not approve of.' It is likely that it was Roger Gadsden who was trying to flirt with Eliza as Thomas King suffered from excruciating shyness. Eliza continued:

> *I told them if they dared to insult me, I would call Mrs Turner, which I did, but she not coming at the instant* [sic] *I went to my own room and, when nearly undressed, Mrs Turner came into the room and asked me what was the matter, I informed her of what had passed, and she said she did not approve of such behaviour.*

ELIZA FENNING

Rather than discipline the apprentices, however, Charlotte criticized Eliza and the next morning told her that if she could not 'behave better' she would have to leave. Eliza came back quickly with a threat of her own:

> *If she did not approve of my conduct when my mistress [Margaret Turner] returned I was willing to leave, at which she was so enraged that she sent for her husband [Robert], and he desired me to leave the house, but the same evening my mistress returned, she asked me kindly how I did, and I told her I was going to leave, and stated the facts to her. She then called her daughter [in-law], and told her I should not leave her house; everything was then settled, and I thought to be comfortable as before. I went on with my business as usual for some time.*

The following day, still a little bruised by the injustice of her accusation, Eliza told Sarah Peer that she no longer liked Charlotte.

This minor conflict, which later formed the motive for Eliza's alleged murderous plot, illustrates perfectly Eliza's personality: confident, assertive and unwilling to subordinate herself, even to her social superiors. She knew she was in the right and that she had been unjustly accused. Perhaps her attitude should not surprise us: she was brought up in a poor family, but it was stable and loving, and she was well educated for a young woman of her rank. Until she was 12, Eliza attended Gate Street Charity School in Lincoln Inn's Fields, which was run by Dissenters, and entered service two years later. She showed independence in her religious choices: the Fenning family was Church of England but Eliza attended the Methodist chapel. She grew into a good-looking young woman and naturally attracted admirers, but by 1815 she had committed to a young man called Edward (whose surname is unknown) and hoped to marry him. Generally, she was seen as good company: personable, friendly and witty. Only one of her former employers, Mr Hardy, a grocer in Portugal Street, had had cause for complaint and after her death said she was 'a hoity-toity, wild, giddy, unsettled sort of girl, curious and inquisitive, and minding what did not concern her'. He strongly disapproved of her habit of reading books.

Her father, William Fenning, had been a bandsman with the 15th Regiment of Foot, having joined the army as a young man to escape a life as an agricultural labourer in his native Suffolk. He was sent to Ireland, where he met and in 1790 married Mary Swayne, a Protestant, the daughter of a slater and granddaughter of a London silversmith. A subsequent posting took the couple to Dominica in the West Indies, where they started a family. Mary gave birth to ten children, of whom Eliza, born on the island in 1793, was the cherished only survivor.

William left the army in 1802 and the family returned to England, eventually settling in London where he worked as a labourer for his brother, a potato dealer, and Mary found employment as an upholsterer.

William perhaps would have had sympathy with the many unemployed soldiers now trickling back into England, especially into the metropolis, who were blamed for a spike in crime. According to the government's figures, the number of committals had leapt twenty-five per cent between 1814 to 1815 after a dip of ten per cent the previous year. The middle classes trembled and muttered. Newspapers reported that 'the increase of crimes in the capital is truly alarming'.

During the years of war, France's blockade had prevented foreign grain imports reaching Britain. Landowners and merchants had grown richer by selling wheat and other grains at a premium and they were not about to allow this to change. The poor, already pushed to breaking point, feared they would starve. In February, Member of Parliament Frederick John Robinson announced that he would bring in a new Corn Law to forbid the import of cheap foreign wheat until the price at home reached eighty shillings (£4) a bushel. Protest was immediate, from farmers, who felt protection did not go far enough, and from the poor, who complained that it kept the price of bread artificially high. When Robinson presented the bill on 7 March, a mob gathered in the streets around the Palace of Westminster with the aim of stopping MPs from entering the House. The protesters were unsuccessful, and afterwards moved on to the homes of supporters of the bill, breaking windows and pulling down iron railings and turning them into spears. Outside Robinson's residence in Old Burlington Street, Edward Vyse, a 19-year-old midshipman who was minding his own business and had no part in the disturbances, was shot and killed by someone firing from inside the house. Disgusted by this callous disregard for life, William Hone, a radical defender of press freedom and persistent thorn in the side of the government, took up the search for the truth of what had happened. He denounced as unconstitutional the coroner's attempts to manipulate the jury's verdict of wilful murder. Later he would turn his attention to Eliza's fate.

Despite the row over her 'indelicate' behaviour, Eliza was content at Chancery Lane. In the kitchen, she made soups, pies and suet puddings, prepared vegetables and joints for boiling or roasting for Mr and Mrs Robert Turner, and for Mr and Mrs Orlibar Turner when they visited, and also cooked separate, cheaper, meals for herself, Sarah and the apprentices. She went to market, shopped and argued about prices and quality with the butcher and the baker. She learned to work around Charlotte's watchfulness.

On Saturday, 18 March, when the brewer's man delivered some beer for Robert, Eliza asked him for some yeast. On Monday he dropped it off with Sarah, who put it in a basin ready for Eliza to use later that day to make dumplings for the two of them. Eliza described what happened the following day, Tuesday, 21 March:

> *I went up for orders for dinner, as usual; my mistress asked me what there was in the house, I told her that the brewer had brought some yeast, at which she seemed pleased...she told me she should have some beef steaks and potatoes for dinner, and dumplings; and to have a meat pie for the kitchen [for the servants and apprentices].*

Charlotte said later that she made it clear that she preferred Eliza to use baker's dough for the dumplings and that Eliza campaigned hard to be allowed to make them from scratch, much to Charlotte's annoyance. Eliza said there was no such insistence.

> *I went down and made the pie and had everything in readiness for making the dumplings; when she came into the kitchen she told me to take the pie to the oven and then to make the dumplings, but to be sure not to leave the kitchen after the dumplings were made.*

At some point that morning, Eliza was interrupted by the delivery of coal to the house. Eliza made the dough with flour, water, salt and yeast, covered it with a cloth and set it to rise by the fire.

> *Then I was sent to the butcher's, for the steaks, when I came back I went into the back-kitchen to clean a dozen and a half knives and forks; during the time I was doing them I heard some person in the front kitchen, and thought it was my mistress, but, on my coming out of the back-kitchen, I saw Thomas King, one of the apprentices coming out: I asked him what he had been doing in the kitchen, he made no answer, and went upstairs.*

At about half past two, Charlotte came down and sent Sarah for some milk as she wanted to make sauce for the dumplings herself. When the dumplings were boiled, Sarah took them upstairs. Then she went out for the afternoon, to see her sister in Hackney. Eliza took the steaks and potatoes up to the table and brought the remainder of the dumplings down to the kitchen. She sat and ate almost all of one and 'when Gadsden, one of the apprentices, came down and asked me to give him some dumpling; I told him they were cold and heavy, but I gave him a piece and some of the sauce; he then left the kitchen.'

Ten minutes later, Robert Turner arrived in the kitchen and said he was ill, and so were his wife and father. They were sick to the stomach, retching, vomiting and in pain. Now Eliza herself began to feel ill ('violent sick, and an uncommon pain in my head'). At half past three Robert told her he was sure she had put poison in the dumplings but that he thought it was accidental. Gadsden had only eaten a small amount of the dumpling and felt nauseous but had not thrown up, so he was dispatched to fetch Henry Ogilvy, an apothecary and friend of the family, who lived a few doors away. That evening at about eight, Thomas King, who had eaten none of the dumplings, was sent for John Marshall, a surgeon living in Piccadilly who had known the family for a decade.

Marshall later described finding Eliza on the stairs 'apparently in great agony, and complaining of a burning pain in the stomach, with violent reaching [retching], head-ach [sic], and great thirst'. He told her to drink milk and water and then proceeded upstairs to attend to the Turners. He treated Robert with laudanum and hot flannels to alleviate his agonizing stomach pain; he had serious fears that Charlotte would lose her baby (she was at the time seven months pregnant). Orlibar also had symptoms but they were not as severe as his son and daughter-in-law's. Throughout the night, at various points, Marshall prescribed sugar water mixed with milk and a dose of castor oil, Epsom salts, mint, saline solution and soda water, remedies he later claimed led to the family's salvation.

Despite her illness, Eliza managed to get a note to her father's place of work near Red Lion Court asking him to come to the house. William Fenning turned up at the Turners between nine and ten, the message having earlier slipped his mind, but he was refused at the door. Sarah Peer, on her employer's orders, lied and said that Eliza was out on an errand.

There were, of course, many instances of genuinely warm, familial attachments between servants and their employers but, more commonly, servants and employers lived together out of necessity rather than affection. The relationship was a fine balance. The middle classes were obsessed with the servant issue and constantly discussed their shortcomings, their betrayals, their laziness, their suspicious behaviour and their sullenness. They were acutely aware that even if servants did not actively harm them or have the effrontery to make their feelings clear, they could frighten and frustrate them with silent contempt and subtle acts of rebellion. What were they really thinking while going through the motions of subservience and obedience? Were they hiding a seething hatred of their masters and mistresses?

A few high-profile cases gave employers real cause for concern and seemed to justify their wariness. No one was immune. The Duke of Cumberland's valet had attacked him one night in 1810, and then slit his own throat in his room (that was the story anyway). Three years before the Turners were poisoned, the Count and Countess d'Antraigues, French *emigrés* living in Barnes, a suburb on the western outskirts of London, were murdered by their mentally unhinged Italian servant. And everyone knew cases in which servants, out of 'envy', thieved and filched from their employers or invited their friends into the house to rob them after dark.

But if there was anything the middle class feared and loathed more than a disloyal servant, it was one with access to arsenic.

In between his ministrations to the victims, John Marshall inspected the dishes in the kitchen. When he saw white particles thickly distributed on the surface of the remaining dumplings in the pan he decided to do some scientific experiments. First he cut a small piece of the dumpling into thin slices, put one on a halfpenny placed on the blade of a knife and held it over the flame of a candle. He detected a garlic smell. When the coin cooled, it was covered in 'silvery whiteness, occasioned by the fumes of the arsenic'. Marshall then examined the knives the family had used at dinner and found them 'deeply tarnished'. It was enough to convince him that the family had been poisoned with arsenic and that Eliza was responsible.

In Marshall's eyes, everything she did was suspect. Despite being in great pain, she refused to take any of the potions he and Ogilvy offered, declaring that 'she had much rather die than live, as life was of no consequence to her.' Eventually she gave in and took them, or appeared to (until Margaret informed Marshall the next day that she had not taken any of them). He interpreted this behaviour as extreme remorse at her unsuccessful attempt to kill the Turners, which had caused her to become suicidal.

By the next day, Wednesday, all the victims had improved but were still bedridden, including Eliza, who was arguably the worst affected. Marshall continued his scientific proofs by looking at the earthen dish in which the dumplings had been kneaded. After scraping it out, he diluted the dough, poured in water, stirred briskly and allowed it to settle. He claimed to have retrieved 'full half a teaspoonful of white arsenic'. He heated some of it between copper plates and detected, again, the odour of garlic and observed silvery whiteness on the plates.

On Thursday, Orlibar checked the drawer in the office where he had kept scrap paper used as spills to light the fire as well as two packets wrapped up and marked 'Arsenic – Deadly Poison'. One packet was missing and no one could remember seeing it since shortly after Eliza's dispute with Charlotte over the 'indelicate' behaviour.

Orlibar paid a visit to Eliza in her room. Arsenic was missing, he told her, and he was sure it was her doing. Then Mrs Turner senior arrived to question Eliza.

'What did you put in the dumplings to make us so ill?'

'It was not in the dumplings, but in the milk Sarah Peer brought in.'

Later Eliza wrote, 'When they say I was sure it was in the milk, I really thought so, for milk is a thing that does not agree on my stomach which made me not know which it could be.' Perhaps Eliza's aversion to milk was why she refused Marshall's remedies.

'Did anyone else have a hand in making the dumplings?' asked Mrs Turner.

'No,' said Eliza. She alone had made them.

The Turners moved swiftly against Eliza. Orlibar and John Marshall went to Hatton Garden Police Office to report the incident and ask for assistance. Marshall wrote later that while they were gone Eliza had tried to dress herself in order to flee but had fainted. Officers arrived to search the house and Marshall alleged later that a book containing information on methods of abortion was found in Eliza's box. After this they put her in a coach and took her to the magistrate at Hatton Garden, where the clerk was a personal friend of the Turners. From here she was transferred to Clerkenwell Prison and a police officer was ordered to watch her.

On 25 March the 'diabolical attempt' was reported inaccurately in *The Globe*, which had already decided that Eliza was guilty: 'A female servant in the family of Mr T—r, in the west end of the town, mixed a large quantity of arsenic in a pie.' *The Globe* took up Eliza's story again on 27 March, remarking that people found it scarcely believable that a servant should poison a whole family and that they 'could not credit it, thinking there could not be such a monster in human nature'. Yet it was the scale of the attack, involving four victims apart from Eliza herself, rather than the attack itself – a servant taking revenge on her employer – that was seen as incredible.

Tantalizingly, *The Globe* report included this sentence: 'We understand that there is some slight suspicion attached to another person.' In reality, however, once Eliza was accused, and certainly once she was arrested, there was no attempt on the part of her prosecutors to look further into the case. Nothing more appears to have been said on this subject, in print at least, and as the records of the case were lost or destroyed it is impossible now to identify this other suspect. Despite this, as we shall see, it is possible to speculate that there were at least two other potential perpetrators.

In Clerkenwell Prison, Eliza was still ill, and while she slowly shook off the effects of the poison, her mental state deteriorated. She was deeply mortified at her predicament. On Tuesday, 29 March she wrote to her 'fiancé' Edward, assuring him that she was innocent and that she expected to be cleared at the next hearing. 'I now lay ill at the infirmary sick ward. My mother attends me three times a day, and brings me everything I can wish for; but, Edward, I never shall be right or happy again, to think I ever was in prison.' On Thursday she appeared before the magistrate again. This time the main witnesses – the Turners, Sarah Peer and Roger Gadsden – gave evidence and she was committed for trial.

ELIZA FENNING

Edward did not write back, so Eliza wrote to him again on Friday. It was a comfort that she had his portrait and previous letters with her, she said, but she had heard from her father that he had gone to a ball with another woman: 'I am glad to hear that you can spend your time so agreeably with another.' She did not tell him that she was due to be transferred to Newgate prior to her trial, which would take place within days. The magistrate had offered her a choice: bail with two sureties of £50 each, a year on remand in Clerkenwell Prison, or a swift trial at the current Old Bailey sessions. The Fennings had no funds for bail and Eliza wanted a speedy resolution to this terrible misunderstanding, so she opted for the Old Bailey.

Forbidding, fortress-like, grim, disease-ridden, grey, noisy, stinking: any number of awful adjectives can be used to describe Newgate in 1815. Writing just over twenty years later, Charles Dickens called it 'the gloomy depository of the guilt and misery of London'. The building was laid out around a central courtyard, and was divided into two sections: a 'common area' for poor prisoners and a 'state area' for those able to afford more comfortable accommodation. Each was further subdivided to accommodate felons and debtors. When the Quaker prison reformer Elizabeth Fry first visited the common area in 1813 she was almost lost for words: 'The filth, the closeness of the room, the ferocious manners, and the abandoned wickedness which everything bespoke are quite indescribable.' Women were living amid urine and excrement, babies were struggling to breathe the fetid air full of tobacco smoke. It was misery incarnate.

Eliza's parents managed to borrow enough money to pay for her to share a cell with another woman away from the hell of the wards, and from here she wrote to Edward again. Her trial would be in a week, she said. She had nothing to fear. She was innocent and would soon be cleared. Her parents had borrowed a further five pounds to pay an attorney to draw up a brief for a barrister to plead for her. She continued to hope for Edward's loyalty, but word had reached her that he was friendly with another young woman: 'I am not apt to be jealous, therefore think no more about it; but I firmly believe you are still true and faithful to me; and as you to me, I have fixed my mind and heart entirely on you.' She asked for a line or two 'if you can spare the time'.

Eliza was tried at the Old Bailey on Tuesday, 11 April 1815. She was prosecuted by her employer, Orlibar Turner, who was represented in court by John Gurney, and he employed as his solicitor the magistrate's clerk who had been at Eliza's examination. Most accused felons were unrepresented, so Eliza was fortunate to have as her defence lawyer Peter Alley, a blunt Irishman known for his experience and all-round competence, but he had been given the brief at the last moment, with no time to prepare. Possibly also he recognized the similarities between Eliza's case and that of another of his clients, the 15-year-old watchmaker's apprentice Henry Wyatt, and thought it would be an easy win.

Defence barristers in felony cases were severely restricted in what they could do or say in court. They could not cross-examine, except on facts, nor could they directly address the jury, but the best of them could undermine the prosecution by putting an apposite question on a matter of fact to a witness. William Garrow made cross-examination, however limited, into an art form. Alley, although praised for his skills, was no Garrow and, it seems, he had more important places to be than in the Old Bailey.

If Eliza had appeared before almost any other judge, she may have been acquitted or her sentence commuted to transportation or prison. It was her misfortune that John Silvester, the 70-year-old Recorder of London, heard her case. He had followed a standard route to the bar: Oxford, admission to the Middle Temple, years as a barrister for prosecution and defence, and had accumulated along the way a reputation for slimy lechery and a fondness for the black cap. The conduct of the trial still has the power to shock, but the half-truths asserted by the Turners, Roger Gadsden and Sarah Peer and the witnesses' obvious collusion were nothing compared to the bias of the Recorder.

Charlotte Turner told the court that on the night of the candle incident she had seen Eliza enter the apprentices' room 'partly undressed', which immediately established Eliza in the eyes of the jury as indecent and immoral. She said that Eliza had persistently begged to let her make the dumplings (Eliza said she had spoken to her about them only on the morning she made them), that no one else had access to the kitchen during the morning they were made (wrong on two counts: the coal had been delivered that morning, which Charlotte and Sarah Peer adamantly denied, and Eliza had gone out to buy steak when anyone could have been in the kitchen without her knowing). She also said the dumplings Eliza served were black and heavy, something she had not noticed enough to mention at the time, and which Eliza later said was untrue. Roger Gadsden swore that he had several times seen Eliza open the drawer in the office where the arsenic was kept, in order to get spills to light the fire. John Marshall, the surgeon, told the court that there was no arsenic in the flour tub but it was present in the dumpling dough. He described his scientific experiments and presented them as incontrovertible proof.

Five character witnesses spoke well of Eliza. Her defence was simple: 'I am innocent of the whole charge. I am innocent. Indeed I am! I liked my place. I was very comfortable.' She also spoke out in court about Charlotte's accusations concerning her 'indelicate behaviour'. Later she wrote:

> *When I heard Mrs Turner speak falsely of me, being in the boys' bedroom, I contradicted her, knowing it to be false; and when Mr Turner said I never assisted them when they were ill, I was going to speak, but everything seemed in such confusion, that I was not heard to speak, and I not knowing the ways of the trial, I did not know hardly what to say, for everyone's eyes were on me, as if I was the greatest criminal on earth.*

Towards the end of the trial, Eliza pleaded to be allowed to call Thomas King, the shy apprentice, 'for he will not dare to deny the truth. He will say I always asked for paper [to light the fire in the office] when I wanted it.'

'You should have had him here before,' said Silvester.

'My Lord, I desired him to be brought, and wish him to be sent for now.'

'No. It's too late now – I cannot hear you.'

Quite against protocol, Silvester then asked Roger Gadsden whether Eliza ever lit the fire in the office.

'Yes. I and my fellow apprentice have seen her go to that drawer many times.' That he was allowing Gadsden to swear to what another person had seen did not bother Silvester.

During the trial, Eliza's father William had tried to get a note to Silvester to say that Eliza had told him before the poisoning that she liked her place. He had rushed away from court to the Pitt's Head public house opposite the sessions house to write it on a scrap of paper, but was so distressed, his hand shaking so much, that he could not manage it. A friend tried to help, but he could not form the letters either and eventually they appealed to a stranger to write it. They managed to get it presented to Silvester, but he would not accept the note. Instead, he announced 'It is too late' and proceeded to sum up. By this stage Eliza's defence barrister, Peter Alley, had left the court on an unknown errand.

Silvester fixed on Eliza's declaration to Sarah Peer that she no longer liked Charlotte Turner, on her alleged repeated requests to make dumplings rather than accept Charlotte's wisdom that the baker's dough was best, and on her warning to Gadsden not to eat the cold leftover dumplings. He pointed out that Eliza would be able to read 'Arsenic – Deadly Poison' on the packets kept in the drawer in the office and that she had not bothered to assist the Turner family when they were struck down. (He did not consider that she herself being poisoned was a reason.) Notably, he asserted that 'although we have nothing before us but circumstantial evidence, yet it often happens that circumstances are more conclusive than the most positive testimony.'

The jury considered and after a few minutes came back with a verdict of guilty. Eliza collapsed screaming and was carried out of court. When she was brought back, the Recorder donned a black cap and pronounced sentence of death. Later, she noticed that the glass in

ELIZA FENNING

Edward's portrait, which she wore on a chain around her neck, had shattered.

Eliza wrote to Edward that evening:

> *They have, which is the cruellest thing in this world, brought me in guilty, because I had the fire to light in the office where the arsenic was kept, and my master said that I went often into the office for things, and so, on that account, they suppose that I must have taken the arsenic out of the drawer, which is the most horrid thing I ever can think of.*

She knew the shame of her conviction would be too much for him. It was easier to let him go: 'Pray make your mind happy, and get someone else that will never bring any reflection on you. I shall never think of marrying any person excepting yourself; but I must for ever give up any thought of such, as it may hurt your character; but I still love and respect you.'

Two days later, in the dismal condemned cell at Newgate, Eliza was receiving visitors and fighting despair. After weeks of silence, Edward had at last written to her. She begged him to visit: 'Pray come, dear Edward, on Sunday, about three o'clock, and you can stop till five, for you can come any Sunday at these hours.' Someone, perhaps Peter Alley, had given her hopes of a reprieve and the prospect of a six-month prison sentence: 'Perhaps it is all for the best, for I am confident that it will make me both steady and penitent the rest of my life; though it's hard to suffer innocent,' she told him.

Edward did not visit. Ten days later, Eliza had sunk into despondency: 'I have no hopes whatever,' she wrote. 'I am making my peace with God and hope to be in a better world, as I shall leave this world innocent of a crime that's alleged against me.' Edward again promised to visit and Eliza sent him detailed instructions on how to gain admittance to Newgate. If he visited at all, it was only once or twice. By 4 May she knew they were finished: 'I should never like a man that would forget me,' she wrote. He responded, excusing his failure: he had no time, he had enemies, he had sent a friend, he had visited her father. Angry, she wrote him a final letter: 'I feel very much hurt at your being out, and could not spare one single hour with me.' She said she was glad he was friendly with her parents 'for you can spend many hours with them, when I am no more.' She expected never to see him again, as 'the Report' was due any day and 'now I wait with impatience to know my fate.' The Report was the list of those convicted felons the Privy Council had chosen for execution.

After Eliza's conviction there was a wave of interest in her case. The Recorder's conduct of the trial and the unfairness of the verdict attracted the attention, not only of the newspapers, but also of influential men. A letter to *The Morning Chronicle* pointed out that one member of the jury was deaf. There were doubts about the evidence given by Marshall. In response, rumours, misinformation and libels about Eliza swilled around the media, probably pushed by the Turners and Silvester. *The Observer* and *The Morning Post*, both in the pay of the government, published outright lies about her: she had been expelled from school for lying and 'lewdness', they said; her parents were – oh, the horrors – Irish Catholics.

In Newgate, Eliza's state of mind veered between despair and hope. She even wrote to Orlibar Turner asking him to sign a petition on her behalf. This would have saved her: the victim's plea for mercy for the guilty, especially for an otherwise respectable young woman with no previous criminal history and convicted on circumstantial evidence alone, would have been irrefutable.

Amongst those who were perturbed by the trial was an anonymous chemical expert who examined Marshall's claims that arsenic made dumplings fail to rise and turned knives black. He asked his own cook to make dumplings and was able to contaminate them with arsenic without her noticing. They rose perfectly and did not change the colour of the knives. He sent his findings to Lord Sidmouth, the Home Secretary, and, bringing his experimental dumplings with him, called on Orlibar Turner, hoping to persuade him to sign the petition to save Eliza. While they were in conversation, Robert Turner and then Marshall arrived at the house, the latter making a speedy departure.

Just as the Turners were won over, declaring that they were ready to sign any petition for Eliza, John Silvester, the Recorder, was announced.

The chemist now attempted to show Silvester his experiments and to explain that arsenic did not tarnish knives. Silvester would not have it and declared that he was leaving. Robert showed him out, and on his return said to his father: 'The Recorder says you must not sign any petition – if you do, it will throw suspicion on the rest of the family!' It was the death blow to Eliza's hopes. Orlibar must have realized that the person most at risk of accusation was his own son.

Among the men of standing who appealed for mercy for Eliza was the former barrister Basil Montagu, co-founder of The Society for the Diffusion of Knowledge Upon the Punishment of Death and the Improvement of Prison Discipline (he wanted to end hanging for all offences except wilful and premeditated murder). He had uncovered evidence that Robert Turner had had a previous episode of mental instability, appearing 'wild' and 'deranged', threatening to kill his wife and himself. He sent his evidence to Silvester, who dismissed it as 'wholly useless'.

In France, on 15 June, Napoleon was defeated at the Battle of Waterloo. A week later he had abdicated. Britain was saved. Eliza, meanwhile, waited in her cell, now shared with Mary Ann Clarke, who had been sentenced to death for stealing in a dwelling house. Eliza was visited by her parents and by a Chelsea doctor, Thomas Wansborough, who provided spiritual comfort.

On 19 July Eliza, along with Mary Ann and the other condemned felons, was called to a ward in Newgate where they were made to kneel on the floor. The Report of the Recorder had arrived and the Reverend Horace Cotton, the zealous Ordinary (chaplain) of Newgate, who was another personal friend of the Turners, went from one prisoner to the next telling each their fate. Eliza's cellmate, Mary Ann, was reprieved. Not so, Eliza. 'Dearest and affectionate parents,' Eliza wrote later, 'Let me entreat your immediate attendance to your lost child. Innocent, dear parents, I am, to God and man. Pray come soon. The Report is come for me to be executed on Wednesday next.' Two days later, in a longer letter to them, she expressed her resignation and told them they would meet in heaven, where her dead brothers and sisters already were. She wished them fortitude to bear the coming trauma.

In the meantime, she had to contend with the attentions of the Reverend Cotton. 'I am surely convinced that Mr Cotton is a great enemy to me,' she wrote on 29 June. His only purpose now was to get Eliza to admit her guilt and go to the gallows visibly and vocally penitent. The government did not want a repeat of the scenes at Newgate in 1807 with convicted murderers John Holloway and Owen Haggerty. Ascending the platform in front of 40,000 people Holloway shouted, 'Innocent! Innocent, Gentlemen! No verdict! Innocent, by God!' The crowd surged and thirty-one people were killed and over forty injured.

Eliza would not go without the last word, however, and would not let her persecutors off the hook. 'I am murdered!' she wrote on 22 July, knowing that her letter would be published by her supporters after her death. She wanted to see the Turners in person, to ensure they were fully aware of the harm they had done her. On the Saturday before her death, she sent a friend, possibly Thomas Wansborough, to ask them to come to Newgate. Robert and Charlotte Turner arrived expecting contrition and a confession but were quickly disabused. Eliza was angry. In her words:

> *When Mr Turner came to me, he said, in the presence of Mr Wansbury [Wansborough], he would do everything in his power to spare my life, but when going I refused my hand. I firmly and most solemnly declare to God and man, I am innocent of the crime, and how was it possible I could do it to a person who swore my life away, but may the Almighty God forgive them; believe me they are almost the death of my dear parents.*

She was avoiding Cotton, not only because she knew him to be allied with the Turners but also because he constantly urged her to confess.

ELIZA FENNING

On the Sunday before her death, she was required to attend the condemned sermon in Newgate Chapel, where she was to take the sacrament. This was always a popular event with the public, and the imminent hanging of a woman made it even more so. A huge number of people queued outside the gates for tickets and the chapel filled quickly. Twenty-one condemned prisoners entered and sat in the black pew set aside for them. Then those who were 'left for execution', Eliza and two others, William Oldfield, a child rapist, and Abraham Adams, convicted of sodomy, were brought in and the service began. When Cotton asked for prayers for 'those about to suffer' she could contain herself no longer and broke down into loud sobs. Cotton had chosen a text from Romans 6: 'What fruit had ye then in those things whereof ye are now ashamed? For the end of those things is death.' He alluded directly to her, saying that she had been persuaded by Satan that revenge was sweet and that he would protect her, but had then abandoned her. Eliza collapsed again. When the sacrament was given, the prisoners went to the altar, with Eliza protesting her innocence.

On Monday evening, the Quaker banker Corbyn Lloyd called on Silvester, asking for a short respite for further investigation as there was no proof that it was Eliza, and no one else, who had poisoned the dumplings. Lloyd related the Recorder's response:

Myself and my friend had done a great deal of harm by interesting ourselves about the girl, as it caused her to persist in denying her guilt; and the reason we felt so much interest about her was only because she was a pretty woman; and he felt so perfectly satisfied of her guilt (there never being a clearer case) that he knew no possible reason for delaying the execution.

On Tuesday, the day before her death, Eliza sent for Thomas King, the nervous apprentice. John Marshall, the surgeon who had attended the family when they fell ill, gave a second-hand account of this meeting, in which he described Eliza accusing Thomas King of the poisoning and King taking an oath in front of Cotton to deny it. Later, Eliza took final leave of her parents. Her father asked her to be strong in the ordeal she was facing; her mother was distraught. In the condemned cell she wrote to Mary Ann Clarke asking her not to grieve as her time 'is but short in this troublesome world, and I will soon be in eternal rest'. She exhorted her to read the scriptures and bequeathed her a lock of her hair. After her parents left, all that was left for Eliza to do was to pray, read her Bible and sleep.

Eliza rose at four to wash, paying particular attention to her feet. She gave a lock of hair to each of the women who attended her. Her chosen minister could not be with her, and she was assigned Mr Vazie, whom she did not know. At six Mr Wansborough arrived to read the Bible with her. She was feeling faint and said she felt it was all like a dream. It was now time to dress. She had chosen to die in a white muslin embroidered gown, tied with a white sash, and a matching cap. She put on lilac boots, laced in front. Shortly after eight, an officer tapped at the door and announced that it was time. Before she left on her final journey, she shouted 'Goodbye! Goodbye to all of you!' to the other prisoners.

She walked to the press room, the space where felons were prepared for the gallows. William Oldfield and Abraham Adams were already there. 'Oh, Oldfield, you are going to heaven,' she said before John Langley, the hangman, started to pinion her arms, binding them by the elbows to her body. As Langley worked, Wansborough, probably by prior arrangement, asked if she was guilty. She announced loudly that 'Before God, I die innocent!' Eventually, a slow-moving and solemn cavalcade set off from the press room: the sheriffs and their officers, Wansborough, Vazie, and others, the Reverend Cotton enunciating the words of the burial service ('I am the resurrection and the life, saith the Lord'). When they came to Debtors' Door, which opened on to the street, Wansborough took his leave. Before doing so, he again asked her about the crime, and once more she said, 'I die innocent.'

It was time. She went through the door. In front of her, filling every corner of the concourse, were thousands of spectators waiting in silence to witness the first execution of a woman at Newgate for three years. Eliza's execution attracted unusually high numbers, and it is likely that many of them believed that she was innocent or at least that she should have been reprieved. Eliza was nubile, attractive and religious. She had the bearing of a martyr. And quite apart from doubts about Eliza's guilt and sympathy for her fate, there would always be prurient interest in the mutilation of the body of a woman.

William Hone, the Radical, was there. 'I got into an immense crowd that carried me along with them against my will,' he wrote years later.

> *At length I found myself under the gallows where Eliza Fenning was to be hanged. I had the greatest horror of witnessing an execution, and of this particular execution, a young girl of whose guilt I had grave doubts. But I could not help myself; I was closely wedged in; she was brought out. I saw nothing but I heard all.*

Thirty-five-year-old Hone was born in Bath although his family soon moved to London. His father, also called William, was a strictly religious Dissenter. At the age of 12, already politicized and with a keen interest in the Revolution in France, the younger Hone published a broadside on the freedoms of the English constitution. Soon afterwards, he began work as a legal copyist, his father's trade, but gradually he lost his religious faith and became involved with the controversial and radical London Corresponding Society (LCS), whose aims, which included universal male suffrage, alarmed the government. After an interlude in Chatham, where he was sent by his father in the hope that he would shake off his increasing radicalism, he returned to London and began several ventures, including opening a bookshop, a partnership with John Bone of the LCS. The business failed, like many of his other commercial projects, and Hone once more diversified, this time into the development of humanely-run asylums for the insane. He also became a campaigning journalist, holding the establishment to account in the murder of Edward Vyse, the midshipman shot outside the house of John Robinson MP, and, notably, the case of Eliza Fenning.

WOMEN AND THE GALLOWS 1797–1837

Eliza was directed to ascend the scaffold first. She walked with purpose and took her place at the furthest end, standing erect and still. Cotton stood in front of her while Langley the hangman was behind her. He had come improperly prepared. He took a white cotton hood from his pocket and tried to put it over her head. It was too small. He tried two others. They were also too small. Then he tied a muslin handkerchief over her face, but thought this would be inadequate and decided to put his own, dirty, pocket handkerchief across her eyes. Eliza's distress was palpable. 'Pray do not put it on,' she pleaded. 'Pray do not.' Cotton insisted: 'My dear, it must be on – he must put it on.' It was tied on. Langley then put the cord around her neck, threw the other end over the beam and secured it.

William Oldfield now climbed the scaffold. He had requested to die next to Eliza and spoke to encourage her. Cotton moved off to attend to him and then to Abraham Adams, while Vazie stayed with Eliza, speaking into her ear. He was attempting to get her, even at this last opportunity, to confess. Cotton also tried again but her last words, before the platform fell, were 'I am innocent!' She was said not to have 'struggled' for long.

The three bodies were left to hang for the usual hour before being cut down. The corpses of murderers were sent to the College of Surgeons for dissection but none of the three had killed. Eliza's parents were at liberty to reclaim her body, provided they paid fourteen shillings and sixpence for 'executioner's fees, stripping the body and the use of a shell [shroud]'. They were now utterly destitute, having sold everything they owned – watch, furniture, best clothes and, in William Fenning's words, 'the last shift from off the back of her mother'. They had even pawned their blankets and bedding and now slept on the floor, but they managed to borrow the fee and Eliza's body was laid out in the back room of their lodgings.

Small crowds of wellwishers assembled outside their home. Some were admitted and allowed to view the body but then police officers arrived. 'The magistrates have ordered that nobody shall go into the house,' they told Hone when he came to pay his respects. He told the officers that the order was illegal and ignored it. Eliza's funeral followed four days later. A hundred mourners accompanied her bier, which was carried to the church of St George the Martyr near Brunswick Square by six young women dressed in white. A substantial crowd gathered at the burial ground but again police officers tried to obstruct the way, insisting they could not go in. Although the ceremony passed off without major incident, the anger of the populace was intense and growing and a thousand people gathered outside the Turners' house in Chancery Lane. There were threats to burn it down. Some were arrested for behaving in a 'riotous and tumultuous manner' and the police were on guard there for days.

Eliza's case continued to trouble and intrigue lawyers and scientists for months, even years, afterwards. Scores of pamphlets were published. Hone started gathering evidence that would make it clear who was responsible for the unnecessary destruction of a young woman in the prime of life. His *Important Results of an Elaborate Investigation into the Mysterious Case of Elizabeth Fenning*, published by John Watkins, was a detailed investigation into the collusion between the Turners and Silvester. Charlotte Turner and her servant Sarah Peer had lied about the delivery of coal to the household that morning, their movements in and out of the kitchen and the appearance of the dumplings. Essential witnesses (Thomas King, the apprentice, and Henry Ogilvy, the apothecary who had first treated those poisoned) had deliberately not been called; John Marshall, a friend of the family, was allowed to give scientific (but totally wrong) evidence; Silvester's extraordinary intervention in the incident with Orlibar Turner and the petition, and Basil Montagu's probing into Robert Turner's mental ill-health were set out in detail.

As Radicals and reformers wrote pamphlets and editorials about Eliza, Silvester, Marshall and the Turner family sought to limit the damage to their reputations. *The Observer* continued to publish more lies about the Fennings. They were said to have put Eliza's body on display in return for money. A turnkey at Newgate was persuaded to sign an affidavit to say that Eliza's father had urged her to protest her innocence, not because he believed her to be blameless but in order to preserve his own reputation. William Fenning was forced to issue an affidavit of his own in answer. Marshall's pamphlet *Five Cases of Recovery from the Effects of Arsenic* described his treatment of the Turners and Eliza on the night of the poisoning and his experiments on the remains of the dumplings, and asserted that Eliza was clearly guilty. Her supporters greeted it with incredulity. Marshall claimed that Eliza had wanted to kill herself after she poisoned the family in order to evade justice and had eaten her dumpling only after Roger Gadsden had eaten his (untrue – she had eaten it before) and that her lack of 'humanity' was shown in her refusal to help the pregnant Mrs Turner after she fell ill. *The Independent Whig* took him to task, calling his assertions 'spurious' and 'flimsy' and it pointed to another disturbing case of a female servant accused of poisoning her employer's family who was currently in prison awaiting trial.

On the evening of 13 September, seven weeks after Eliza Fenning was hanged, Anne Newman, accompanied by her maid Mary Eades, took her two young daughters for a walk near her home in Kennington, south London. Anne was married to Richard Newman, a butcher, who had lately had a problem with rats, which plagued his house and the adjacent slaughterhouse. His rat-catcher put arsenic behind the skirting boards, under the flagstones and in the suet drawer. When Mary Eades came across a twist of paper on a window sill, one of Mr Newman's slaughtermen told her it was poison and not to touch it.

After their walk, Mrs Newman asked her second servant, 19-year-old Elizabeth Miller, to bring some watery gruel upstairs for the children's supper, which she did. Mary Eades added magnesia and rhubarb to it. Although the toddler, Elizabeth Ann, was quite well, Mary, the baby, had been sickening and the hope was that this would settle her. Both little girls drank the gruel and Mary Eades had some of it too but as she dressed the baby for bed, she felt sick, with a burning sensation in her throat and stomach. Very soon, highly distressed, little Elizabeth Ann ran in to her mother. She climbed into her lap for comfort and started vomiting, as did the baby.

Soon after, Richard Newman, the children's father, came up.

'What have you been doing with the gruel?' he demanded of Elizabeth Miller.

'Nothing,' said Elizabeth and continued to vehemently deny doing anything wrong. Eventually she burst into tears.

The basin of gruel was brought from the kitchen and Mr Newman challenged her to drink it, but by then she had seen that the children and Mary Eades were ill and refused. Mr Newman sent her for the apothecary, Mr Dixon. During their journey back to Kennington Lane, Elizabeth told Dixon that she had made the gruel and thickened it with oatmeal she had found in a jar in the kitchen cupboard. One of the men employed by Mr Newman had bought it about a month before to treat a cold, she said. Dixon ordered the basin of gruel and all the equipment and utensils involved to be locked up for future examination. (He analyzed the contents of the basin in the presence of 'four [natural] philosophical gentlemen', who found that it was 'strongly impregnated with arsenic' – but, like Marshall's, this was worthless science). As both children continued to deteriorate, Elizabeth was sent out to fetch medicine. At nine o'clock the following morning, after fitting several times, Elizabeth Ann died.

Mary Eades went up to the room she shared with Elizabeth. 'Is the child gone?' asked Elizabeth, and when told that she was, said, 'Good God! What shall I do? What shall I do with myself?'

'What would you wish to do with yourself if you are innocent?' said Mary Eades.

If she did not already know the story, Elizabeth would have been told about what had happened to Eliza Fenning.

An inquest was held at the White Hart pub, a few doors away from the Newmans' home, in front of Charles Jemmett, the Surrey coroner. Mrs Newman told the jury that Elizabeth Miller was a bad-tempered girl who was often cross with the children, and that Elizabeth Ann had not liked her. The previous Monday, she said, she had scolded her twice for 'suffering the men in the shop to take improper liberties with her'. These were echoes of the accusation against Eliza. Did a humiliating telling-off provoke a murderous resentment of her mistress?

The case came to trial the following April at Kingston, Surrey and was heard by Charles Abbott (who went on to become a Lord Chief Justice). William Hone was among the observers. Elizabeth was defended by Mr Nolan, whose bill was being paid for by a subscription donated by the public; a solicitor gave his services for free. Isaac Espinasse, representing Mr Newman, described the abuse the butcher had suffered for his prosecution of Elizabeth. He had been 'assailed on all hands' and had been 'foully traduced, and vitally injured in his trade', precisely because of what had happened to Eliza Fenning.

Elizabeth was acquitted. Justice Abbott stated that the child had died as the result of an accident. Elizabeth had simply mistaken arsenic for oatmeal. Had justice been done? It is impossible to know but no one had seen Elizabeth add arsenic to the gruel. Perhaps mindful of the catastrophic verdict against Eliza, the jurymen were cautious.

For Hone, the acquittal of Elizabeth Miller was an opportunity to remind the public of the behaviour of Orlibar Turner and his family towards Eliza Fenning. He published his account of Elizabeth Miller's trial in several forms, including the pamphlet *Four Important Trials at Kingston Assizes, April 5th 1816*, in which he detailed thirteen examples of Mr Turner's deliberate concealment of pertinent facts during the Fenning case. These included his refusal to allow her father to see her when she was suffering the effects of arsenic poisoning; his decision to employ as his solicitor the magistrate's clerk who had taken Eliza's deposition; and his failure to inform the court of a possible suspect within his own family, his son Robert.

At this distance of time, we cannot be sure that arsenic killed Elizabeth Ann Newman just as we cannot be sure it was in the dumplings Eliza made, although it was a strong possibility. As Marshall's experiments showed, the science of detecting poisons was rudimentary; Eliza's prosecution provided a salutary lesson in its limitations. It would be another twenty years before an effective test for arsenic became available.

Eliza Fenning's memory lived on for decades, in stage plays and books. Struck by the similarities between her story and the plot of *La Pie Voleuse*, a melodrama then playing to enthusiastic audiences in

ELIZA FENNING

London, Hone wrote a prose version, *The Narrative of the Magpie, or the Maid of Palaiseau*. Eliza inspired other characters too: Mary Shelley may have used her as a model for Justine Moritz, a servant girl in her gothic novel *Frankenstein*, who is unjustly accused of a murder the monster has committed, is pressurized into confessing and hangs, condemned by a cold-hearted judge. Plays such as *Eliza Fenning, the Persecuted Servant Girl* were being performed well into the 1850s and in 1867 Charles Dickens commissioned seasoned journalist Water Thornbury to write about the case. He concluded that Eliza was an 'entirely guiltless young creature'.

By contrast, the reputations and fortunes of her accusers suffered. In 1825 Orlibar Turner was declared bankrupt. In 1828, John Gordon Smith, the University of London's first professor of medical jurisprudence, noted a claim in the *Morning Journal* that Robert Turner had died in an Ipswich workhouse after confessing that he had put arsenic in the dumplings. Robert was certainly living in Ipswich in 1820 (his wife Charlotte was originally from Suffolk), but we know no more than that.

In 1829 *The Examiner* reported that William Fenning, Eliza's heartbroken father, was still living in London. 'The unfortunate girl was his favourite child,' they said, forgetting that in 1815 she was also his only surviving offspring. A man called William Fenning died in Holborn in 1842. If this is 'our' William Fenning, he would have been 91.

We cannot know what really happened in the kitchen of 68 Chancery Lane that day in March 1815 when the coal man called and Eliza was making dumplings. Perhaps Thomas King, the apprentice so shy he could barely speak, thought it would be fun to observe the effects of a few grains of arsenic on the stomachs of his master's family. Perhaps Robert Turner, in one of his periods of instability, slipped into the kitchen while Eliza went to the butcher's to fetch the steaks and wrought the damage. It doesn't really matter who did it. It is enough to know that Eliza probably did not.

Eliza had the misfortune to be accused at a time when the middle class were on high alert. On the day the dumplings were poisoned,

WOMEN AND THE GALLOWS 1797–1837

Bonaparte was reported to be on his way to Paris and Wellington was making for Belgium to coordinate the Allies' response. The old certainties, of a safe, free and stable Britain looked suddenly in doubt. The middle class were gripped by a loss of confidence, seeing danger everywhere, in the Corn Law rioters ripping out iron railings and turning them into spears, in the Radicals and their clamour for reform and change, and in an impudent servant in Chancery Lane who could read the writing on a packet of poison.

CHAPTER 2

Ann Heytrey
Warwick, 12 April 1820

*

Murder and Petty Treason

A charge of treason was laid when people challenged the fixed order of society. While high treason concerned the betrayal of the sovereign, petty treason concerned the betrayal (usually murder) of a husband, employer or ecclesiastical superior. A servant murdering a master or mistress could be charged with petty treason but not the other way around, and while the murder of a woman by her husband was simply murder, a man killed by his wife was both murder and petty treason.

Petty treason carried a special punishment for women. They were drawn or dragged to their place of execution on a sledge or wattle hurdle tied to the back of a horse – their position near the ground symbolizing their disgrace – and then burnt at the stake. From the middle of the eighteenth century, unofficial acts of mercy saw them being strangled by the executioner before the flames got to them. In 1793 burning was abolished, the result of growing disgust at the gruesome practice. After this date women were merely dragged to the gallows and hanged.

Sunday, 29 August 1819 in the small Warwickshire village of Ashow was glorious: blue skies, baking hot, still and silent. From the kitchen of Dial House, the Dormers' farmhouse, all you could hear were the birds, the gentle rustle of trees and the animated voices of passers-by on their way to the annual village fair, a thanksgiving festival known in that part of the world as a 'wake'.

WOMEN AND THE GALLOWS 1797–1837

Joseph Dormer, his six children, three servants and two business friends who had earlier taken lunch with the family, were out enjoying the musicians, the fun and jollity, leaving Ann Heytrey, the maid, alone at home with her mistress, Sarah Dormer. Together they picked cucumbers in the kitchen garden. Then, following Mrs Dormer's directions, Ann took the cucumbers into the pantry, filled a bowl with water and washed them. Just as she was finishing, Mrs Dormer's young nephew and niece arrived at the back door, pink-faced and breathless from running in the heat. Ann fetched her mistress, who gave them some of the cucumbers and a drink of elder wine and water before they ran off back to the fair.

In the pantry Ann cut onions while Mrs Dormer put on her reading glasses and settled down by the kitchen window with her Bible. Then Ann came into the kitchen and stealthily approached Mrs Dormer. As she looked up, Ann suddenly punched her full in the face. Bleeding and bewildered, Mrs Dormer tried to speak but, understanding now that she was in real danger, made for the stairs. Ann grabbed a knife from the pantry and followed. Mrs Dormer had just managed to reach her chamber when Ann pushed her into a corner. She turned round and Ann landed two good slashes to the jaw. Mrs Dormer fell to the floor and, while Ann hacked at her throat, desperately tried to catch at the knife.

Once Mrs Dormer was quiet, Ann wiped her hands on her apron, took one of her mistress's black caps and placed it under her shoulder and, thinking that this would make it look like Mrs Dormer had killed herself, positioned the knife near her hand. She went downstairs, put her bloodied apron in a wash tub to soak, wiped away some of the spatter on the floor and the walls in the hall, and awaited the return of the Dormer family.

At around ten past seven, she heard the chatter of the children as they approached the door. It opened and she saw the four oldest – the other two and their father would be home soon, they said. Ann broke out into a sweat. Sensing that something was not right, 17-year-old Elizabeth asked her if anyone had called at the house. 'No, nobody,' said Ann, and went out to the wood yard. The children were disconcerted. They had expected their mother to do as she usually did, to call to them from the kitchen or come out and greet them. Elizabeth asked Ann to come back into the house.

'What's this on the floor? It looks like wine,' she said, pointing to a spray of blood. 'What have you been doing?'

'Oh, nothing.'

Elizabeth told her to bring a mop and clean it up, which she did.

The Dormers were prosperous farmers living in comfort. Dial House was a handsome redbrick residence on the Kenilworth road just outside Ashow, five miles north east of Warwick. They kept three male servants and young Ann Heytrey, who had been with them for a little over a year.

Ann had the most difficult job in the house, with the longest hours. She rose before everyone else in order to light the fires in the kitchen range and boil the water, and spent the day cleaning the dressers, shelves and tables, keeping the hall, passages, living rooms and bedrooms clean, making the beds, and preparing plain meals for the family and her fellow servants. In the absence of a scullion, it was also her job to scour and wash the saucepans, pots, kettles and utensils, pick, trim, wash and boil the vegetables; all in all, to fetch, carry, scrub and assist. For all servants, life was a constant battle with dirt in which victory was fleeting: as soon as something was washed it was dirty again. It was endless, wearying and tedious, simultaneously boring and important, for if the basic tasks were not done a household could not function.

Not long after Ann's arrival at Dial House, the Dormers came close to dismissing her. They caught her stealing bank notes. Mrs Dormer pleaded with her husband not to prosecute, because that would have led to the gallows or to transportation, which would break Ann's mother's heart. This woman, the widow of an agricultural labourer, lived fifteen miles away at Charlecote and already had to contend with the delinquent behaviour of Ann's brother Thomas, whom the Dormers suspected was behind the bank note incident.

Despite the work and the humiliation of performing all the lowliest jobs, and of not being entirely trusted by the Dormers, Ann was grateful for her place. It provided safety and warmth, with food and clothes found, and a small wage (probably about eight guineas – £8.40 – a year, much less than a male employee would be paid). For servants, the money was not just for their own personal upkeep but also a supplement to their family's finances, especially if a parent was absent or dead, as in Ann's case, or unable to earn through pregnancy or disability.

Women's lives in the country were hard; if they worked outside the home, it was usually on a family smallholding or in the fields, which was seasonal, insecure and left them at the mercy of the elements. Jobs in domestic service, in households such as the Dormers', were thus to kill for, sometimes literally. In summer 1818 in Litton, near Derby, only eighty miles to the north of Ashow, 16-year-old Hannah Bocking became so resentful of Jane Grant, who had been given the domestic job for which she had been rejected, that she invited her rival on a friendly walk and gave her cake laced with arsenic. Jane died in agony a few days later and Hannah went to the gallows the following spring.

Twenty years before Ann Heytrey took the kitchen knife and pursued Mrs Dormer up the stairs, another maid took deliberate revenge on her employer. In 1799, the Proctors, living in the town of Royston, Hertfordshire, engaged 15-year-old Ann Mead to care for their children, including Charles, then only a few months old. Her duties would have included bathing the children, preparing their meals, taking them for walks and getting them ready for bed. She ensured their beds were clean and dry and that their chambers were well ventilated. She had to make, or at least maintain, the fire. A nursemaid would also have to safeguard them against the dangers of the house, especially in the kitchen, and watch for illness; if her charges succumbed to sickness, she must nurse them, doing all the fetching and carrying: cold compresses, clean linen, chamber pots, and food from the kitchen. Her skills were not just physical. She was obliged to show a mature understanding of her place in the family by offering appropriate guidance to the children while never overstepping her

ANN HEYTREY

mark. At times she would need to discipline the children but as a social inferior she was not allowed to physically chastise them – that was the province of the master or mistress. In some households, servants could be directly disciplined by the children. For those, the injury to their self-esteem must have been devastating.

While the children were toddlers, much of the nursemaid's work was spent dealing with excrement and dirty nappies. She had to scrape faeces off soiled clouts (nappies) and wash them. Washing was backbreaking work, which involved lifting and carrying large pails of water, lighting fires for the copper boiler, and scrubbing with harsh substances such as lye soap, chalk, brick dust, pipe clay, alcohol and stale urine (a natural disinfectant). Clothes would then be put through the mangle, spread on bushes in the fields or hung on racks or lines to dry before, finally, being ironed. It goes without saying that the more numerous the family the more work for the nursemaid.

In June 1800, in a moment of anger, Mrs Proctor called Ann a slut, perhaps not for the first time. She could not have predicted her reaction: Ann went to the local chemist, bought some arsenic and gave a spoonful to baby Charles. It killed him. At first Ann loudly denied everything, but after the coroner's inquest admitted what she had done. She was committed to Hertford Gaol to await her trial.

There is almost nothing in the records about Ann Mead. Newspapers reported scant details of her trial at the Hertford Assizes in front of Lord Justice Kenyon, although there was a tiny expansion on the reason for her fury with Mrs Proctor in the *Bath Chronicle* on August 7, 1800: 'It seemed she had been induced to commit this horrid act, merely in malice to her mistress, who had found fault with her for not keeping the child so clean as she ought to have done.'

Perhaps the endless rounds of washing clouts, cleaning the children and obeying her mistress became too much to bear. She probably did not think through the full consequences of that spoonful of arsenic: death, discovery, grief, accusation, arrest and her own ignominious end. All she had in mind was punishing Mrs Proctor. Five weeks after she took her revenge, on 31 July 1800, Ann went to the gallows at Hertford.

* * *

WOMEN AND THE GALLOWS 1797–1837

In Ashow, while Elizabeth Dormer spoke to Ann Heytrey downstairs, Mary Dormer went upstairs to find her mother. Her screams on finding her bloody corpse were heard in the road by a surgeon, Mr Bodington, who happened to be riding by and was so alarmed by the noise that he took his horse right up to the front door, dismounted and rushed into the house. There he found the children in deep shock, although 18-year-old John Dormer had the presence of mind to be guarding Ann. Bodington soon saw that it was too late to help Mrs Dormer so he closed up the chamber and sent for Thomas Bellerby, the constable from Kenilworth, about two and a half miles away.

Ann was the only suspect. There was blood on her hands and under her nails and she was behaving strangely; she was diffident and quiet – 'sullen' according to those who dealt with her. Before Bodington's arrival John Dormer had dragged her into the wood yard and slapped her, but she merely responded with, 'You have no occasion to pull me, I'll go where you have a mind to take me.' When Bellerby arrived and asked whether she was the 'servant who had killed her mistress' she said, 'They say so, but I am not.' Later, after her brother Thomas was arrested as a suspect, she said to Bellerby, 'What a thing it is to bring my friends into trouble. Neither my brother nor no other man had to do with the murder' and went on to admit she had done it. As Bellerby related later her explanation was merely, 'A thought struck her that she would murder her mistress.'

An inquest jury brought in a verdict of wilful murder against Ann and she was conveyed to Warwick Gaol to await the next assizes. As she had already admitted her guilt, it was now the duty of the prison chaplain to help her prepare for her future, which would be short, and to this end the Reverend Hugh Laugharne 'spared neither time or trouble to bring her to a true sense of her awful situation'. He also tried to discover what had triggered Ann's derangement.

'Had your mistress done or said anything in the course of the day to offend you?'

'She had not given me an angry word.'

Ann burst into tears and said, 'I liked my mistress so much, I would have got up at any hour of the night to serve her.' It was, she said, a sudden inexplicable impulse, with no intention of robbery in it.

In Warwickshire, not long before Ann launched her attack, there had been another extraordinary saga with a highly disturbed and violent female as its protagonist. In April 1818, Rebecca Hodges was indicted for setting fire to hayricks at Ward End near Ashton and appeared before Judge William Garrow at the Warwick Shire Hall. It was a notable case, not because rural arson was especially unusual but because of the long and disturbing history between the accused, Rebecca Hodges, a servant, and Samuel Birch, her former employer.

Sixteen years previously, on a Saturday in 1802, Rebecca left Birch's farmhouse, ostensibly to fetch water, and went missing. On her return on the Monday, she was dismissed for being absent without permission. After this she determined to take revenge. Over the next seven years, disguised in men's clothes, she stalked Birch as he went about his business. Finally, on 27 February 1809, having bought a horse pistol and moulded her own bullets (she pressed the lead with her fingers), and once again dressed as a man, she travelled to Ward End. That evening she secretly followed Birch around his farm, hiding in an outbuilding until the moment was right. At around ten o'clock, she peered through the kitchen window to check that his housekeeper and niece Sarah Bradbury had gone up to bed, lifted the latch of his farmhouse door, crept up behind him as he slept in a chair and shot him twice, with one of the bullets lodging in his head.

Birch did not at first realize he had been wounded, but Sarah Bradbury, alerted by the gunshot, came downstairs and saw immediately that his head was 'all over blood'. Mr Vickers, a surgeon in Birmingham, was fetched. He trepanned Birch's skull and retrieved the bullet. The patient survived but suffered lifelong effects.

Still dressed in male clothes and carrying a loaded pistol, Rebecca was arrested in Birmingham, probably because she was showing some form of erratic behaviour, and taken to the town gaol where William Payn, the gaoler, assumed she had 'broken out of a place of confinement'. He offered to send for her relatives in order to get her properly cared for, but she said it would be no use as she would just be arrested again.

'For what?' asked Payn.

'For shooting a man,' she replied.

In the courtyard she walked obsessively in a figure of eight and hung her head.

Later, once the connection between her confession and the assault on Birch became known, she was brought to the Birmingham Police Office, where she encountered Vickers, the surgeon who had treated Birch. She said, 'He [Samuel Birch] is not dead, I hope?' and when asked whether her former employer had ever ill-treated her, replied, 'No, never.' She claimed that they had once had a romantic relationship and that she liked her master very much.

Rebecca was tried in front of Judge John Bayley. It was clear that she had committed the deed and that it had involved a considerable amount of planning and intention, but the real question was whether she was in her right mind. Francis Woodcock, a Worcestershire magistrate, told the court that when Rebecca lived in his household she had shown symptoms of insanity, talking to herself, dancing alone in barns and fields and picking up sticks in one place and laying them down in another. In his opinion she was 'virtuous and harmless'. Rebecca's sister also gave evidence, describing her walking without shoes or wearing only one of them, going out with few clothes on and on one occasion trying to hang herself. Judge Bayley told the jury that if they had any doubt about her sanity they should acquit her, which they did. She was ordered to be incarcerated in Warwick Gaol as a criminal lunatic and in 1816 was transferred to Bethlehem Hospital (Bedlam) in London, where after fourteen months she was discharged, the doctors there declaring her to be cured.

After her return to Birmingham in early 1818, Rebecca lived a hand-to-mouth existence of casual employment, possibly combined with part-time prostitution. She often got drunk and was locked out of her lodgings. She still harboured resentment of Birch and after writing letters to him, pleading and threatening by turn, she once more travelled to the farm at Ward End intent on revenge. This time she set fire to his haystacks, another capital offence. She was soon arrested and the circumstantial evidence against her was overwhelming. Witnesses spoke of a woman wearing a long dark cloak and bonnet; similar clothes were found in her lodgings. A linen draper, called as an expert witness, confirmed that a section of purple-spotted scarf found near the fire matched one in her possession. A tinderbox that had been discarded on the road contained small pieces of cotton resembling one of her gowns.

During the trial she loudly and repeatedly berated and insulted the witnesses, each time Judge Garrow patiently exhorting her to wait until it was her turn to question them. But despite his instruction to the jury to 'keep in mind...the dreadful punishment that must necessarily follow a conviction' they did not even pretend to discuss her possible innocence and within three minutes delivered a guilty verdict. While Rebecca screamed for mercy ('My Lord, have mercy upon me!...Oh spare my life! Only spare my life, my Lord! I'm innocent! I'm innocent!') the judge sentenced her to death and warned her not to entertain hopes of a reprieve.

Rebecca did not go to the gallows. The authorities made the pragmatic decision to ship her out of England; from then on she would be someone else's problem. In 1819 she was transported for life on board the *Lord Wellington* in the company of two other Warwickshire women, Elizabeth and Rebecca Bamford, who had themselves narrowly avoided execution. They had been deeply involved in the family business of forgery and their 60-year-old mother, Ann Bamford, had been hanged the previous year.

It helped that Rebecca Hodges's actions had not led to a loss of life, of course, but leniency and understanding could be shown even when someone died. Possibly the Georgian era's most famous killing resulting from a temporary loss of control was that of Elizabeth Lamb by her daughter Mary, a young seamstress caring for her infirm parents, her aunt and her brother John and with responsibility for training a young apprentice. One afternoon in September 1796 at the family's lodgings in Little Queen Street near High Holborn in London Mary, mentally fragile at the best of times, had an altercation with the apprentice, who was helping Elizabeth with some needlework. In front of her father, Mary picked up a knife and stabbed her mother through the heart. Afterwards she was confined to Fisher House, a private mental home in Islington, and a few days later a coroner decided that Mary was suffering from lunacy. Her brother Charles managed to persuade the authorities to release her into his care rather than face a trial and possible incarceration in a gaol as a lunatic or in a public hospital such as Bethlehem. Charles looked after Mary for the rest of his life, never marrying. While her father was still alive, she lived in lodgings but after his death she moved in with her brother, and remained there except during recurrences of her mental illness, when she returned to the asylum. She led a useful life with Charles. They collaborated on writing *Tales from Shakespeare* and were at the heart of a literary circle that included William Wordsworth and Samuel Taylor Coleridge.

Why were Rebecca Hodges, Mary Lamb and Ann Heytrey treated so differently? The British legal system at the time recognized four kinds of insanity: perpetual infirmity of mind from birth; the result of sickness, grief or other accident; intermittent mental illness (classed as insanity when it manifested); and a state arising from 'vicious acts' such as drunkenness. Ann Heytrey did not fit any of the categories. Her explosion of anger was so sudden and over so quickly that it seemed not to be insanity but wickedness. Unlike with Mary Lamb, there had been no previous recognizable signs of mental instability. She had simply had an impulse and acted on it. Rebecca Hodges's attack on Birch may have been planned well in advance (it took place seven years after her dismissal from Ward End farm) but her erratic behaviour before this – dancing and singing in fields and obsessively moving objects from one place to another – showed that she was not in her right mind and was enough to convince the judge of her incapacity.

One of the few available contemporary explanations for Ann's actions was her appearance. Just as mental illness was thought to arise from infirmity of the body and produced acts such as Rebecca's, a

ANN HEYTREY

criminal's physical appearance both indicated and determined her innate wickedness. These assessments were, of course, always made in hindsight. Ann was described in newspaper reports as generally unremarkable (she was a 'middle-sized woman, and stoutly made' with high cheek-bones and dark brown hair and eyes) but her 'physiognomy [was] well calculated to conceal a criminal heart.' In other words, she had a face that cleverly hid her true nature.

Ann's rank in life, near the very bottom, also played a part in how she was viewed. Uneducated, poor, and connected by blood to an acknowledged malefactor (her brother Thomas), she would have been regarded as dangerous and expendable. In addition, she had not killed a family member, as Mary Lamb had done, but her social superior, a worthy and respected member of society.

Powerless Ann, who was beholden to the kindness of the Dormers, who was denied permission to go to the wake with the other young people, who was the lowest in the household and who could be bossed by everyone, even the Dormer children, made something happen. Ann had loved her mistress. After all, this kindly woman had gone out of her way to help and protect her. Was it possible that it was not Mrs Dormer but her children who were the true object of Ann's fury? Did Ann anticipate and relish their dismay when they expected to be greeted by their mother at the door after a day at the fair and instead discovered her mutilated body?

On Monday, 10 April 1820, Ann Heytrey appeared at the Warwick Assizes before Judge Best, charged with murder and petty treason, which she denied.

Four of Sarah Dormer's children, John, Elizabeth, Harriet and Mary, related the events of the day of the Ashow wake. The constable Thomas Bellerby told the court of Ann's confession. In the dock, Ann appeared calm, her only sign of agitation was that she held a bottle of smelling salts to her nose and occasionally adjusted her shawl 'in a manner indicative of internal restlessness, seemingly remote from fear'. Her face betrayed 'undaunted firmness'. She was unrepresented and did not call character witnesses or even make a defence statement. After the evidence and summing up, the jury consulted for a few minutes and found her guilty of both murder and petty treason. Judge Best passed the death sentence on her and ordered that she be dragged through the streets to the place of execution and her body be handed over to surgeons for dissection. There was no question of a reprieve. While awaiting execution, Ann wrote to Elizabeth Dormer:

I am heartily sorry for the sorrowful misfortune as has happened which I hope the Lord in his mercies will forgive me and I was very sorry to see you look so bad [in court]. I did not know you when you was called up. I hope you will forgive me for what I have done as my life will pay for the unfortunate deed, Oh may the Almighty be your comfort and may he pardon me my sins.

And to Mr Dormer:

Dear Master, Before I leave this world, permit me to declare again, that I had no ill will towards my beloved Mistress. I am sorry for the distress I have brought upon you and your children. I hope you will forgive me, and the Lord also. I wish you health and happiness, trust I shall meet my Mistress in glory.

On Wednesday, Ann was tied to the hurdle outside Warwick Gaol and drawn to the scaffold where she was asked what evil thoughts led her to kill Mrs Dormer. She replied, 'I cannot tell – I had none, but I thought I should murder my mistress.' As the rope was placed around her neck, she told the Reverend Laugharne that she hoped God would forgive her, and soon afterwards the signal was given and she fell. Two local surgeons, one of whom was Mr Bodington, who had burst into Dial House when he heard Mary Dormer's screams, were given her body. Mr Bodington took the body to his house and dissected it there.

Both before and after Ann's execution, theories about the motive for the crime swirled around. *The Warwick and Warwickshire General Advertiser* published an intriguing paragraph admonishing local rumour-mongers for spreading the lie that Ann had killed an illegitimate child while in prison ('Let justice be done even to a murderer'). From this small clue we can speculate that she was pregnant when she committed the crime and suffered a miscarriage while in prison. Some, even to this day, doubt Ann's guilt, pointing instead to her brother Thomas and his associates.

Two further deaths form postscripts to Ann's story. Less than a year after her execution Ann's mother 'died of a broken heart.' Not only had she endured the shame of her daughter's crime, trial and execution, but now her son Thomas was in prison awaiting his own trial. Days later, on 14 April 1821, he and three others were hanged in Warwick for robbing and murdering William Hiron on his way back from voting in the county election.

The crime of petty treason was abolished in 1828 as part of the consolidation of criminal laws in the Offences Against the Person Act. One of the objections to it was that defendants charged with petty treason were allowed to challenge up to thirty-five jurors (normally it was twenty) and two witnesses had to swear to the crime. In truth, however, it was recognized that there were no real grounds for distinction between the murders of husbands and wives, clergymen and their superiors and servants and employers, and that the premortem punishment of drawing on a hurdle was unnecessary and archaic, a relic of a medieval, bygone age.

CHAPTER 3

Esther Hibner
London, 13 April 1829

*

Murder

The system of parish apprenticeship will be familiar to readers of Charles Dickens's *Oliver Twist* (published 1837–9), which he subtitled *A Parish Boy's Progress*. After having been in the care of a baby farm, and returning to the workhouse where he is half-starved, Oliver is indentured to an undertaker, whose wife mistreats him.

While the system of parish apprenticeship was, on the face of it, a way of educating poor children in a trade, in practice it was often little better than slave labour. Not all parish apprentices were abused, but all were vulnerable. Few checks were made on the conditions they were sent into or on their welfare after they left the workhouse. The potential for disaster should have been obvious, especially in the industries that were known for the ill treatment of juvenile indentured labour.

The tambour industry in which Esther Hibner and her daughter made their living consisted of small workshops, typically run or owned by women and employing large numbers of parish apprentices. For these young girls, the day involved standing, often for many hours at a time, at a round frame (the tambour) over which Brussels or Nottingham net was stretched and using a pointed, hooked needle to embellish and embroider it. It was a skilled, labour-intensive process. With margins tight and competition fierce, conditions for workers in the industry were tough and the wellbeing of the young parish apprentices was therefore very much at risk.

ESTHER HIBNER

According to an eyewitness writing in 1830, crowds at Newgate executions regularly sympathized with the criminal, murderers included. They would shout 'God bless you!' and 'Shame! Shame!' even when murderers were being hanged. The only recent exception had been Esther Hibner, condemned to death for the murder of a parish apprentice in her care. While the executioner wagged his finger at her and pointed down to hell, the spectators, most of them female, abused and derided her, clapping and shouting 'Bravo!' as he put the rope around her neck and again on the fatal drop.

There was one man in London who was troubled by this 61-year-old grandmother's fate and the day before she died, he tried, in vain, to save her. On 12 April 1829, Mr W. Brown, a lawyer whose first name is unknown, wrote to Robert Peel, the Home Secretary, pleading for a stay of execution. He felt strongly that there had been a miscarriage of justice. Esther Hibner was guilty of something, for sure, but it was not murder; her conviction was the result of violent and unfair prejudice, a 'flagrant violation of evidence, law and justice'. In Brown's opinion, Frances Colpitts, the 10-year-old victim, had died from mortification of the feet and abscesses on her lungs, caused by the immersion of her head in a pail of water, for which Esther's daughter had admitted responsibility, compounded by want of food and exercise – not because Esther Hibner had murdered her.

It had been over sixty years since a woman had been executed in London for a crime of this notoriety against a child. In 1767, Elizabeth Brownrigg, who was a midwife to St Dunstan's Workhouse in Fetter Lane and herself the mother of sixteen children, murdered 14-year-old Mary Clifford, an apprentice from the Foundling Hospital. For trying to abscond, Mary was kept naked, forced to sleep in a coal hole, beaten while chained to a roof beam in the kitchen and fed on bread and water. Concerned neighbours alerted the Foundling Hospital and Elizabeth Brownrigg and one of her sons went on the run but were soon caught. By the time they stood trial at the Old Bailey, Mary had died of infected wounds. Mrs Brownrigg was hanged at Tyburn.

Generally, when the ill treatment of apprentices was prosecuted, punishment was light, unless a child died. In 1780 Catherine Parker, a weaver, was executed at Northampton for the murder of parish apprentice Thomas Cottingham. However, sixteen years later Elizabeth Hale, who was prosecuted by parish authorities at Surrey Quarter Sessions for beating and starving two female apprentices aged nine and eleven, was merely fined three shillings and fourpence and imprisoned in the house of correction for six months.

In 1801 an extreme case of ill treatment within the tambour industry came to the attention of the authorities. Mr Jouvaux from Stepney in east London was sentenced to a year's hard labour for his treatment of seventeen female apprentices. Fifteen-year-old Susannah Archer, whose case formed the indictment, was 'famished almost to death'; in addition, the premature deaths of five other apprentices were attributed to Jouvaux's harsh treatment. All of the girls were beaten regularly. They were allowed no meal breaks – their meagre rations were brought up to them while they continued to work at their frames. At times they were so hungry they ate from the pigs' trough or neighbours took pity and gave them what they could afford. Judge Grose, while upbraiding the defendant, also blamed the parish officers for their negligence.

The Jouvaux case did not lead to improvements in working conditions for parish apprentices. More than twenty-five years later, Frances Colpitts had the misfortune to enter a world with absolutely no protection of her welfare. She was born in 1819 into a poor family in the parish of St Martin in the Fields in Westminster, orphaned (or her parents were otherwise unable to care for her) and handed into the custody of the overseers at Castle Street Workhouse in Westminster, who sent her to their infant poorhouse at Highwood Hill in Mill Hill, ten miles north of London. It cannot have been an idyllic childhood but Frances would have been fed and clothed. As soon as she was old enough, she would have been put to work helping to care for the younger children at Highwood.

Frances was not totally without family. Her maternal grandmother, Frances Gibbs, after whom she was named, visited when she was able. Mrs Gibbs was probably relieved when her granddaughter, at the age of nine, returned to Castle Street Workhouse in late 1827 as it meant she no longer had to travel to Mill Hill to see her. At some point, probably after her return to London and before the child was due to start her apprenticeship to Esther Hibner, she gave Frances a dress, a petticoat and a green baize cloak.

In early 1828 Frances was sent out as a parish apprentice. Her employer was Esther Hibner, born Esther Read in about 1769 in the parish of St Giles Without Cripplegate in the east of the city. At the age of 26 Esther married John Ellis Hibner, a butcher, in St Andrew's, Holborn. She was subsequently kept busy with at least five surviving children, including twins. We do not know when Esther was widowed, but it is likely that she started her business of tambour-making after John died in order to provide an income for herself and her daughter, also called Esther, who was unmarried with a child. They lived and worked at 13 Platt Terrace, off St Pancras Road.

Frances was taken 'on liking' meaning that there was a probation period of three weeks, during which both sides would see if they were suited and, if all went well, Frances would sign the indenture papers in front of a magistrate and be bound to Esther for seven years. In return for feeding, clothing and housing Frances, the parish would pay Esther a premium of £10. It was a mutually advantageous system for parish and employer. There were no wages for Frances and Esther would have the benefit of the child's labour. The parish, meanwhile, was able to shed its financial obligations towards her. Although in theory Frances had to give her consent, in reality she and her grandmother had little say in the arrangement.

On joining the Hibners' business, Frances was introduced to Mrs Hibner's daughter Esther and to the general servant Ann Robinson, a young woman whose job was to assist her mistresses and manage the workers. Frances was probably heartened to see some familiar faces from Highwood Hill and Castle Street. Five of the other apprentices, who were aged between 6 and 10, came from her own parish of St Martin's, including Mary Ann Harford, her senior by a year, who had also been at Highwood Hill as a young child, and who had been apprenticed to Mrs Hibner a few months previously. Two others were from Esther Hibner's own birth parish, St Giles Without Cripplegate.

WOMEN AND THE GALLOWS 1797–1837

Frances was bound on 29 April. The work was hard but conditions were bearable. There was just enough food. Then things took a steep downward turn. After October, the apprentices were given little to eat. That winter was especially cold but the apprentices, who slept in a huddle on the floor of the workshop, were protected only with a thin blanket and wore their clothes to bed. They had no stockings and no clean linen. They were woken at two or three in the morning and worked until ten or eleven at night. Breakfast was a five-minute break for a slice of dry bread and watered milk but on the days when a dinner of potatoes was served there was no breakfast. Meat was given once every two weeks. The worst of it was that if the girls did not produce enough tambour, their meagre rations were cut. Sometimes they were so hungry they stole bits of fish and bone from the pigswill brought in for the dog by Esther's butcher son. One of the apprentices said later that Frances would eat candle ends and grease.

The privations the girls endured were appalling and they were crowned with physical abuse. For not working fast enough both the Hibners and Ann Robinson beat Frances with a rod, cane or slipper, or knocked her to the floor with their fists. She developed sores on her feet. On one occasion, when ordered to clean the stairs, she fell to the floor. Then she was hauled up and beaten 'under her clothes' according to one of the other apprentices. When she was sent back to the stairs to continue cleaning, she wet herself and the younger Esther pushed her nose into the urine, afterwards holding her up by the heels and plunging her face first into a pail of icy water, with Robinson shouting 'Curse her, dip her again, and finish her.' Frances later told the other girls that she was 'ill in her inside'.

The Hibners may have taken Frances on to replace another apprentice, Margaret Hawse, who had become sick and died earlier in the year. One morning, complaining of headache, underfed and exhausted, Margaret was so weak that she was unable even to get out of bed. When Ann Robinson dragged her upstairs and tried to make her stand, she collapsed. Eventually Mrs Hibner pushed her downstairs, where she lay on the floor.

'Let her lay there and die; she will be good riddance,' said Mrs Hibner.

ESTHER HIBNER

Margaret, by now unable to speak, died at seven the next morning.

That evening the Hibners and Robinson participated in a macabre celebration. After a good dinner of meat and pudding they toasted Margaret's death with a pint of gin. Meanwhile, two of the apprentices were given the task of washing and laying out Margaret's body, a job more usually done by 'searchers', middle-aged women of the community whose job was to report on cause of death to the authorities. The Hibners could not risk anyone outside the premises seeing the state Margaret died in, so they bought a coffin and nailed Margaret into it before having it carted off to the undertaker, Mr Hamp, who later said that he peeked in to check, saw an emaciated child and assumed that she had died of tuberculosis.

Mrs Gibbs usually visited her granddaughter every few weeks. In late September, five months after Frances went to the Hibners, she was turned away at the door. One of Mrs Hibner's other daughters had died (this much was true) and it was not possible to see Frances. On 3 January, she came again and was told that the girls were 'being washed' and could not see visitors. A few months later, Miss Hibner told her that Frances had spoiled her work and was being punished. Eventually, on 11 February, Miss Hibner told her, 'You will see a pretty thing when you do see her, she is in a deplorable state', adding that the child had been ill. What Mrs Gibbs found shocked her so profoundly that she went straight to the Castle Street workhouse and returned the following day with John Blackman, the overseer.

He later described the scene. Frances was on a filthy mattress on the floor, covered only with a small woollen cloth. She was skeletal, covered in bruises and her feet were gangrenous, with the toes almost dropping off. Blackman insisted on taking the girls to the workhouse but Mrs Hibner resisted. He came back the next day with Charles James Wright, the parish surgeon, and together they took five of the children to the workhouse, one to St Pancras Infirmary and Frances straight to St Martin's. Wright said later that Frances was 'merely skin and bone, her lips contracted a great deal, the teeth much exposed, a redness about the eyes'. She was not expected to live.

Blackman had counted the children and worked out that one was missing. Initially, at the house, the girls told him that Margaret Hawse had gone to her aunt in the country but he suspected they were lying. Now, after their removal from Platt Terrace, they told him that they had feared the Hibners would flog them and keep them without food if they told him the truth. They described how Margaret had died and was buried in secret.

Four days later the Hibners and Ann Robinson were brought before Sir Richard Birnie at Bow Street Magistrates and charged with extreme cruelty towards the girls and starving them almost to death. The magistrate was particularly upset to hear that Frances's face was forced into her urine. Miss Hibner interjected. 'The truth is, Sir, she wet the bed repeatedly, and I rubbed her nose in it.' 'You had better say nothing for you are doing yourself no good,' he responded.

Birnie committed the prisoners and recommended the parish officers apply to have the body of Margaret Hawse exhumed as soon as they could. At an inquest at the Elephant and Castle public house in St Pancras Road her body was found to be a 'mere skeleton' and a surgeon confirmed that she had died of starvation. The coroner's jury concluded that Mrs Hibner was guilty of wilful murder and that her daughter was an accessory. Five days later they and Ann Robinson pleaded not guilty at the Old Bailey, but barrister Peter Alley, for the prosecution, asked for a postponement as he had only just been given the brief. The judge, Stephen Gaselee, agreed and moved the case to the next sessions.

On 15 March, Frances Colpitts, who had been removed from the Hibners' premises in a critical condition, died in the infirmary, and another inquest took place at the Elephant and Castle. The jury again found Mrs Hibner responsible, with her daughter an accessory. It is unclear when or why the principal charge against the Hibners and Robinson was switched to the murder of Frances Colpitts rather than that of Margaret Hawse. Perhaps the prosecuting team felt that Frances's case had more chance of success. Whatever occurred, on 9 April 1829 the three women stood trial in front of Judge William Garrow at the Old Bailey.

The surviving apprentices gave evidence against their former

ESTHER HIBNER

mistresses: Susan Whitby, Mary Ann Harford and Eliza Loman told the court about the starvation rations, overwork, punishments and abuse. Charles Wright, the surgeon, described the state in which he and Mr Blackman found Frances Colpitts and how the postmortem had discovered that she had tuberculosis and abscesses in her lungs. Thomas Gosling, another surgeon with long experience of treating workhouse patients, agreed that children of 'diseased and weak parents' were more liable to consumption but said that dipping Frances's head in cold water had aggravated her underlying disease.

Mrs Hibner, who was unrepresented, merely said, 'I leave my defence to my daughter' and her daughter asserted that, 'My mother was a very good mistress to them', adding that the apprentices would wet the bed two or three times a night and that her mother had borrowed £200 in order to feed and clothe them. Robinson said she never saw any of the ill treatment described by the girls. The accused called only one witness in their defence: John Steed, whose stepdaughter was an apprentice, but he turned against them and said that when she came home on Sundays he could see that she was underfed and gave her food to take back with her.

The jury retired at half past six and after just over an hour returned a verdict of guilty against Mrs Hibner. Her daughter and Ann Robinson were acquitted.

Judge Garrow addressed Mrs Hibner. He spoke of her duty of care to the children and the 'want of feeling' she had displayed, for no other reason than her own profit. She should have seen that the health of Frances Colpitts was deteriorating. Her status as a mother herself compounded her guilt: 'You saw her sufferings without any of the feeling which one would imagine could never have been absent from a female breast.' He urged her to use the time she had left to her to ask heaven for mercy, as she would find none on earth.

When he ordered her to be hanged on Monday she showed no emotion. Even when arraigned on the second indictment, the murder of Margaret Hawse, she remained stony-faced and pleaded not guilty with, as a broadside later described, 'all the firmness of conscious innocence, although as the poor child's death had been the result of the same dreadful course of treatment adopted towards Colpitt [sic], there could be no doubt of her legal and moral responsibility for the crime which had hurried the wretched being from the world.' She only broke down when told that her body would be dissected.

The authorities were determined that Esther Hibner the younger and Ann Robinson should not escape punishment and they were ordered to be detained for trial for assaulting Margaret Hawse, Susan Whitby and others. Miss Hibner was sentenced to twelve and Robinson to four months' imprisonment.

In Newgate Mrs Hibner continued to display 'the most hardened disposition'. *The Morning Post* reported that she complained about the food and demanded mutton chops (she was refused and told that she could have only bread and water, the standard fare for prisoners awaiting execution). Reverend Horace Cotton, the Ordinary of Newgate, advised her to read her Bible but she said she knew it already. She asked to see her daughter, and then affected not to care when she refused to come ('It don't signify,' she shrugged). Cotton managed to persuade Miss Hibner to change her mind and she was brought from her house of correction to the condemned cell at two o'clock in the afternoon but the meeting at first was 'cold and indifferent' with mother and daughter behaving like 'perfect strangers'. After a while they bonded with some 'most abusive vituperations against the witnesses'. 'Well, all I am sorry for is that I did not rush from the dock, and tear the wretches to pieces,' Mrs Hibner was reported to have said. At the end of the encounter, suddenly grief-stricken, her daughter wept bitterly.

At about four o'clock on Sunday, Mrs Hibner made an attempt at self-harm. In the privy she jabbed at her throat with a blunt dinner knife she had hidden in her stockings. Meanwhile, Mr Brown, the solicitor convinced that her crime should be downgraded to manslaughter, was writing his last-ditch appeal to the Home Secretary. He had in mind the trial's failure to directly link Esther Hibner's cruelty with Frances Colpitts's death but he would also have had in mind the general hypocrisy of a society in which the casual exploitation of children was commonplace, only remarked on if sensational cases came to public attention.

ESTHER HIBNER

The Hibner case highlighted the evils of parish apprenticeship at a time when other forms of slavery were a political issue. Less than a month after Mrs Hibner was executed, 'A Country Clergyman' wrote to *The Exeter and Plymouth Gazette*: 'The sooner the Apprentices are emancipated the better; and whilst our Philanthropists are anxious to do away with negro slavery, I would beg to call their attention to a system of domestic slavery, pursued at home, and which ought immediately to be corrected.' The reformer Edward Gibbon Wakefield, who had had direct experience of Newgate after he was sentenced to three years' imprisonment for abducting a 15-year-old heiress and forcibly marrying her at Gretna Green, pointed out the irony that children were available for sale for £50 in America as slaves, while in London they were given away as apprentices for £10.

Even as 'A Country Clergyman' was composing his letter, another case of cruelty towards an apprentice came to light. On 1 May 1829 *The Stamford Mercury* reported that the town of Alford in Lincolnshire had been 'for several weeks in a state of excitement' over the case of a young woman whose treatment echoed Frances Colpitts's. The 12-year-old victim, who was apprenticed to a dressmaker, was not expected to live after 'a series of ill-treatment and want of air and exercise'.

CHAPTER 4

Mary Thorpe
York, 17 March 1800

*

Mary Voce
Nottingham, 16 March 1802

*

Mary Morgan
Presteigne, 14 April 1805

*

Infanticide

Of the ninety-one women hanged for murder between 1797 and 1837, thirty-five were convicted of the murder or attempted murder of their own infants. Infanticide usually involved the death of a newborn baby but occasionally of an older child. Most of those prosecuted were unmarried domestic servants who had concealed their pregnancies and given birth in secret.

Infants had a high mortality rate and this must have hidden numerous deliberate killings with many partners, parents, employers, surgeons and coroners colluding discreetly to register the deaths as natural. Overall, only a few women were prosecuted and if they did appear in court they were likely to be acquitted. However, the authorities could not ignore infanticides with manifestly aggravated features – violence or deliberate neglect – and a death sentence sometimes resulted.

MARY THORPE, MARY VOCE, MARY MORGAN

Seventeen-year-old Mary Morgan worked as an under-cook at Maesllwch Castle, just over a mile from Glasbury in Radnorshire, Wales, where she was brought up by her parents, Rees and Elizabeth Morgan, who were known as poor but respectable people. The castle was the home of Walter Wilkins, the Whig MP for Radnorshire and a former High Sheriff of Radnorshire and Breconshire, his wife and two adult sons, Walter and Jeffreys. It was a large and busy household, and the kitchens were a hub of activity, so much so that on the afternoon of Sunday, 23 September 1804, when Mary said she was too ill to work and crawled upstairs to her bed, the housekeeper was left short-handed and had to call in Margaret Havard to replace her.

The servant women were concerned about Mary, and probably not a little suspicious of the reason for her sudden inability to carry out her duties. They went up to her quarters to check on her. The housekeeper arrived at the door of her chamber with some warm wine and at some time between six and seven Elizabeth Evelyn, the cook, brought tea, returning half an hour later with Margaret Havard. The minute the women came in to the room their suspicions were confirmed. 'From some particular circumstance which [Elizabeth Evelyn] saw' they knew that Mary had given birth, and said so. 'Mary strongly denied it with bitter oaths for some time,' said Margaret Havard later. Eventually, Mary admitted that it was true and told them that the baby's body was buried in the mattress, and there they found her 'amongst the feathers', her head nearly separated from her body. A penknife Mary used for cutting up chickens was discovered under the pillow.

A coroner's inquest held two days later decided that Mary, 'not having the fear of God before her eyes, but moved and seduced by the instigation of the Devil', had assaulted her child and made a 'mortal wound of the length of three inches and the depth of one inch' with her knife and that the child had died instantly. Mary was arrested but remained a few days at Maesllwch until she had sufficiently recovered from the birth to make the twenty-five-mile journey to the county gaol at Presteigne to await her trial at the next assizes.

Mary Morgan started work at the castle at about the age of 15 or 16 and seems to have soon attracted the attention of Walter Wilkins the younger. George Hardinge, who tried Mary at Presteigne, later claimed that Walter was 'intrigued with her'. Although female domestic servants were admonished to be careful around their masters – 'A young girl will have occasion to resist temptations from debauched superiors who glory in the demolition of female virtue,' intoned the *Westminster Magazine* in 1780 – in reality they were more vulnerable to their fellow servants. While Mary may well have had some sort of liaison with Walter, she later said the father of her child was an unnamed waggoner (he probably worked on the estate or had business with it). This man refused to marry or support her.

What were Mary's choices? The waggoner offered her 'herbs', abortifacients to terminate the pregnancy, but she rejected them. Abortion was a felony crime, and at this stage it is unlikely that Mary had decided to kill her child. Probably, like many women in her situation, she simultaneously looked forward to the coming child and dreaded its impact. As her time approached and certainly after labour started, she must have come to accept that her situation was desperate: a baby would mean the end of everything. Even if she managed to avoid the workhouse, a life of shame and poverty was ahead.

Where a pregnancy was the result of a casual coupling, a woman's reputation would be ruined: sexual incontinence was seen as one step away from prostitution. However, social ostracism did not always follow an illegitimate birth. It was accepted that if the pregnancy arose from a longstanding relationship and that there would eventually be a marriage (or at least a settled constancy), unmarried parents were granted a degree of tolerance. The poor could only do what was necessary rather than what they wished and sometimes a young couple had to wait years before they could afford to marry or even to set up home together, because that meant paying rent and outlay on furniture, linen, pots and pans. Sympathy was also expressed for women who had been deserted or deceived. However, matters were more difficult where a child was disowned by the father, if only because the mother and child might then become a burden on the parish.

Servants, hired on condition they were single and childless and of good reputation, were in a special position. A baby born out of wedlock meant instant dismissal and a humiliating return to their families. They could no longer work and were unable to contribute their wages to their family. They and their baby became dependants, extra mouths to feed.

Before Mary Morgan's trial on 11 April 1805 at Presteigne, Charles Rogers, the high sheriff, took pity on her and appointed and paid for a defence counsel. The trial itself was a straightforward affair. The servant women who had given evidence at the coroner's inquest, including Elizabeth Evelyn and Margaret Havard, repeated their testimony. Mary was entitled to speak in her own defence but there is no evidence that she did so and no record of any defence presented by the barrister.

The jury returned a guilty verdict. Possibly they assumed that Judge Hardinge would recommend Mary for a reprieve. In this they were wrong. Only a week previously a similar case at Brecon had a very different outcome. The jury there found Mary Morris guilty only of the crime of concealment, even though she had killed her child with scissors. Hardinge imprisoned her for two years, the maximum allowed. The verdict against Mary Morgan was his opportunity to make a point.

Hardinge was known for his emotional speeches to the convicted, many of which were later published. His words to Mary Morgan were carried in newspapers across Wales. He spoke about the murder of the child ('the offspring of your secret and vicious love'), Mary's likely reasons for killing her ('Had it lived, you might have lost your place.... You might have lived in poverty as well as shame') and included numerous admonitions of her 'criminal intercourse', 'criminal passions' and 'depraved self-indulgence' which had led her first to 'the sin of imposture' (concealing her pregnancy) and then to the murder of her baby.

She was to be made an example. 'Had you escaped, many other girls, thoughtless and light as you have been, would have been encouraged by that escape to commit your crime with hope of your impunity. The merciful terror of your example will save them.' He ordered her to be *taken from hence to the place from whence you came, and from thence to the place of execution, the day after tomorrow. You are there to hang by the neck till you are dead: your body is then to be dissected and anatomised. But your soul is not reached by these inflictions. It is in the hand of your God – may that fountain of love show mercy to it when it shall appear before him at the day of judgement!*

Hardinge was in tears as he spoke, as was everyone else in the court, except for Mary herself.

Hardinge later wrote about the case to his friend the Reverend Dr Horsley, Bishop of St Asaph. He said Mary was

pretty and modest; [her countenance] even had the air and expression of perfect innocence. Not a tear escaped from her, when all around her were deeply affected by her doom; yet her carriage was respectful, her look attentive, serious, and intelligent... It appeared she had no defect of understanding, and she was born with every disposition to virtue.

Mary had the bad luck to appear before a judge who, despite his apparent admiration for her, felt strongly about punishing infanticide.

The law had been changed only two years previously to accommodate juries' refusal to convict women for killing their illegitimate babies. Lord Chief Justice Ellenborough had taken the pragmatic view that trials of these women were a waste of time because there was so little likelihood of conviction, and in 1803 proposed the repeal of the 1624 statute (The Act to Prevent the Destroying and Murthering of Bastard Children) as part of a package of changes. This law held that an unmarried woman whose illegitimate child was found dead was automatically assumed to have killed it. It was up to the woman to prove that she was innocent, rather than for the prosecution to prove that she was guilty. Of course, the law did nothing to deter unmarried women from falling pregnant and, when they found themselves facing destitution, from doing away with their babies.

MARY THORPE, MARY VOCE, MARY MORGAN

Ellenborough, by no means a liberal (his Offences Against the Person Act introduced many new felony crimes punishable by death), wanted to ensure that women who killed their babies were punished in some way. His new law treated the murder of legitimate and illegitimate infants as the same, requiring the same standards of evidence, but he also introduced a new crime: concealing the death of a child, a misdemeanour punishable by a fine or imprisonment for up to two years or a combination of both.

For Hardinge, Ellenborough's reforms were a step backwards. 'In our part of Wales it is thought no crime to kill a bastard-child,' he wrote, bemoaning the fact that 'there has not been a conviction at the Old Bailey for this crime during a period of twenty years.' In Ireland, he said, 'the habit of exposing children...rages like a pestilence.' Through tears, he berated Mary in court: 'There is not a more sacred object of that parent's love (whose children we all of us are) than a new-born child' but he was unable to show mercy to her, scarcely more than a child herself. Hardinge gave no consideration to the desperate situation she was in, in labour, alone and seemingly friendless, nor to the possibility that she had suffered a mental breakdown at the time of her delivery. Her demeanour in court was interpreted as sullenness, a refusal to engage, rather than the manifestation of a state of deep denial by someone very young and in shock.

She was led away back to Presteigne Gaol, to the accommodation for condemned prisoners on the first floor. Here her composure disappeared and, according to *The Chester Courant*, she became 'much agitated'. The following day, Friday, her father visited and she seemed calmer. Hardinge told Bishop Horsley that 'Mary took it for granted that she would be acquitted' and that she had ordered 'gay apparel' in the expectation that Walter Wilkins (the 'young master') would write to the judge and bring about a reprieve (according to Hardinge, Wilkins refused to help her). Probably only when all hope had expired did Mary accept the consolations of the chaplain, the Reverend Smith, admit her guilt and prepare for the Christian death Hardinge wished for her. The archives reveal no trace of a petition for mercy, either from the judge or from Mary's friends and family.

WOMEN AND THE GALLOWS 1797–1837

Newspaper reports stated that Mary was 'truly penitent' when she walked the few yards from the gaol to the gallows tree at Presteigne the following day. She was buried in St Andrew's churchyard in Presteigne, her body not having been dissected. It is likely that the surgeon to whom it was donated returned it untouched to her family.

It was highly unusual to hang women, especially for infanticide. To take Wales as an example, of the 149 women indicted for murdering their babies between 1730 and 1804 at the Court of Great Sessions, only seven were convicted and two executed, the most recent in 1739. After Mary Morgan's case, up to 1830, forty-six were indicted and none was convicted.

Judge Hardinge was much criticized for Mary's harsh punishment and it is not difficult to see why. He insisted that she had to die at a time when compassion was routinely shown to unmarried women, especially those in service whose babies were found dead in suspicious circumstances. Hardinge was fighting a trend. Between 1797 and 1837 at the Old Bailey in London, forty-eight trials for the manslaughter or murder of a baby were heard. Thirteen ended in a conviction for the lesser crime of concealing a birth (these were after the 1803 Act), for which the defendants were given prison sentences ranging from fourteen days to two years. In thirty-three cases the defendant was acquitted.

Judges and juries generally tried hard to find grounds for acquittal and might accept any one of a variety of arguments. A woman could be found not guilty if she brought forward a witness to show that she had planned for a live birth. The possession of baby linen or merely asking to borrow it would suffice (this was known as the 'benefit of linen' defence). In 1833 Catherine Weeks was accused of killing her newborn baby girl, who had been delivered in the privy of St Giles workhouse. She claimed the child was stillborn. Three respectable tradesmen and a local washerwoman in whose house the body was later found, probably hidden there by Catherine herself, gave her a good character at her trial, but it was her sister's evidence that tipped the balance. She told the court that Catherine had come to her lodgings and borrowed baby linen. Catherine was found guilty of concealment but the jury recommended mercy and she was punished with fourteen days' incarceration.

Where the woman gave birth alone, unaided and unfamiliar with the mechanics of birth, she might say that she made a mistake during the delivery, failing to catch the baby while it was being born or neglecting to tie the cord, or that she had suffered a fainting fit. Sometimes judges made pointed remarks, particularly to the medical witnesses, in order to acquit women. The following exchange is typical. In 1802 (before Ellenborough's law), Elizabeth Harvey, who had denied to her friends that she was pregnant but who later gave birth alone in her lodging room in Tottenham, north of London, leaving her bed drenched in blood, was later seen putting the body of her child into a pond.

Judge: Might not the navel cord, not being properly attended to, of itself occasion the death of the child?

James Sheffield, assistant to a surgeon: It would undoubtedly.

Judge: I believe it is a very frequent thing for the child to die in the birth in the very act of delivery?

Sheffield: Most assuredly.

Judge: Even where a skilful practitioner attends the birth?

Sheffield: Yes.

Judge: It is the more likely when an ignorant woman delivers herself?

Sheffield: Yes.

Judge: And you yourself can form no judgment how the child came by its death?

Sheffield: No.

There were no marks of violence on the body and Elizabeth was acquitted.

A midwife or surgeon might testify that the child was premature, stillborn or too ill to survive. In 1837 Sarah Blacklock was accused of killing her six-week-old baby boy, who had died shortly after Sarah had flitted from her lodgings owing rent, which gives a clue to her circumstances. Her new landlady testified that the baby had been 'sickly and poorly' and 'did not cry' and after surgeon James Carter gave evidence that the baby 'died of convulsions occasioned by a slow inflammation of the lungs, occasioned by a cold or want of food, and other things' the jury exonerated Sarah.

Occasionally in the nineteenth century the long discredited hydrostatic test, first devised in the seventeenth century, was used to prove stillbirth. This involved removing the lungs and plunging them into a pail of water to see if they sank (stillborn) or floated (live, because they had previously been inflated with air). As late as 1836 George Box Drayton performed this test on 18-year-old Jane Hale's tiny baby (born at less than one kilogram), who had been found with a gash in his neck. 'I did not perceive any air in the lungs,' he told the Old Bailey and gave his opinion that the wound had not caused death: the child had already died. Jane was acquitted of murder but found guilty of concealment and imprisoned for two years. In Devonport in 1832 Mary Kellaway was not so lucky. A surgeon used the hydrostatic test to prove that her baby, found with tape wound tightly around the neck, was born alive. Mary had no linen to prove that she had anticipated a live birth and despite the jury's pleas for mercy was hanged.

There was also the defence of temporary insanity. In 1800 Elizabeth Jarvis, an unmarried servant described in court as 'very poor indeed', appeared at the Old Bailey. She had been in deep denial about her pregnancy, even in the middle of 'strong labour'. Elizabeth tried to suffocate her baby boy with a cloth and hid him in a bundle in the corner of her room, where he was discovered close to death. Robert Whitfield, a surgeon, gave evidence.

Defence counsel: A woman in strong labour is not always possessed of her faculties of reason?

Whitfield: Not always.

Elizabeth was acquitted.

Mary Frances Jones was charged with the murder of her infant daughter in 1808. She was working as a nursemaid for Mrs Birkett at Catherine Court in Tower Hill when she became ill and took to her bed, where she delivered a 'very large child' who was later found dead in a trunk, wrapped in one of Mary's gowns. Her throat had been cut. Under cross-examination, Mrs Birkett described Mary's state after the child had been discovered: 'She appeared to be in a stupid state; she hardly appeared to be alive', and Mary herself told the court, 'It was in my extremity that it happened.' She was sentenced to a year in the house of correction and fined a shilling.

A woman could lose her reason from extreme labour pain, but an insurmountable sense of shame might have the same effect. In 1784 the physician, surgeon, anatomist, surgeon and man-midwife William Hunter reminded his colleagues that the death of an infant was not murder unless it was 'executed with some degree of cool judgement, and wicked intention. When committed under a phrenzy [sic] of despair, can it be more offensive in the sight of God, than under a phrenzy from a fever, or in lunacy?' Rebecca Merrin's behaviour before and after her child was born indicated a disturbed state of mind. Her fellow lodger Mary Hoskins told the Old Bailey in 1809:

The prisoner came into my room with the child in her hands. I said: 'What have you got there, Beckey?' She said: 'A child.' I said: 'Take it away, I will have nothing to do with it.' She made answer: 'I will put it in the closet'...She wanted to put it in my bed.

She had previously denied to everyone who asked not only that she was pregnant but also that she had ever had sex. She had even consulted John Wallis, a surgeon and man-midwife, complaining of 'the dropsy' (oedema). The jury found Rebecca guilty of concealment and she was fined a shilling and sent to the house of correction for six months.

Of the forty-eight Old Bailey cases, only two resulted in a conviction for murder. Neither was commuted and the defendants were hanged. What made them different to the others? Like many in her predicament, 33-year-old Sarah Perry denied to all that she was pregnant. She worked as a cook for the King family in Manchester Square, London in 1817 and claimed to be married although no husband was identified. Early one morning she was taken ill in the scullery in the basement. Her sceptical fellow servant Charlotte Armstrong tried to help her but Sarah refused to let her in and then, when Charlotte was called away by her mistress, locked the kitchen door. After a while the footman heard the cry of a child. Charlotte later found blood in the scullery, on the floor of the bedroom she shared with Sarah and on Sarah's nightdress. When Sarah told her the stains were from a calf's heart, which the household had not ordered for months, Charlotte knew Sarah was lying and told her mistress, who reported her to the authorities. After two searches of the house the body of a baby girl was found buried in the coal cellar, wrapped in Sarah's petticoat. Her mouth had been stuffed with a dishcloth. The surgeon Edward Leese told the court that the child was certainly born alive. Sarah's defence explained the dilemma of the pregnant domestic servant – 'The prisoner never had a child before, and being inexperienced, thought she had two months of her time to go. Her reason for not making her situation known was that she might remain in her place as long as she could' – but it did not explain the dishcloth in her baby's mouth. Sarah was executed outside Newgate on 24 February 1817.

The other case that ended in execution is much less clear cut. Twenty-four-year-old Catherine Welch's baby was found in a watery ditch in a field in Parsons Green, west of London, on 2 March 1828. He was over a month old when he died and, according to surgeon Joseph Holmes, he had sustained a wound to his temple and blood vessels in his eyes had burst. Holmes told the court he thought the child had been strangled. Witnesses said they had seen Catherine nearby with a bundle under her clothes. Her defence was that her child had been born in Saffron Hill, died and was interred in the old burial ground in Marylebone High Street but Catherine could provide no details of the woman whose son she said had taken the baby for burial. 'I am as innocent as a baby unborn and leave it to the gentlemen of the Court to look into my case, for I have not a person in the world to do anything for me,' she told the court. The jury found her guilty and the judge sentenced her to death. Three days later she was hanged outside Newgate, having confessed that she had intended to kill her child because she had no way to feed him. Her husband had abandoned her when she became pregnant by another man.

MARY THORPE, MARY VOCE, MARY MORGAN

As we have seen with Catherine Welch, not all the victims of infanticide were minutes or hours old. Sometimes they had been fed and cared for by their mothers for some time. A woman charged with murder in this circumstance might claim to have suffered from milk fever at the time of the killing. Well into the nineteenth century it was believed that breast milk – the lack of it or its inability to flow properly – could cause severe illness. If it became congested in the breast it caused mastitis; if it diverted to other areas of the body, the thighs and pelvis, for instance, it could lead to abscesses and inflammation. It could also, without displaying other symptoms, affect a woman's rationality.

On 12 May 1822 Ann Mountford, the wife of a weaver living in Bethnal Green in east London and mother of a delicate and sickly nine-month-old daughter Lucy, who was still on the breast, suffered a sudden and catastrophic breakdown. Covered in blood, Ann ran to her neighbour, Mary Ireland, screaming, 'I have done it! I have done it! Send for an officer. I want to be hung. I must be hung. I have done it to be hung!' She had decapitated Lucy. Mary Ireland told the court at the Old Bailey:

> *She had been attempting to wean the child for three weeks – it often happens that at that time women have a milk fever... Giving the milk now and then would cause the milk to flow into the breast, and keep it fuller than if she suckled it entirely. The fever would be more or less violent according to the quantity of milk. I told her I thought she was hurting herself, by suckling it.*

It was a theory backed up by surgeon Joseph Dalton, who told the court:

> *I have known an attempt to wean a child and not accomplishing it, produce insanity. If it was lurking in the habit it would be more likely to break out at that time. When I attended her in 1819, she repeatedly made use of the words, 'I*

have no peace at all...' I was not at all surprised when I heard she was the subject of insanity. At the time of weaning, the breast remains extremely full of milk, which always produces a degree of irritation.

Ann was found not guilty, 'being insane'.

A crisis affecting 21-year-old Mary Thorpe in 1799 was very different. She had been in service for six or seven years when she became pregnant. She concealed her condition and eleven weeks before her due date left her employment to travel to Sheffield where, pretending to be a married woman, she took lodgings at the house of Mrs Hartley, a widow, and gave birth. At about five o'clock one afternoon in December she wrapped her eight-day-old baby boy in cloths and left her lodgings, telling Mrs Hartley that she was taking him to her sister in Derby to be wet-nursed. Instead, she wound a length of tape around his neck three times, attached a large stone and put him in the river. His body, found the next morning near a bridge about a mile from the centre of Sheffield, not far from the spot where she had left him, was soon identified.

Mary travelled on to her family home in the village of Ecclesfield, where she was arrested a short time later by Samuel Hall, the Sheffield constable. When she flatly denied ever having had a baby, he had a woman examine her breasts; they were pronounced 'full of fresh milk'. Mary was taken into custody and imprisoned in York Castle, charged with the wilful murder of her male bastard child. At the coroner's inquest she said she had given the child to a man living in Milk Street, Sheffield and had not seen him since, but the evidence of several witnesses that the tape of the type found around the baby's neck had been seen in her possession was compelling. In March 1800 she appeared before judge Giles Rooke at York. The general consensus was that she was 'a decent respectable looking young woman' and that 'her appearance and deportment excited the warmest sympathy'. Her defence was that she was 'ill and delirious, and knew not what she did' and although it was accepted that she was indeed suffering from milk fever, the court decided that it was 'not sufficiently

MARY THORPE, MARY VOCE, MARY MORGAN

to destroy her sanity.' The premeditated steps she took to kill her baby were considered proof of that.

She was found guilty and bore the verdict 'with the greatest firmness', curtseying to the court before she left it and expressing contrition. On 17 March she and Michael Simpson, who had been convicted of poisoning his employer at the same assize, were taken to the Knavesmirc Tyburn near York and hanged. Simpson protested his innocence; Mary did not.

Although most of the victims of infanticide were illegitimate babies born in difficult circumstances, a few were born to married women. Some of them were the products of illicit relationships. Unlike unmarried women, who until 1803 were subject to the 1624 Act to Prevent the Destroying and Murthering of Bastard Children, married women who killed their babies were charged with murder and the proofs required were the same as for an adult victim.

On the morning of 10 November 1801, shortly after breakfast, Mary Voce, a young married woman 'in the prime of life and comeliness of person', living apart from her husband in Fisher Gate, a poor district of Nottingham, mixed arsenic with water in a teacup and carefully poured it into the mouth of her six-week-old baby Elizabeth. The child screamed in agony, distressed beyond description. Despite being the author of her daughter's pain, Mary was heartbroken, shocked and frightened, and paced back and forth, wringing her hands and wailing. Neighbours soon came to help but within a couple of hours it was all over. The baby was dead.

After the coroner's inquest Mary was taken up and committed for trial at the next Nottingham Assizes to answer charges of murder. In prison she was regularly visited by Methodist preachers John Clarke, Miss Richards and Elizabeth Tomlinson, who prayed with her and tried to get her to accept her guilt. She stuck to her assertion that she was innocent.

She admitted that she had not led a blameless life, and latterly, after trying to find work carding cotton, had turned to 'other methods which it is too painful to relate' by which she meant prostitution. Born Mary

Hallam in 1778 in Sneinton, not far from Nottingham, she had been brought up in poverty. Her unmarried parents had died young and she was passed into the care of relatives. She had seen her marriage to Thomas Voce as a path to stability, but it had been a disaster, blighted by his violence and her infidelity. When Thomas was required to travel 160 miles to Chatham in Kent to confirm his entitlement to a military pension, she had taken a lover, not her first, and become pregnant with Elizabeth. The couple separated, Mary taking their five-year-old son with her. Mary's lover abandoned her before Elizabeth's birth and, at her wits' end, she begged Thomas to accept her back, which he did for a while, but left her soon afterwards, convinced that the boy was not his. Mary was now penniless with two children.

Mary told her prison visitors that she had obtained the arsenic intending to kill herself and not the baby. Her story was that she put it in a teacup on the hob but on the morning of the tragedy a neighbour asked her to breakfast. She left the baby in her lodgings and while she was gone a child must have slipped in and mistakenly thought to have done the baby a service by giving her water, little realizing that the cup contained poison.

On 12 March 1802 Mary Voce appeared at the Nottingham Lent Assizes before Sir Robert Graham, a judge known for his humanity. When he asked Mary if she had anything to say, she handed him a piece of paper refuting the charge and blaming the neighbourhood children. She stated again that she had bought the arsenic intending to poison herself and that Thomas Voce had been abusive to her. Graham gave this careful consideration and a witness was called who confirmed that Mary had indeed taken breakfast with a neighbour that morning. He accepted that she may have been abused by her husband but 'motive and cause for such treatment, was, alas!, too apparent', that is, Mary's infidelity had given him justification. However humane Graham was, it did not extend to an understanding of the corrosive effects of domestic abuse.

In summing up the case, Graham 'took particular notice of every circumstance which had appeared in her [Mary's] favour' and 'called the attention of the jury to her apparent state of mind during the illness

MARY THORPE, MARY VOCE, MARY MORGAN

of her infant.' Wringing her hands and weeping was, he said, a genuine display of grief, but Mary was not insane and there were no special grounds for mercy. The jury deliberated for ten minutes and declared her guilty. During the sentencing, 'His Lordship and the whole court were deeply affected.' Mary herself was scarcely able to stand and announced that she wanted to die. She was removed from the bar and taken to Nottingham Gaol to await execution. Someone was with her at all times to prevent her suicide.

In the condemned cell, she continued to deny her guilt, until finally persuaded by her Methodist visitors that telling the truth would relieve her suffering. At two o'clock on Saturday she confessed, crying out, 'Oh my heart will break! My heart will break!' She sent a message to her husband to say she did not want to see him again but hoped he would forgive her. She had a final meeting with her young son.

By Sunday she was 'quite comfortable and resigned'. The next day, 16 March 1802, at ten o'clock the under sheriff and his constables arrived to take her to Nottingham's Gallows Hill and she took her last leave of the gaol governor, his maid and other female prisoners. Then she and her empty coffin were placed in a cart, and her Methodist advisers climbed in next to her. She told them: 'This is the best day I ever saw. I am quite happy. I had rather die than live' and 'I am so happy I cannot cry. I cannot shed one tear.' When they reached their destination, Miss Richards said: 'We are got there, Mary.' She replied, 'Well bless the Lord.' She greeted the executioner with a smile and gave him her hand. 'Bless you, I have nothing against you. Somebody must do it,' she said and assisted him in placing the ropes. As the hood was put over her head, she exclaimed, 'Glory! Glory to Jesus! I shall soon be in Glory. Glory is indeed already begun in my soul, and the angels of God are about me!' She dropped and her body was left to hang for an hour, and then handed to surgeons for dissection. Her remains were publicly displayed.

Two years later, Elizabeth Tomlinson, who had counselled Mary, married Samuel Evans. Elizabeth went on to have three children, and was also a beloved and devoted aunt. Her niece Mary Ann, the daughter of Samuel's older brother Robert, was particularly fond of her, and listened attentively to her recollections. When Mary Ann was 20, Elizabeth told her about sitting with Mary Voce before her trial and in the condemned cell and the efforts she and her companions made to bring her to confess. Twenty years later, Mary Ann Evans, writing under her pen name George Eliot, published *Adam Bede*, which featured the beautiful but morally vacant Hetty Sorrel, who was sentenced to death for infanticide.

We do not know how common infanticide was. The earliest official statistics available show that between 1839 and 1840, the first year for which there are official data, seventy-six children under the age of one were murdered, but the true number must have been much higher. How much did people care about these lost children? Juries, and the wider public, did not often regard the murder of a baby as deserving the death penalty and were content to find the woman temporarily insane and therefore not responsible for her actions, or to accept one of the array of defences presented to the court, or to downgrade the charge to concealment. They understood that the decision to kill a child was usually the result of mental disturbance, shame, fear or poverty rather than because the woman had a naturally murderous nature. They recognized that infanticides were rarely a threat to wider society.

Judge Hardinge, who condemned Mary Morgan, did care. He called infanticide 'the vice of the poor' and blamed their lack of religion and education. 'In proportion to the undisciplined and savage characters of the poor, this offence is more or less prevalent,' he wrote. Regarding Mary Morgan his opinion was that 'there was not a single trace of Religion to be found in her thoughts. Of Christianity, she had never even heard, or of The Bible; and she had scarce ever been at Church.' Hardinge was known as a charitable man. He was a successful fundraiser for good causes and became vice chairman of the Philanthropic Society, which sought to help the young homeless children begging and stealing on the streets of London by training them in cottage industries. However, he appears to have had no insight into Mary Morgan's state of mind at the time she committed the crime. In his view, there were some cases where capital punishment was judged unavoidable, where the crime was too heinous or an example was required, and Mary Morgan's was one of them. Hence, Hardinge's words to her: 'The merciful terror of her example' would save other girls from a similar fate.

On his subsequent visits to Presteigne, Hardinge made repeated visits to Mary Morgan's grave, where he shed real tears. He did not blame himself for her death. Rather, he was keen to show that he had the appropriate levels of sensibility, that peculiar Georgian spin on sentiment and sentimentality, and employed his much-lauded facility for poetry to memorialize the young woman he sent to the gallows:

> *Flow the tears that Pity loves*
> *Upon Mary's hapless fate;*
> *It's a tear that God approves:*
> *He can strike, but cannot hate.*
> *She for an example fell,*
> *But is Man from censure free?*
> *Thine, Seducer, is the Knell,*
> *It's a messenger to thee.*

As a further response to public feeling, his friend Thomas Brudenell-Bruce, Earl of Ailesbury, erected a stone on Mary's grave, the inscription perfectly reflecting Hardinge's opinions and eulogizing him as a 'benevolent judge'.

> *To the Memory of Mary Morgan who young and beautiful endowed with a good understanding and disposition but unenlightened by the sacred truths of Christianity become the victim of sin and shame and was condemned to an ignominious death on the 11th April 1805 for the Murder of her bastard child. Rousd [sic] to a first sense of guilt and remorse by the eloquent and humane exertions of her benevolent judge, Mr Justice Hardinge, she underwent the sentence of the Law on the following Thursday with unfeigned repentance and a furvent [sic] hope of forgiveness through the merits of a redeeming*

intercessor. This Stone is erected not merely to perpetuate the remembrance of a departed penitent but to remind the living of the frailty of human nature when unsupported by Religion.

Local people felt differently. An anonymous donor countered Brudenell-Bruce's stone with another, simply inscribed:

*In Memory of
MARY MORGAN
who Suffrd April 13th 1805
Aged 17 Years.
He that is without sin among you
Let him first cast a stone at her
the 8th Chapr of John part of ye 7th VI.*

In 1818, over ten years after Mary was killed and two years after Hardinge died, Thomas Horton, a playwright, made use of her death. In *Elegy Written in the Church Yard of Presteign* [sic] in emulation of Thomas Gray's 1750 work, he aimed to impress on 'young females in the same sphere of life in which poor Mary Morgan moved' the 'dreadful consequences a single deviation from the path of virtue may ultimately lead to.' This was in the belief that young girls would be mindful that one episode of sexual intercourse could, and probably would, lead directly to the gallows. The poetry is indifferent (Mary was 'sweet as the sunshine sparkling on the stream') but serves to illustrate the invidious position of women. They had little or no power over their own lives, about a third of a man's earning power, and no position in the structure of society, yet they must also be super-angelic: good, submissive ('virtuous, lovely', 'meek as the daisy' in Horton's phrases) and, above all, careful to 'shun the poison of a flatt'ring tongue'. There was no mention of the responsibilities of the owner of the flatt'ring tongue nor of his role in pushing young women towards the waiting noose. The pamphlet attracted over 300 subscribers, no doubt many of them also congratulating themselves on their sensibility.

CHAPTER 5

Mary Bateman
York, 20 March 1809

*

Murder

In an age when the educated classes were increasingly fascinated by scientific discoveries and prided themselves on their own rational and enlightened religion, the case of Mary Bateman, the so-called Yorkshire Witch, exposed the persistence of deep superstition among the working classes, and some more educated people too, as well as their belief that magic charms could bring about changes in their lives. Mary Bateman was not a witch in the conventional sense, but presented herself as having access to the 'cunning folk', white witches who used herbal medicine and folk magic to help their sick or distressed neighbours or to cast spells on their enemies. She probably had no belief in supernatural powers, religious or otherwise, but was astute enough to take advantage of those who did.

Her career, during which she cynically gulled her neighbours into handing over goods and cash in return for the working of magic, found a strange parallel with that of the self-proclaimed prophetess Joanna Southcott, who convinced thousands that the 'seals' she issued would ensure their place in heaven and that she would bear a child who would be the Second Christ. Both Bateman and Southcott were derided for preying on the credibility of the poor and ignorant, but while Bateman was obviously criminal – and deadly – opinion on Southcott was divided and she retained supporters well beyond her death in 1814.

After Mary Bateman's execution, parts of her body were sold or given away by surgeons involved in her dissection and made into ghoulish relics. There is a certain irony that she should, in this way, have become something of a magic talisman herself.

On 20 October 1808 William Perigo and Mary Bateman arranged to meet by a bridge on the Leeds and Liverpool Canal. Perigo, a clothier in Leeds, had brought two men with him but they had agreed to stay out of sight while he and Mary talked. As she saw Perigo approach, Mary, holding a glass medicine bottle, turned towards the bankside and pretended to vomit. 'That bottle you gave me last night has made me ill,' she said. 'You have poisoned me.'

At this, Perigo's witnesses emerged and one of them laid a hand on Mary. One of them, William Duffield, the Chief Constable of Leeds, announced that he was arresting her on suspicion of the murder of William Perigo's wife Rebecca. Mary and her husband, who was tracked down and arrested too, soon found themselves in front of a magistrate, suspected of killing Rebecca Perigo. The pair were committed to York Castle. Mary's youngest child, who was still on the breast, went with her.

What had Mary done to attract the interest of the chief constable himself? Two years previously, 46-year-old Rebecca Perigo, who lived with her husband in Bramley, a few miles outside Leeds, had started to complain of discomfort, a fluttering in her chest, when she lay down. She consulted a doctor who, rather unhelpfully, told her she was under a spell. This diagnosis spurred her to follow up her niece Sarah Stead's recommendation of Mary Bateman, whose powers to help the afflicted get rid of 'evil spirits' were well known locally. The first thing, Mary said to Sarah, was to bring a petticoat or other item of underclothing. She needed this for Miss Blythe, who lived in Scarborough. Mary admitted that she herself had no special abilities but was a mere conduit for Miss Blythe's power to 'screw down' the 'evil wish' that was upon Rebecca. The Perigos did as requested and some time later, arranged to meet up with Mary at the Black Dog public house near Mary's home. She impressed them as a respectable and modest matron (she was married with three children), and her sympathetic face and soft manners put them at ease. They had no qualms about doing what she advised.

MARY BATEMAN

Miss Blythe then wrote to the Perigos with instructions for what they must do next: allow Mary to sew four guineas in notes and coins in silk bags into the corners of their bed and leave them in place for eighteen months. Then they were to give Mary four guineas, which she would send to Miss Blythe. They were forbidden to talk to anyone about this magic charm; if they did, it would be ruined. Over the ensuing months there were numerous further requests from Miss Blythe, for cash, large quantities of cheese and pieces of furniture. Mary promised that all the money they had paid to Miss Blythe would be returned eighteen months after they gave it over. As part of the charm, they were to burn Miss Blythe's letters in Mary's presence.

In early May 1808, as the due date for the first repayment to them approached, the Perigos were alarmed to receive a letter from Miss Blythe warning that they would soon become seriously ill but that they would survive if they ate honey to which Mary Bateman would add a magic potion. She would also give them six powders wrapped in paper, which they were to add to Yorkshire pudding, which they must eat for six days. They were not to call a doctor. That would break the spell.

For the first five days there were no problems and the Perigos thought nothing of the fact that the sixth powder was much larger than the others, so they added it to the batter and made the Yorkshire pudding as usual. It was only when they started vomiting that they knew Miss Blythe's prediction was coming true. They started eating the honey, but this only made it worse. Both of them were now seriously ill with headache, pain and diarrhoea, and their vomit was yellow and green froth. Rebecca had eaten more of the pudding than William and her tongue was so black and swollen she could hardly breathe.

On 24 May, as Rebecca deteriorated, William grew desperate and sent for Thomas Chorley, a local surgeon; while Chorley was on his way to them he received word that Rebecca had already died and turned back. The next day, he received a grieving William, who complained of numbness in his hands and feet, feverishness and pain in the bowels. Chorley immediately suspected poisoning and when William told him about Mary Bateman and Miss Blythe's instructions, he sent his assistant to retrieve the honeypot. Unfortunately, at this point the matter was dropped, possibly at William's request because he had upset Miss Blythe. Through Mary Bateman she had accused him of almost killing her by consulting a doctor and predicted that Rebecca would rise from the grave, stroke his right side and paralyze him. To appease her spirit, he should send her one of Rebecca's gowns. Still in Miss Blythe's thrall, he did so, but she replied that it was too shabby, and that he must send a better one, as well as the family Bible. Demands for money, food and coal followed.

Doubt about the existence of Miss Blythe was slow to take hold of William but eventually, because he was in deep debt, having given so much money to Mary for Miss Blythe, he made the decision to open the silk bags sewn into the bed, hoping to retrieve the money. He found that the notes were nothing but waste paper and the gold was pennies and farthings. When he confronted Mary, she said, 'But you have opened them too soon!' He knew then he had not opened them soon enough and threatened to come to her place with two or three friends to settle the matter, which was when she suggested they meet on the canal bank. He went to the police and the chief constable agreed to come with one of his constables to make the arrest.

Mary Bateman was born Mary Harker in about 1768 in Asenby, five miles from Thirsk in Yorkshire, to respectable farmers, one of at least four children. According to the anonymous author of *Extraordinary Life and Character of Mary Bateman, the Yorkshire Witch*, written after her execution, her criminal career started early. Aged five, she stole some Moroccan slippers, hid them in a barn for weeks, and then claimed to have found them. Having gone to school until the age of 12, she could read and write well. Then she moved to Thirsk to work as a domestic servant but repeatedly lost her place, each time leaving under a cloud of suspicion. At 19, she moved to York, again working as a servant, but was sacked for pilfering. Finally, she went to Leeds to apprentice to a dressmaker. Here, in 1792 she met John Bateman, a wheelwright, and within three weeks married him.

Her life of petty crime continued. She broke open a box belonging to her lodger and stole his watch, silver spoons and cash. She was forced to return them. She did the same with the next lodger. Then she tried a different tack, ordering silk from a linen draper and charging it to someone else. She even dunned her husband by sending him a letter telling him his father was dangerously ill and in his absence sold their furniture. In 1796, after a major fire at a Leeds flax factory which had resulted in ten deaths, she went from door to door claiming to be a nurse at the Leeds General Infirmary and asking for contributions of linen so that poor families could lay out the dead and for bandages for the injured. She pawned the sheets.

A pattern was emerging: she would identify an easy theft or fraud, pay back the money if caught, and when her *modus operandi* was no longer lucrative think of something new. By 1799, the Batemans were living in the Timble Bridge area of Leeds. It was during this period that Mary first conjured up an alter ego. She targeted vulnerable young women, telling them that her close acquaintance, Mrs Moore, could read the future and cast love spells for money. She then identified another type of victim, the insecure wife, and offered a new twist on her services, the 'screwing down' of 'evil wishes'. She convinced a Mrs Greenwood that she was in danger of suicide and told her that only Mrs Moore could prevent it. Then she informed her that Mr Greenwood, who was working away from home, had been arrested for a serious crime. Mrs Moore would be able to 'screw down' the men guarding him and prevent him from being killed or hanged, and Mrs Greenwood from destroying herself, if she had four pieces of gold, four pieces of leather, four pieces of blotting paper and four brass screws. Mrs Greenwood was a poor woman and when Mary suggested that she should borrow or steal the money she realized that it was a scam and saw her off.

The same happened with Barzillai Stead and his wife. Mary got him out of the way by convincing him that bailiffs were after him and that he should join the army (she got a part of his bounty). Then she told Mrs Stead, who was pregnant, that her husband had gone off with his pregnant mistress and that Mrs Moore could 'screw down' her rival if she provided three half crowns and two pieces of coal. The hapless woman sold all her possessions to pay Mrs Moore and, now with a baby, was driven to attempt suicide. When the Leeds Benevolent Society stepped in to support her, Mary appropriated most of the cash. She was exposed when she persuaded one of Mrs Stead's young female relations that the father of her unborn child would never return but that the son of the household where she would soon get a place would marry her, but only if she were childless, and gave her abortifacient herbs. After the young woman died (we don't know whether Mary's ministrations were responsible), Mrs Stead began to doubt her, but Mary swiftly paid her off and moved on.

There followed a series of petty robberies, cruel deceptions and bizarre fakery, including a religious miracle. Inspired by the activities of Joanna Southcott, the controversial self-styled religious prophetess who sold paper 'seals' guaranteeing a place in heaven as one of the elect, Mary pushed eggs bearing the words 'Crist [sic] is coming' into the cavity of a hen and charged visitors a penny each to see them emerging. She also attended one of Southcott's meetings in York, bought a seal and identified her next mark, an old widow woman, following her home. She knocked at her door and announced herself as a fellow follower of Southcott, emotionally blackmailing the old lady into offering her a bed for the night. That evening Mary insisted on cooking meat, pressing the woman to drink the leftover broth, and when she left, took her money and some of her clothes with her. When Mary's crimes became known, the widow became convinced that the broth Mary had urged her to take had been poisoned. After Mary's trial in 1808 newspapers alleged that she adopted other aspects of Southcott's campaign, affecting to have religious trances and visions and to be gifted with second sight.

This was Mary's practice period and although some of her schemes were unsuccessful she was always quick to adapt and improve them. It is impossible to know when she first killed for profit but by 1803 she had embarked on a scheme to appropriate the property of two Quaker sisters, the Misses Kitchin, who ran a linen shop near St Peter's Square in Quarry Hill, Leeds. She ingratiated herself by helping out in the shop, and soon the sisters were acquainted with the existence of the

MARY BATEMAN

mysterious Mrs Moore and her powers. After Mary gave them medicines from a 'country doctor' they fell ill and within a week one of them was dead. Their distressed mother arrived from Wakefield but before long both she and the other sister also died. Neighbours assumed, or were persuaded by Mary, that they had contracted cholera and as a result, their property was shut up for weeks. When it was eventually opened, it was discovered to be empty and the accounts were missing.

The sisters were probably the last victims of Mrs Moore. In her place, Mary brought in Miss Blythe, who would remove an 'evil wish' for five guineas. When the Batemans moved to Meadow Lane in 1807 and later to Water Lane, Mary targeted the families of her poor and illiterate neighbours. Each time, she identified a vulnerability, usually a worry about a child or grandchild. In order to secure their health and wellbeing, to keep them from drowning or from the gallows, all Mary's victims had to do was provide cash. Then she would write to Miss Blythe for them and forward the cash.

She worked several scams at once. While she was managing the Perigos, she was also playing another family. She told Mrs Snowden that she could prevent her daughter becoming a prostitute by sewing her husband's silver watch and twelve guineas into the bed, with Mary's help of course, and then move to Bradford. At Miss Blythe's urging, they took the bed but left the furniture, and the key to their home, with Mary. When the Snowdens heard that Mary had been arrested for the murder of Rebecca Perigo, they returned to find all their possessions gone.

Despite plenty of evidence of Mary Bateman's wrongdoing, building the case for murder was not easy. As *The Leeds Intelligencer* put it:

> *against sifting at all into this matter there are the strongest bars: the length of time since the woman's [Rebecca Perigo's] decease; the total want of medical deposition how she came by her death; in short almost everything of proof is wanting but that she did die, for the evidence of her husband can only be considered as presumptive.*

Nevertheless Mary Bateman was tried at York Castle on Friday, 17 March 1809 in front of Judge Simon Le Blanc and many observers. The courtroom was packed and newspapers reported that inns and hotels were 'full and crowded' with visitors who had come to the city specifically to see the trial. By now the case against Mary's husband John had been dropped for lack of evidence. Most of the testimony against her came from William Perigo who stood in the witness box for over four hours. An 11-year-old boy told the court that he and Mary's son had gone to a chemist to get fourpence worth of arsenic on her behalf but had been refused. William Duffield described how he had arrested Rebecca at the canalside and found a bottle on her, later confirmed to contain arsenic. The surgeon Thomas Chorley described his analysis of the honey, which he found to contain corrosive sublimate of mercury. He had made pills out of it and given them to a dog, which died.

Mary was unrepresented and after she made her defence, which was simply to deny the crime, the judge summed up, instructing the jury to consider whether she had contrived 'the means to induce the deceased to take [the poison]' for, of course, she was not there when the Perigos ate the Yorkshire pudding and the honey and did not administer it herself. The jury conferred for 'a moment' and returned a guilty verdict. When the judge passed sentence on her, including the order that her body be dissected, she immediately 'pleaded her belly', that is she declared herself to be pregnant. As the judge ordered the sheriff to assemble a jury of matrons, the women in the court hurried to leave – they wanted nothing to do with the 'witch'. Le Blanc ordered the doors be locked.

A jury of matrons, consisting of twelve married women who had given birth, would examine the prisoner in private and produce a verdict on the pregnancy. To be temporarily reprieved, a capitally-convicted woman had to be 'quick with child', that is, the child had to have moved, usually in the fifteenth or sixteenth week of pregnancy. To be merely pregnant was not enough. By the 1830s the role of the jury of matrons was beginning to lapse in favour of doctors and surgeons, who were horrified at the prospect of making a mistake over a pregnancy verdict, as indeed were judges (see Chapter 7). In 1843 the British Medical Association passed a resolution condemning the law that allowed a distinction between 'with child' and 'quick with child'. Although by the end of the 1830s it was standard practice to pardon or transport women who had successfully pleaded their belly and had subsequently given birth it was not until 1931 that the Sentence of Death (Expectant Mothers) Act was passed, which stipulated that a woman capitally convicted who was found to be pregnant on medical evidence must be sentenced to life imprisonment rather than hanged.

The reluctant jury of matrons examined Mary. They returned to court saying that she was neither quick with child nor even pregnant and she was remanded back to York Castle to await her execution.

After the trial, on the Saturday and Sunday before her death on Monday, 20 March, Mary was reported to have behaved 'with decorum' and attended services in the chapel, but showed no real repentance and continued to deny murder, conceding only that she had been involved in fraud. It seems that in her last hours she could not abandon her habits: she was alleged to have told the fortune of one of her female attendants and persuaded a fellow prisoner to sew a guinea into her stays in order to ensure her sweetheart visited.

Her husband refused to visit. One of the astonishing aspects of Mary's life was her relationship with this man who seemed to tolerate her behaviour, even if he did not become directly involved in her more heinous crimes. Although the prosecution against John Bateman was not pursued, he certainly knew that some of the items Mary appropriated from her victims were stolen. He collected a bedstead left at a public house to be forwarded to Miss Blythe, took it home and told people he had bought it. It is likely that he was the perfect front for her – he was 'sober and industrious', a steady worker who had been employed in the same business for more than fifteen years – and she was able to manipulate him as successfully as she had others.

On the morning of Mary's execution, a crowd of over 5,000 gathered in front of York Castle. Mary was taken from her cell, leaving her sleeping baby ('without a pang!' according to *The Leeds*

Intelligencer), pinioned and marched in process through the gate and out to the New Drop, where the hangman was waiting for her and for Joseph Brown, another poisoner. The atmosphere was tense, the audience subdued. She pleaded for mercy and declared herself innocent before the lever was pulled and her life ended.

The two bodies were left for the usual hour, cut down and sent to Dr William Hey at Leeds General Infirmary for public dissection. It was Mary's that attracted most attention. On the first day, it was laid out to be viewed by the public (over 24,000 people paid threepence each to see it) and later by medical students (each paying ten shillings and sixpence), who witnessed the first phase of the dissection. On day two, the educated elite or professionals of the town (men only) came to see the spectacle and were charged five guineas, with ladies attending in the evening to observe the dissection of an eye. This was deemed suitable for their genteel sensibilities – it was not proper for them to see naked body parts. On the final day, the medical men and their apprentices watched the full-scale dissection, which concluded with a complete dismemberment of the body. *The Leeds Intelligencer* reported that this event afforded 'much edifying and useful information to a very numerous and respectable auditory' and that Mary's plea of pregnancy was entirely unfounded. In all, the dissection raised over £80.

The Chester Courant alleged that Mary was a 'follower of the principles of Joanna [Southcott]' and that, like Southcott, her claims were an imposture. Reports of the execution alleged that many Southcott followers attended the execution. 'The more simple part... really imagined that some miracle would be worked in her favour, and that she would fly off the scaffold in a cloud, or on a broom, and be saved by the interposition of Heaven.' For Joanna Southcott herself, the association in the public mind of her predictions of the Second Coming and a Heaven on Earth with Mary Bateman's outlandish promises was a deep embarrassment. Her supporters were forced into print in order to deny allegations that Mary was a follower and to reassert the sincerity of Southcott's Divine Mission.

MARY BATEMAN

Postmortem punishment of the bodies of murderers was meant to obliterate them, but Mary Bateman's did not disappear entirely. Her skeleton was cleaned and wired up for use in anatomy classes at the infirmary and until recently was exhibited at the Thackray Medical Museum in Leeds. Her body parts were highly prized. The corpses of criminals were believed by some to have special healing powers. When Henry Hollings was hanged in 1814 at Newgate for the murder of his stepdaughter, three women asked to receive a touch from 'the dead man's hand', which was believed to remove birthmarks and wens, and after the execution of Ann Norris at Newgate in 1821 men rubbed their necks and faces with her hand. Some of those who filed past Mary Bateman's body in Leeds Surgeons' Hall touched it 'to prevent her terrific interference with their nocturnal dreams', as *The Leeds Intelligencer* put it. The educated classes, even if they did not subscribe to this superstition, still coveted parts of her body as keepsakes. Thomas Chorley, who had given evidence at the trial, took part in the dissection and afterwards gave some of Mary's 'tanned' skin to William Elmhirst, the Deputy Lieutenant for the West Riding of Yorkshire, who made it into a folding cup and commissioned the binding of books in her 'leather'. Another gentleman received her pickled tongue.

CHAPTER 6

Eliza Ross
London, 9 January 1832

*

Murder

In November 1818, Mary Redmond, a poor Irishwoman, appeared before magistrate Joshua Jonathan Smith, accused of threatening to kill Dr Chumley at Guy's Hospital, London. She had been enraged that the doctor had, without her permission, autopsied the body of her young son, who had died of fever at the hospital. Despite Chumley's protests that 'the examination of the human body is attended with admirable effects known only to medical men,' the magistrate told him that 'this thing ought not have been done' and dismissed the case against Mary, to the vociferous approval of her supporters.

Strong beliefs persisted about the need for the body to remain whole in order to reach Paradise on Resurrection Day, despite there being no Christian spiritual teaching, either Catholic or Protestant, that required it. Among the poor there was, in addition, a sense that the least they were entitled to was a 'decent burial', that is, in one piece. Those at the bottom of the heap, for whom the destruction of the body was a final indignity in a life full of them, were especially horrified by the activities of curious doctors keen to take a knife to their deceased loved ones and also by the so-called resurrection men, who dug up or otherwise acquired bodies to supply the voracious needs of the rapidly-expanding anatomy schools.

Eliza Ross was the last person convicted of 'burking', the murder of a person in order to sell their body to surgeons. Her victim's body was never found. It was probably annihilated by anatomists, as was

ELIZA ROSS

Eliza's own body, which was destroyed as a postmortem punishment. She was among the last to suffer this fate, as soon after her execution new laws were put in place to provide anatomy schools with the bodies abandoned in poorhouses and infirmaries, their relatives and friends unknown or too poor to afford funerals.

A report on the execution on 9 January 1832 of 33-year-old Eliza Ross in *The Morning Advertiser* opened with her description as a 'large, raw-boned coarse-featured Irishwoman' and claimed that she sometimes worked as a porter 'for which her masculine proportions and strength well qualified her' and that by using her 'superior size and strength' she was able to reduce her partner, 50-year-old Edward Cook, to subjection. According to the paper, she also ran a sideline in cudgeling cats to death (for which she had previously been prosecuted) and decoying children in order to steal their clothes.

The physical form of criminals was of intense interest to the public; during this period and beyond, it was believed to have a direct bearing on the degree of their wickedness. Because women were relatively rarely convicted of murder, and because they were so often judged and ranked on appearance in the normal course of life, their looks gave rise to the most comment and often led to a discussion of their traits and characteristics. If a woman behaved 'like a man' she was automatically perceived to be more masculine than other women and any unusual physical characteristics were shoehorned in to fit the theory. The face of Kezia Westcombe, who in 1829 was convicted with her lover of the poisoning murder of her husband, was 'marked with all the outward signs of a ferocious disposition' according to *The Western Times*, which added that 'she had extraordinary high cheek bones, a sharp-pointed, indented nose, dark hazel eyes, and large black eye-brows. In stature she was about 5ft. 3in. high, her figure was good, and her general appearance partook of what she really was, a strong, robust, vicious, cruel woman.'

In December 1831 Eliza Ross and Edward Cook were charged with the murder of 84-year-old Caroline Walsh, a street seller of sewing threads, tapes and laces, who was lodging with them at their garret at Goodman's Yard, Whitechapel on the night of 19 August.

WOMEN AND THE GALLOWS 1797–1837

According to Walsh's devoted granddaughter Ann Bruton, Walsh was a 'very tall, hearty woman' in excellent health. When Ann attempted to visit her grandmother at the lodgings, by arrangement, the day after she moved in, Eliza told her that she had just missed her. Ann noticed a bundle of her grandmother's possessions in the corner of the room. Eliza then persuaded Ann to stand her for some gin, so they departed for a public house, where Ann expressed puzzlement that her grandmother had decided to go out when she knew she would be stopping by. 'You seem to think from what you say, that we have murdered the woman... From what you seem to say, you think we have destroyed her at our place,' said Eliza. She invited Ann home to have something to eat and urged her to stay the night. Wisely, as it turned out, Ann refused.

Ann and her sister Lydia Basey made tireless enquiries at workhouses and hospitals looking for their grandmother but there was no sign of her. Finally, they went to the police, whose investigations revealed that within days of Caroline Walsh going missing Eliza Ross had sold her clothes and stock of sewing notions to second-hand dealers at Rag Fair in the East End.

Eliza and Edward were arrested, along with their 12-year-old son, also called Edward. At their committal by the magistrate at Lambeth Police Office on 23 December, Eliza said, 'I am glad we have not to come up again, for we run the risk of being torn to pieces by the mob and gang brought to the office by some of the witnesses.' The magistrate assured her she would be protected. Public awareness of burking was high; three years previously, William Hare and William Burke, whose name had been adopted to describe the practice of murdering in order to supply fresh bodies for sale to surgeons, had committed at least sixteen murders in Edinburgh. They sold the bodies of their victims to Dr Robert Knox for his dissection lectures. Burke was executed. More recently, the horrific crimes of the so-called London burkers had hit the headlines. Less than three weeks before Eliza Ross and Edward Cook senior were committed for trial, John Bishop and Thomas Williams (aka Head), members of a gang of resurrection men, were executed at Newgate for the murder of 14-year-old Carlo Ferrari, who became known as the Italian Boy. A crowd of 30,000 watched them die. Bishop and Williams had kidnapped and killed Ferrari and then tried to sell his body to surgeons at King's College Anatomy School in the Strand, where doubts were immediately raised because it showed no signs of ever having been buried. Ferrari was not the only victim and before their execution Bishop and Williams confessed to murdering more than sixty others.

On 5 January, Edward Cook junior gave evidence at the Old Bailey at the trial of his parents for the murder of Caroline Walsh – but his account put the weight of blame firmly, and only, on his mother. He told the court that he had watched as she suffocated the drowsy or sleeping Caroline Walsh (he implied that the cup of coffee Eliza gave her had been drugged) by putting her hand over her mouth and pressing on her chest. His father, he said, had stuck his head out of the window while it was done and had not seen the murder or taken part. Then Eliza had lifted the body off the bed and carried it downstairs. The following day young Edward found a sack in the cellar with hair poking out of the top; in the evening, from the window of the garret, he saw his mother carrying the sack across her shoulders through the yard. He said she told him she had taken it to either Guy's or the London Hospital, he couldn't remember which. Eliza Ross was found guilty and sentenced to death and dissection. Edward Cook senior was acquitted but retained in custody as he was to be charged with other offences.

Was there a miscarriage of justice? Did Eliza, unassisted, really heft a 'very tall, hearty' woman over her shoulder in a sack? We cannot know for sure. It is troubling that apart from young Edward's account, there was nothing to show that Caroline Walsh was dead or that Eliza had killed her. There is also the possibility that Edward Cook senior, far from being henpecked, as the newspapers alleged, was himself physically intimidating. In the account Ann Bruton gave to the court, she said she saw 'red marks' around Eliza's face and that Eliza had told her that her husband 'had beat her most unmercifully' after they went out for gin together. For her own part, Eliza loudly protested her innocence until the very end. As she was being pinioned at Newgate prior to her execution, she said, 'I declare before God and man that I am innocent. Oh, why did I come to this country [from Ireland] to be butchered?.... They have persecuted my poor boy to forswear himself, and give false evidence against me.' She told the Reverend Cotton, the Ordinary of Newgate, that she had committed many crimes, but not this one.

Meanwhile, outside in the street, a large crowd had gathered. They certainly believed that Eliza was guilty. When she mounted the scaffold and became visible to them a 'deafening yell and shout' burst out and when she was 'turned off' a cheer went up. Her body was left to dangle for the usual hour, after which it was stripped and carted off to the College of Surgeons for dissection. The hangman, William Calcraft, was entitled to her clothes as part of his payment.

A month after Eliza Ross's death, in an unsubtle challenge to the famous *emigrée* and wax modeller Madame Tussaud, the proprietor of Simmons's Waxworks in Finsbury Square, London published an advertisement in the newspapers in which he offered to pay fifty guineas if she could produce a better likeness of Bishop and Williams, the burkers of the Italian Boy, and of Eliza Ross, the female burker. He boasted that his own wax figures were dressed in the very clothes in which the murderers were executed. He must have bought them from Calcraft, who had executed them all.

Females were of particular interest to anatomists. Doctors rarely had access to the live bodies of female patients (decorum demanded that they performed examinations 'blind', under the bedclothes) so Eliza's freshly dead corpse was a rare opportunity. Only seven bodies of female murderers were received by the College of Surgeons between 1800 and 1832. One of them was 24-year-old Catherine Welch, 'a fine young woman of stout and particularly healthy appearance', who was accused of murdering her six-week-old son in 1828. Fulham surgeon Joseph Holmes gave evidence at her trial:

> *I had seen the prisoner at the workhouse at Fulham...the first thing I asked her was, if she had been suckling a child lately. She said she had not for two months. I asked her then to let me*

ELIZA ROSS

look at her breasts. She showed me her breasts – I pressed on both her breasts and milk spurted out of both of them.

When Catherine's body reached the college, Holmes extracted milk from those breasts and then gifted her remains to Charles Bell, who ran a West End anatomy school. Bell amputated the breasts and sent them back to the Hunterian Museum for display. The butchering of Catherine's body was an example of the astonishing emotional distance surgeons were capable of in their pursuit of the 'admirable effects known only to medical men'.

Eliza Ross's body was initially given to William Clift, the chief dissector at the college. Although not a surgeon himself he had been an assistant to the surgeon and anatomist John Hunter and was highly skilled. He was also an accomplished artist and drew remarkable sketches of the bodies on the dissecting table. There exists in the archive of the Royal College of Surgeons a collection of his fine illustrations of executed subjects, including those of Bishop and Williams and of Eliza Ross. The pre-dissection illustration shows not only the piercings in her ears but also the mark the rope had made on her neck. Overall, the impression is of a person who looked older than her 33 years but who was not especially muscular or likely to possess masculine strength.

Before Clift started the dissection, he would have had to make sure that Eliza was fully deceased. Just as the condemned were terrified by the prospect of being dissected alive, surgeons were horrified at the thought of anatomizing a live body and performed tests to ensure that the subject was well and truly dead. Clift described inserting needles into the eyes of the corpse of Martin Hogan in 1814, but there were less gruesome methods such as putting a hot wet cloth on the face and tracing a swan's feather along the neck. If there were no signs of life, a small cut was made at the breastbone so that the surgeon could observe the heart and lungs. If blood was still flowing, he would wait until life signs stopped.

Eliza Ross's body was amongst the last dissected as postmortem punishment. By the time she was hanged, the campaign against the dissection of murderers was well under way. The number of corpses provided by this channel was tiny compared to the demand for bodies by the medical profession. In 1828 it was estimated that 1,500 bodies a year were needed to supply 500 medical students. The shortfall was made up of unclaimed bodies from workhouses and infirmaries, and from bodysnatchers. The authorities recognized that the lack of bodies was actively encouraging burking and the activities of resurrection men and that the punishment of murderers' bodies after death did nothing to discourage murder. It merely increased sympathy for the hanged. In future, murderers would be buried within the grounds of the gaols where they were killed, their remains still out of reach of their friends and families but no longer obliterated in the name of science.

Ten days after the execution of Bishop and Williams, the MP Henry Warburton introduced the Anatomy Bill, which was given Royal assent in August 1832. From now on, it was not murder that would bring bodies to the surgeons but poverty. That led to a different set of moral questions and, of course, objections.

After his acquittal, Edward Cook senior was accused of being an accessory before the fact, but charges were eventually dropped and he was released. He protested his innocence to any and everyone, blaming schoolmasters and police officers for tricking or bribing his son into giving false evidence at the trial. The authorities at Whitechapel workhouse, who now had care of the boy, wanted to close the issue by testing Edward Cook junior's truthfulness, so they organized a meeting between father and son. Despite his father's imprecations, Edward junior stuck rigidly to the evidence he gave in court ('I said it because it was true') and denied that he had been pressurized in any way. He managed to maintain his sangfroid until his father took out a small packet and handed it to him saying, 'There, there is your poor mother's hair; your poor mother...your poor murdered mother', but he still refused to retract.

The parish authorities arranged for Edward Cook to be placed in a charitable institution, given a year of education and then sent to sea. He was advised to change his name.

CHAPTER 7

Catherine Frarey and Frances Billing
Norwich, 10 August 1835

*

Sophia Edney
Ilchester, 14 April 1836

*

Murder

Until divorce became widely and cheaply available, the options for ending a marriage were limited. In the period under discussion, an annulment was sometimes used to dissolve a union, but that had problems, not least of which was that it rendered the woman a concubine and her children illegitimate. A man could sue his wife's lover (if there was one) for 'criminal conversation' (effectively, damage to his property) and then apply for a church divorce ('separation from bed and board'). Then he could petition parliament for a bill of divorce. But divorce was both reputation-shredding and prohibitively expensive, and therefore an option only for people of means.

Of course, a woman, rich or not, could simply run away from home. However, she could be coerced into returning as her husband was entitled to send a sheriff to track her down. Even if she managed to stand her ground, she lost any claim to maintenance and had no rights whatsoever to her children.

For many women, death, however achieved, was the only respectable end to a troubled union.

In 1809 Mary Bateman was convicted of poisoning with arsenic without any scientific evidence at all and in 1815 Eliza Fenning was found guilty of the attempted murder of the Turner family in Chancery Lane, partly on the strength of John Marshall's spurious scientific experiments. By the early 1830s courts required much more sophisticated tests for arsenic and juries rejected evidence they did not consider reliable. In 1832 chemist James Marsh's analytical evidence failed to convince the jury that John Bodle had poisoned his grandfather and Bodle, who was indeed guilty, escaped justice. Marsh went back to the lab determined to develop an infallible test.

Arsenic, a metal, is not toxic. It is the compound arsenic trioxide, or 'white arsenic', that was used widely to poison rats, and a substantial number of people. In minute doses it had other uses, to treat menstrual pain, worms, fevers, typhus and asthma, although its efficacy was never scientifically proved. An abundant byproduct of the iron smelting process, white arsenic was cheap, widely available and tasteless, which made it easy to disguise in food. It was only once it was ingested and absorbed into the bloodstream through the stomach and oesophagus, usually thirty minutes to two hours after being taken, that the victim showed signs of illness. The symptoms were dramatic: retching, nausea, vomiting, diarrhoea and dreadful pain. There was no antidote. A manual from 1810 recommended butter and milk 'taken in large quantities' but that was probably useless. Other treatments included vinegar, linseed, sugar water and egg whites, bleeding or leeches. Recovery was possible when very small amounts were involved, as the Turner family and Eliza Fenning found in 1815, although their doctor, John Marshall, congratulated himself that it was his remedies that had saved their lives (see Chapter 1). Usually, perhaps after a day or so but sometimes longer, arsenic damaged the heart, and death followed. It was a hideous way to die.

In 1834 a sensational arsenic poisoning case hit the headlines. Penelope Bickle, 54, was tried at Exeter Assizes for murdering her husband John, who died in agony after a prolonged illness suddenly worsened. She was known to have bought arsenic for killing rats and later told her daughter that she had mislaid it. After a surgeon testified that none of the tests normally used was infallible, the jury deliberated for a quarter of an hour and returned a verdict of not guilty.

CATHERINE FRAREY, FRANCES BILLING, SOPHIA EDNEY

The following year a spate of poisoning deaths in Burnham Westgate in north Norfolk came to light. A baby, the husband of one woman and the wife of the lover of another had died in short order. The murders had some unusual features: there were two alleged perpetrators, both of them female, who were friends and neighbours; and, to the astonishment of the locals, not only was it the second poisoning case in a tiny geographical area it was also the second to have involved Hannah Shorten, the 'cunning woman' whose spells involved the burning of arsenic.

Burnham Westgate, these days known as Burnham Market, is now a bijou holiday retreat referred to only half jokingly as 'Little Chelsea'. Two centuries ago, it was a small village with a church, a doctor and a few shops where most of the inhabitants were poor people living as steadily and respectably as they could without the benefit of education. The church played an important part in their lives, as a place for baptisms, marriages and burials. Nevertheless, belief in magic, charms and spells persisted.

In 1835 Frances (Fanny) Billing, a 46-year-old washerwoman, her husband James, an agricultural labourer, and eight children lived at one end of a terrace of three cottages in North Street. Fanny had once had a good reputation as a steady sort, a churchgoer who regularly took communion, but she had recently started an affair with her neighbour, Peter Taylor, who lived with his wife Mary in the middle cottage. Taylor had worked as a journeyman shoemaker but he suffered from bad health and was now casually employed as a barber, pub waiter and singer. Mary was a shoebinder. The Taylors had no children. The relationship between Fanny Billing and Peter Taylor soon became the subject of village gossip. Fanny's husband became aware of it and beat them both. Fanny later went to the local Petty Sessions complaining of his abuse and had him bound over to keep the peace. She denied that there was any wrongdoing with Peter Taylor.

Catherine (Kate) Frarey, a 40-year-old childminder, and her husband Robert, 33, who had once been a fisherman and was now an agricultural labourer, and their three children, all under the age of eight, were in rooms above Thomas Lake's carpenter shop at the other end of the terrace. Like Fanny, Kate had once had a good name but there were rumours about her relationship with a Mr Gridley. She was known to believe in fortune-telling and charms and to associate with Hannah Shorten, a 'witch'.

One of Kate's infant charges was Harriet Southgate, whose unmarried mother Elizabeth worked on a farm. On 21 February, Elizabeth received a message that Harriet was very ill. She rushed to North Street to find the baby in great distress and Kate's husband Robert, who had been ill for two weeks with an inflammation of the stomach, in bed, groaning in agony. Elizabeth gave her child warm water sweetened with sugar but she died in her arms in the early hours of the following morning.

The day after little Harriet's funeral Elizabeth visited the Frareys to see how Robert was faring. While she was there, Fanny Billing came in with a jug of porter and offered her some in a teacup but when Elizabeth spotted white sediment in the bottom ('like undissolved lump sugar') she handed it back. Fanny gave it instead to Robert Frarey, telling him, 'Drink it up. It will do you good.' Later Elizabeth found Robert retching into a basin, begging her to hold his head for him. Two days later, he could no longer speak, and on 27 February he died and was buried soon afterwards in St Mary's churchyard in Burnham Westgate.

Gossip must have started immediately. On a trip to Wells-Next-the-Sea with Kate Frarey, Elizabeth Southgate brought up the subject of Robert's demise:

'If I were you, Mrs Frarey, I would have my husband taken up [disinterred] and examined, to shut the world's mouth.'

'Oh, no,' replied Kate, 'I should not like it. Would you?'

'Yes, Mrs Frarey, I would like it, for it will be a check on you and your children after you.'

During the period when Robert was ill, Kate, accompanied by Hannah Shorten, bought arsenic from Mr Nash, the chemist in Burnham Westgate. Barely a week after Robert was put in the ground, Fanny Billing persuaded a neighbour to accompany her to buy more arsenic, saying it was for a villager called Mrs Webster (who later denied all knowledge). Inspired by the successful dispatch of Robert, Fanny and

CATHERINE FRAREY, FRANCES BILLING, SOPHIA EDNEY

Kate had fixed on a new victim: Mary Taylor, Fanny's lover's wife.

With the arsenic bought, all that was needed was opportunity. On 12 March, while Mary Taylor was out at work, Fanny or Kate or Mary's husband Peter poisoned the dumplings and gravy she had left out for the evening's supper. When Mary fell ill, she had the misfortune to be nursed by Kate. People came and went, and neither Fanny nor Kate seem to have been careful in what they did or said. William Powell, the village blacksmith, stopped by to get a haircut and shave from Peter Taylor. He saw Kate bring in a bowl of gruel and, using the tip of a knife, add to it what looked like powdered sugar. Phoebe Taylor, married to Peter Taylor's brother, visited to tend to Mary and care for Peter. She saw Fanny take a paper out of her pocket and pour its contents into a teacup and then throw the paper in the fire. Eventually, with Mary suffering convulsive fits, Phoebe Taylor and Kate Frarey summoned a doctor. By now Mary's pulse was feeble and she died while he was in the house.

This was the third death in the terrace within a month. The doctor alerted the coroner, and Mary Taylor's body was opened in her own kitchen and her stomach taken to a nearby pharmacist, where it was pronounced to be riddled with arsenic. Next it was taken to Norwich where more tests were conducted by surgeon Richard Griffin, who also confirmed arsenic. Soon after, James Billing, in an unguarded moment, accepted a cup of tea from his wife. He became very ill, but recovered.

Fanny Billing was arrested on 18 March and taken to Walsingham Gaol. Kate Frarey then asked Fanny's sons to take her to the town of Salle in order to consult another 'witch' (not Hannah Shorten this time), telling them that she needed a spell to ensure that the gaoler at Walsingham would not question Fanny. The indiscreet comments did not stop. When Peter Taylor was arrested, Kate shouted out to him, 'There you go, Peter, hold your own, and they can't hurt you.' She could not have been more wrong.

Kate Frarey and Hannah Shorten were arrested and Robert Frarey's and Harriet Southgate's graves opened. Peter Taylor's house was searched and he was taken into custody. All three suspects, Fanny, Kate and Peter were committed for trial at the Lent Assizes at Norwich but charges against Hannah Shorten were dropped and after a grand jury chose to throw out Peter Taylor's indictment as an accessory before the fact, he was released. No one was charged with baby Harriet's murder as no discernible traces of arsenic were found in her body.

On 17 August, in a packed courtroom, a jury returned guilty verdicts against Kate and Fanny for the murders of Robert Frarey and Mary Taylor. Judge William Bolland declared that poison 'was one of the worst acts that can be resorted to, because it is impossible to be guarded against such a determination, which is but too often carried into effect, when no one is present to observe it but the eye of God'. As he condemned the two women to death, Bolland referred to their morals. They had pursued a 'profligate, vicious and abandoned course of life' full of 'guilty lusts'. He urged them towards repentance and sincere contrition. Kate, often agitated during the trial, went into 'strong hysterics' and her shrieks could be heard after she was removed from court. Fanny showed no emotion.

The women's execution in Norwich on 10 August attracted vast crowds from the surrounding villages. All routes leading to the castle were packed with 'persons of various ages and of both sexes (the weaker vessels being the more numerous)'. At noon the great gates opened and the Reverend James Brown emerged, prayer book in hand, followed by the 'two unfortunate beings', Kate dressed in mourning for her husband and Fanny in 'coloured clothes', white handkerchiefs covering their faces. The apparatus had been moved to the upper end of the bridge, which had the effect of both reducing the distance the women would have to walk to the gallows and enabling more people to see them die. Fanny walked with 'a firm step' but Kate was on the point of fainting and had to be carried up the steps of the scaffold. The executioner William Calcraft was in attendance. 'It was a sight which no one but an alien to humanity could look on unmoved,' reported *The Norfolk Chronicle*. The ropes were adjusted and, hooded and holding each other by the hand, the friends were 'launched into eternity'. The crowd fell silent. Kate was 'much convulsed' but Fanny's neck broke and she suffered less.

Amongst the spectators, someone recognized Peter Taylor. The crowd turned on him and he fled, only just managing to make it to his home village of Whissonsett. He was not safe there, however. Before their executions, the women had implicated him in their fulsome confessions. The investigation was reopened and on 29 August, scarcely three weeks after Kate and Fanny were executed, he was committed for trial as an accessory before the fact to his wife's murder. He was found guilty and on 23 April the following year, insisting on his innocence to the last and in 'a state of the greatest prostration of strength, both mental and corporeal', he was hanged at Norwich Castle.

Serial poisoning is generally a solitary crime, characterized by subterfuge and secret triumph over the victims. It is not often conducted in pairs or trios, which makes Kate Frarey and Fanny Billing (with or without Peter Taylor) so unusual. Were they emboldened by the acquittal of Penelope Bickle who was accused of poisoning her husband the year before their murdering spree started? Even if they were not, they must have known of the conviction three years previously of Mary Wright for the arsenic murder of her husband in the village of Wighton, less than eight miles from Burnham Westgate.

Mary Ann Darby was born in Wighton in 1803. At 26 she married William Wright, a 34-year-old teamerman (he worked with farm horses), and together they set up home with Mary's father Richard, a widowed agricultural labourer. Mary was so badly affected by the loss of a three-year-old son that she was 'never in her right mind' afterwards, according to a neighbour. When she started behaving oddly, setting fire to a tablecloth and chairs, the villagers agreed amongst themselves that madness ran in the family. Mary's now-deceased mother had spent eighteen months in a lunatic asylum.

The Wrights were unhappy in their marriage, or at least Mary was. She started exhibiting signs of extreme jealousy concerning William. After she was arrested, magistrates heard that she had made previous attempts on his life and on her own and that she had paid for the services of the 'witch' Hannah Shorten, who had cast spells for her during which she burned arsenic with salt.

Mary appears to have planned the murder of her husband carefully.

She persuaded a young girl called Sarah Hastings to walk with her to Wells, telling her on the way that the local rat-catcher had advised her to get arsenic. She also asked Sarah how much arsenic she thought it would take to kill a person. While she was in Wells, Mary also purchased currants and told Sarah she was going to make cakes.

A few days later, on 1 December, William rose early. His employer had asked him to take a load of grain to Cley, ten miles away. Mary gave him the cakes for the journey and her father Richard Darby helped him prepare the waggon and horses, after which the two of them went to a public house for beer. They also ate the cakes. Richard went home and William travelled on towards Cley with William Hales, another farm worker. At first William Wright seemed fine but later became so ill that there was no question of returning home. Instead, William Hales took the team back to Wighton and William Wright was carried to a public house where Charles Buck, a local surgeon, examined him. Mary was sent for. William died on Sunday night. As was often the case with arsenic, cholera was blamed; the villagers were terrified and kept away. There were more shocks for them, and especially for Mary when she returned to Wighton. Her father, who had shown similar symptoms, had died. Both men were buried in the graveyard at Wighton Church on 4 December.

It was a chance remark by Sarah Hastings, that Mary had recently bought arsenic, that led to the suspicion of foul play. Four days after the funerals, the bodies of William Wright and Richard Darby were exhumed and autopsied by Charles Buck in the chancel of Wighton Church; the stomachs were sent to Mr Bell, a chemist at Wells, who performed four separate tests before he was confident that the men had consumed arsenic.

Mary was committed to Walsingham Gaol for trial at the Lent Assizes, where she was prosecuted for the murder of her husband only, possibly because it was accepted that she had not intended the death of her father. She had already confessed, but justice demanded a full hearing, so at her trial before Judge William Bolland, who later tried Fanny Billing and Kate Frarey, she pleaded not guilty. Witnesses from Wighton testified to William Wright's sudden illness and Sarah

CATHERINE FRAREY, FRANCES BILLING, SOPHIA EDNEY

Hastings told the court about Mary's expedition to buy arsenic; Charles Buck described William's death and Mr Bell his chemical tests. Mr Crosse, a surgeon from Norwich, giving evidence on Mary's mental state, declared that 'child bearing is apt to produce insanity [but] insanity from child bearing is mostly temporary.'

Mary was found guilty and Judge Bolland sentenced her to death. She had an 'hysteric fit' in court after which she declared she was pregnant. The judge followed standard procedure to determine whether she was telling the truth and hastily assembled the twelve women required for a jury of matrons to examine her. After an hour they returned to court to declare that she was not pregnant. Perhaps prompted by Mary's vehemence, Bolland ignored them and then asked the opinion of three 'eminent *accoucheurs*' [man-midwives], including Mr Crosse, who declared that Mary was indeed 'quick with child'.

Five months later, in Norwich Castle, she gave birth to a healthy girl, Elizabeth. Mary's execution was scheduled for 17 August but at some point before this date her sentence was commuted to transportation for life. She never reached Australia, however, dying in Norwich Castle in November, the cause of death determined to be 'the visitation of God'. She was buried at the Church of St Michael at Thorn in Norfolk. The fate of her baby is unknown.

'In the black catalogue of human crimes, none manifested so much depravity as that of poisoning. It was one of those of which the commission was most easy and the prevention most difficult,' said prosecution barrister John Hardy, addressing the court at the trial of 'sorceress' Mary Bateman in 1809. Poisoning, with all its connotations of simmering resentment and secret planning, was long associated with women, especially domestic servants and wives. The kitchen was the one area of the house where women had dominion. They shopped, they cooked and they served meals.

Of the twelve women convicted of murder in the five years after 1832 nine used poison to kill. Some of the anxiety around women and poison was based on age-old misogyny. Yet the idea that gained currency from the 1840s onwards – that women were increasingly murdering their husbands with rat poison – probably arose from the fact that the women who were hanged after 1832 were more likely to have been convicted of the murder of another adult than of anything else (because the 1832 Punishment of Death Act reduced the number of capital offences from over 200 to about sixty) and were more likely to use poison to do so.

Undoubtedly, cases of poisoning escaped detection, the deaths assumed to be the result of organic disease or infection. Many an apparently grieving widow must have breathed a secret sigh of relief when their husband was deemed by the coroner to have died from gastroenteritis or cholera.

Men killed their wives in much greater numbers than women killed their husbands, but men more often used fists and implements than poison. They could argue in court that the killing was manslaughter, and that they were provoked into acting aggressively but had no intention to kill. Not so the women, for whom those methods were rarely possible. They tended to use a more subtle method: a trip to the chemist for rat poison, a smiling face, and a carefully-prepared supper.

Sophia Edney, who was hanged in Taunton in 1836, said that she was influenced by the notorious case of Mary Ann Burdock, who had poisoned Clara Ann Smith in 1833 to get her hands on her money and was hanged in Bristol in 1835. The lesson Sophia may have taken from that case was that Burdock had very nearly got away with her crime. It was only the suspicions of Smith's heirs, two years after she died, that led to Burdock's undoing. Sophia knew that arsenic was cheap and highly effective but it is likely that she and other illiterate women were not fully aware that, unless expertly administered, arsenic left specific and tell-tale traces.

In 1836 in Compton Bishop, a small village near Axbridge in Somerset, John Edney's neighbour Elizabeth Dunn became concerned about him. John's much younger wife Sophia had stopped by and told her that John was in so much pain with his old stomach complaint that she wished, for his sake naturally, he was in heaven. John was indeed extremely unwell, with a terrible pain in his insides. Elizabeth and

CATHERINE FRAREY, FRANCES BILLING, SOPHIA EDNEY

Sophia gave him orange juice, milk and mutton broth but nothing worked – he just brought everything up. He told Mrs Dunn that the gruel and ginger Sophia made for him burned his mouth and that he had a raging thirst. None of the powders or mixtures Edward Wade, the local doctor, prescribed seemed to improve matters. In fact, they made things worse. John thought he was dying and wanted to send for the doctor again, this time to sell his corpse so that his wife and children would have some money after he was gone.

The Edneys were an ill-matched couple. They had met six years previously, when Sophia Vane was 16 and in domestic service in Bath. John, a 61-year-old widower, delivered eggs, butter and poultry to the household. According to newspaper reports after Sophia's conviction, she was persuaded by her friends to marry John, which might indicate that she was parentless, either an orphan or a parish apprentice. Later, the couple settled in Compton Bishop, where John continued with his eggs and butter business and also gathered watercress. They had three children but lately there were rumours that Sophia had wanted to be rid of her elderly spouse in order to marry a younger man.

Mrs Dunn witnessed one of the last conversations between the Edneys. Sophia brought John some milk in a teacup.

'Have you put the powder in it?' he asked, meaning the doctor's remedy.

'No, I have not.'

He asked to have the candle brought nearer, and then put his finger into the milk.

'Have you put it in?' he asked again, and Sophia repeated that she had not.

He drank some and vomited.

Elizabeth Collins, another neighbour, also looked in on John. He complained to her that the doctor's medicine had 'burnt his inside out' and that his throat felt raw and 'on fire'. In dreadful agonies, twisting and turning himself about, 'very agitated and his features very much discoloured', according to Mrs Collins, John died after a few hours. When Edward Wade, his suspicions forming, wished to autopsy the body straight away Sophia objected, but he proceeded anyway. John had told the doctor that he had had a 'slight gnawing pain' for some time and the ulcer Wade found easily accounted for that. But John had also told him that the burning sensation had become acute after eating fried potatoes. Wade, thinking that John may been poisoned with arsenic, decided to take the contents of John's stomach to William Herapath, Professor of Chemistry at Bristol Medical School who had given evidence the previous year at the trial of Mary Ann Burdock. Before he left the house, Wade also collected scrapings from the skillet in which the potatoes had been fried.

On 12 April 1836, a month after John's death, Sophia stood trial at Taunton Assizes in front of Judge Joseph Littledale. Elizabeth Dunn gave evidence that Sophia told her that Mr Wade had diagnosed inflammation of the kidneys. A druggist from Axbridge said that he had sold Sophia arsenic for killing rats. Mr Wade outlined his suspicions at the time of John's illness and death (and denied mentioning inflammation of the kidneys). Professor Herapath described his tests on the contents of John's duodenum, which confirmed the presence of arsenic, and stated that he had found a small amount of arsenic in the scrapings from the skillet. Sophia's defence was to blame John's death on his ulcer.

After the jury had consulted for less than half an hour, Sophia was found guilty and Judge Littledale sentenced her to death. In prison she was said to have conducted herself 'with great propriety' and to have confessed to the crime. It was reported that few spectators witnessed her hanging.

Sophia, the last woman executed in England before Victoria ascended the throne, was also the last woman hanged within forty-eight hours of conviction before the Offences Against the Person Act of 1836 repealed immediate execution for murder. Henceforth murderers were to be treated like other capitally-convicted felons and allowed an interval between conviction and execution. There was growing unease about the possibility of making an irrevocable mistake on the basis of 'erroneous or perjured evidence' by executing too precipitously.

Part 2

Property

When a crime was committed, whether it was a felony or a misdemeanour, it was usually up to the victim to prosecute and, in most cases, to bear the cost of bringing the case to court. It could be an expensive process. For prosecutors of felony crimes there was also an ethical, even religious, issue: the risk that the defendant would be capitally punished. While murder was viewed as the most heinous crime and almost universally seen as deserving the death penalty, property cases put prosecutors in an unenviable position. Did they really want to be responsible for ending someone's life for a crime which harmed no one physically? It was not unknown for shopkeepers to plead for mercy for the criminals who had stolen from them or for prosecutors to decide not to turn up at court, automatically causing the case to fail.

In areas where there was a persistent problem with a particular type of crime, prosecutions might be brought not by an individual but by a group or association. Local farmers sometimes banded together and contributed through subscriptions to the cost of prosecuting sheep-rustlers (usually men), for instance. Institutions also brought cases. Those who were caught manufacturing and distributing false currency or fraudulently trading financial instruments were prosecuted by the Royal Mint, the Post Office or the Bank of England.

CHAPTER 8

Sarah Lloyd
Bury St Edmunds, 23 April 1800

*

Melinda Mapson
London, 13 June 1810

*

Elizabeth Fricker
London, 5 March 1817

*

Theft

'The breach of confidence on the part of servants has been recently so repeated, and reached to such an alarming extent, that it was considered necessary, for the prevention of the offence, that the wretched beings should pay forfeit of their lives,' wrote a journalist in the 18 December 1826 edition of *The Courier*. While servants lived adjacent to privilege and luxury, dusting precious items, brushing down costly clothing, tidying away fancy jewellery and preparing expensive dishes, they were expected to suppress any feelings of covetousness. They must be content with their lot and stay in their God-given rank.

Of course, not all stealing occurred within the home. Pickpocketing and shoplifting were both capital offences when the value of goods stolen was more than five shillings and one shilling respectively.

SARAH LLOYD, MELINDA MAPSON, ELIZABETH FRICKER

However by the beginning of the nineteenth century the usual sentence was imprisonment or transportation and in 1808 these crimes, along with stealing from a bleaching ground and begging by soldiers and sailors without a permit, were removed from the capital code.

This chapter focuses on stealing in a dwelling house, a crime the middle class viewed with special horror, an attack on them at their most vulnerable. Thefts after dark were seen as particularly serious. Any theft of goods worth forty shillings or over attracted a death sentence. Even so, most of the convicted, whether male or female, had their sentences commuted to transportation, which had dual benefits: it reduced the number of hangings (the authorities felt there was a limit to the amount of capital publishment the public would tolerate) and fed the demand for labour in New South Wales. Young women were especially valuable there, for their supposedly civilizing influence and to produce children.

Eleven of the 131 women executed between 1797 and 1837 were convicted of theft charges. Of these, two were convicted for stealing sheep, the last of whom, Diana Davies, was hanged in Presteigne, Radnorshire in 1802 after being tried by the hardliner George Hardinge (see Chapter 4). Why were these eleven not deemed to deserve the mercy of transportation? Some, like Diana Davies, were inveterate recidivists. Others, like Melinda Mapson and Elizabeth Fricker, stole goods worth huge sums. Occasionally, someone was chosen to serve as an example to deter others. That was the role of Sarah Lloyd, who was hanged in Bury St Edmunds in Suffolk in 1800.

'It was not me, my Lord, but Clarke that did it.' These words were Sarah Lloyd's meagre defence when she appeared on capital charges at the assizes at Bury St Edmunds. She could not call witnesses to her good character, as the only person who could have attested to it was her employer, who was both victim and prosecutor.

Sarah Lloyd, who was illiterate and did not even know her own age (judged to be somewhere between 18 and 23), worked as a maidservant to Sarah Syer, an elderly widow, who shared her home with a companion, Elizabeth Hoborough, in the tiny hamlet of

Hadleigh, near Ipswich. Unknown to Mrs Syer, Sarah had started a relationship with Joseph Clarke, a plumber and glazier who was known locally to have a bad character. One night in early October 1799, while Mrs Syer was asleep, Sarah and Joseph sneaked into Mrs Syer's bedroom. Sarah carefully reached behind the bedhead and from their hiding place between the bolster and the pillow slid out Mrs Syer's pockets (detachable bags usually worn under the petticoats) where she kept her valuables. Altogether, the haul included clothes, handkerchiefs, a watch and ten guineas in cash.

After setting fire to an outhouse as a distraction, Sarah and Joseph went to the Lloyd family home at Naughton, five miles away, where they hid their stash. Joseph told Sarah that she was sure to be accused and advised her to say that some soldiers billeted nearby had inveigled her into the crime. She tried to keep a low profile but a few days later, while out walking, she was recognized by a local man and ran away across the fields. She was caught hiding in a ditch and taken to a local tavern to await the constable. Then she made a fundamental mistake: she confessed and revealed the location of the stolen goods (the cash was never found). Soon Joseph was arrested too and, after their indictment by a grand jury, he and Sarah were committed to Bury St Edmunds Gaol to await their trial.

On 20 March 1800 Joseph and Sarah were arraigned on charges of feloniously and burglariously breaking and entering and stealing goods over the value of forty shillings (£2) and of setting fire to Sarah Syer's dwelling house. They pleaded not guilty, in Sarah's case a formality as there was no doubt that Sarah had robbed her mistress: her affidavit stated it. Georgian justice demanded that even the guilty deny their guilt, in order that the court properly explore the extent of it and whether they were deserving of mercy. However, after describing the crime and outlining Sarah's confession, the prosecutor, Mr Harvey, announced that there was no evidence against Joseph.

The witnesses – Mrs Syer, her companion Elizabeth Hoborough, the schoolmaster who was alerted on the night of the crime by cries of 'Fire!', the local man who recognized Sarah and the constable who arrested her – gave evidence. It was an open and shut case, at the end

SARAH LLOYD, MELINDA MAPSON, ELIZABETH FRICKER

of which Sarah was found not guilty of burglary, which by definition has to take place at night and to involve breaking *into* a property rather than out of it, but guilty of stealing in the dwelling house to the value of forty shillings, a capital offence. Joseph Clarke had not confessed to the crime and as there was no direct evidence against him, he was acquitted and discharged.

In the opinion of Judge Nash Grose, as a female and a servant, Sarah had transgressed on many levels:

> *A servant robbing a mistress is a very heinous crime; but your crime is greatly heightened; your mistress placed implicit confidence in you; you slept near her, in the same room, and you ought to have protected her...and though this crime was bad, yet it was innocence, compared with what followed: you were not content with robbing your mistress, but you conspired to set her house on fire, thereby adding to your crime death and destruction not only to the unfortunate Lady, but to all those whose houses were near by.*

He exaggerated her guilt – she was not convicted of arson and the fire she and Clarke set was minor – but Grose saw no grounds for a recommendation for mercy and advised her to repent and seek God's forgiveness before her inevitable death.

Events would have proceeded along the normal course, with Sarah being hanged within forty-eight hours of conviction, but for remarks she made to the Reverend Hay Drummond, the rector of Hadleigh, when he visited her in the condemned cell at Bury St Edmunds. She told him she had been seduced by Joseph Clarke, who was in the habit of visiting her for sex, and that she had regarded him as her husband. On the night of the crime, she had told him that she was pregnant and he had promised marriage. (She appears to have been mistaken about the pregnancy or to have subsequently lost the baby.)

This disclosure caused Drummond to adjust his view. Sarah was less a sinner who had acted as a free agent and more Joseph Clarke's object, who had been made to do his bidding; so he set about organizing a petition for mercy from the king and asked Capel Lofft, who had been on the grand jury that indicted Sarah, for help. Educated at Eton and Cambridge, Lofft was a one-time Radical barrister who had opposed the American War and supported the aims of the French Revolution. In middle age his revolutionary fervour had cooled and he was now a Suffolk magistrate, but he retained a humane approach to his social inferiors.

Lofft visited Sarah in prison and immediately took up her cause with an enthusiasm bordering on obsession. His description of her would not have been out of place in a novel:

> *She was rather low of stature, of a pale complexion, to which anxiety and near seven months' imprisonment had given a yellowish tint. Naturally she appears to have been fair, as when she coloured, the colour naturally diffused itself. Her countenance was very pleasing, of a meek and modest expression, perfectly characteristic of a mild and affectionate temper. She had large eyes and eyelids, a short and well-formed nose, an open forehead, of a grand and ingenuous character, and very regular and pleasing features; her hair darkish brown, and her eyebrows rather darker than her hair: she had an uncommon and unaffected sweetness in her voice and manner. She seemed to be above impatience or discontent, fear or ostentation, exempt from selfish emotion, but attentive with pure sympathy to those whom her state, and the affecting singularity of her case, and her uniformly admirable behaviour, interested in her behalf.*

Together with Mr Orridge, the prison chaplain, and the governor of the gaol, Lofft asked the Suffolk Under Sheriff to delay the execution, citing legal precedent. He also wrote to the Home Secretary, the Duke of Portland, and the former prime minister, the Duke of Grafton. His efforts were unsuccessful. Portland angrily rejected Lofft's interference in the process of execution and declared that Sarah Lloyd would hang on 22 April.

Before 1790 women were burnt at the stake for crimes of treason, most often for the murder of a husband or employer (petty treason) or for coining offences (high treason). As traitors their punishment was to be dragged behind a horse to the place of execution; they were usually strangled before the flames were lit.

'Dr. Syntax Attends the Execution' by Thomas Rowlandson (1820) shows the traditional mode of transport to the gallows, on a cart accompanied by coffins. In 1829 Jane Jamieson was taken to Newcastle Town Moor in this way.

Until 1783, the main place of execution in London was Tyburn, shown here in William Hogarth's 'Idle Apprentice executed' (1768). Execution days were often regarded as a chance for chaotic revelry.

A *North Quad: of Newgate.*
B *A Screen from ye Penthouse to the Prison door.*
C *The Penthouse.*
D *Entrance on the Scaffold.*
E *Boxes or seats for the Sheriffs.*
F *The Scaffold.*
G *The Platform.*
H *The Gallows.*
I *The Pin which loosens the Platform and lets it fall in.*

London's place of execution was moved from Tyburn to Newgate in 1783. The gallows, known as the New Drop, was erected for execution days and later dismantled and stored.

Despite the efforts of the authorities to instill order and solemnity at executions, in 1807 about 31 people were crushed to death at the execution of John Holloway, Owen Haggerty and Elizabeth Godfrey (on the right of the platform) after a surge in the crowd.

'The Condemned Chapel at Newgate' by Thomas Rowlandson (1809). Prisoners under sentence of death were obliged to attend a Condemned Sermon, for which tickets were sold to the public, and to sit around an empty coffin during the service.

Right: The condemned cell at Newgate, where condemned felons were allowed a final interview with their loved ones.

A few years after her first visit to Newgate in 1813 the Quaker Elizabeth Fry initiated a programme of improvements in the condition of female prisoners, including education and religious instruction. She took a special interest in women condemned to death, including Charlotte Newman, Harriet Skelton and Mary Ann James, who were convicted of fraud and forgery.

Eliza Fenning in Newgate, from a print by George Cruickshank. After Fenning's death in 1815, William Hone (top right) campaigned against the corrupt forces that led her to the gallows.

Right: A poster for the Pavilion Theatre in Whitechapel Road, east London, in 1854 shows that Eliza's story continued to appeal to audiences decades after her death.

Judge Hardinge (above, as a young man) ordered the execution in 1805 of teenage servant Mary Morgan for the murder of her newborn illegitimate baby but regularly visited her grave at Presteigne, Radnorshire. Hardinge's friend the Earl of Ailsbury erected a headstone to Mary in an attempt to improve Hardinge's reputation but local people put up another expressing a different viewpoint.

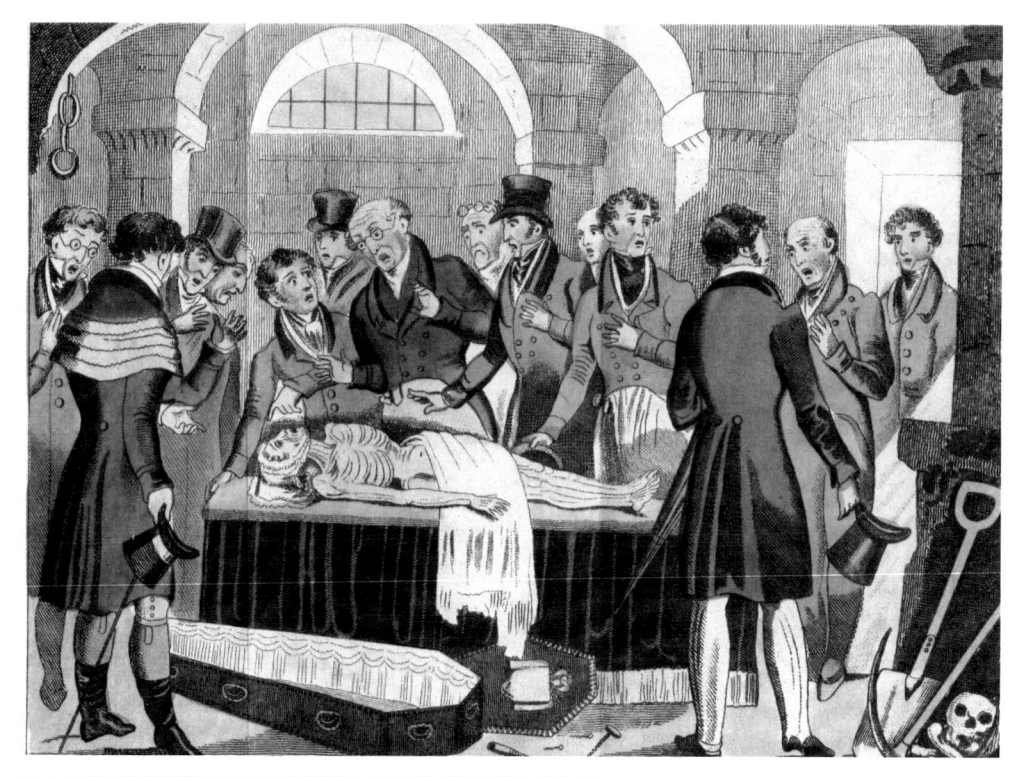

Above: In 1828 the Coroner's Jury viewed the disinterred body of 13-year-old Margaret Hawse at the Elephant and Castle pub in north London. Esther Hibner and her daughter were later charged with the murder of 10-year-old Frances Colpitts, another of their workhouse apprentices. Hibner was compared in the press to the notorious Elizabeth Brownrigg (left) who was hanged at Newgate in 1767 for the murder of her apprentice Mary Clifford.

February 1804: Ann Hurle seated with Methuselah Spurling in the cart on their short journey from Newgate to the gallows outside the church of St Sepulchre in 1804. The execution was notable because they were hanged using the old 'horse and cart' method rather than the New Drop.

A Bank of England £1 note from 1798, the year after the Bank Restriction measure was introduced to stabilise the currency.

The work of counterfeiters from 1799.

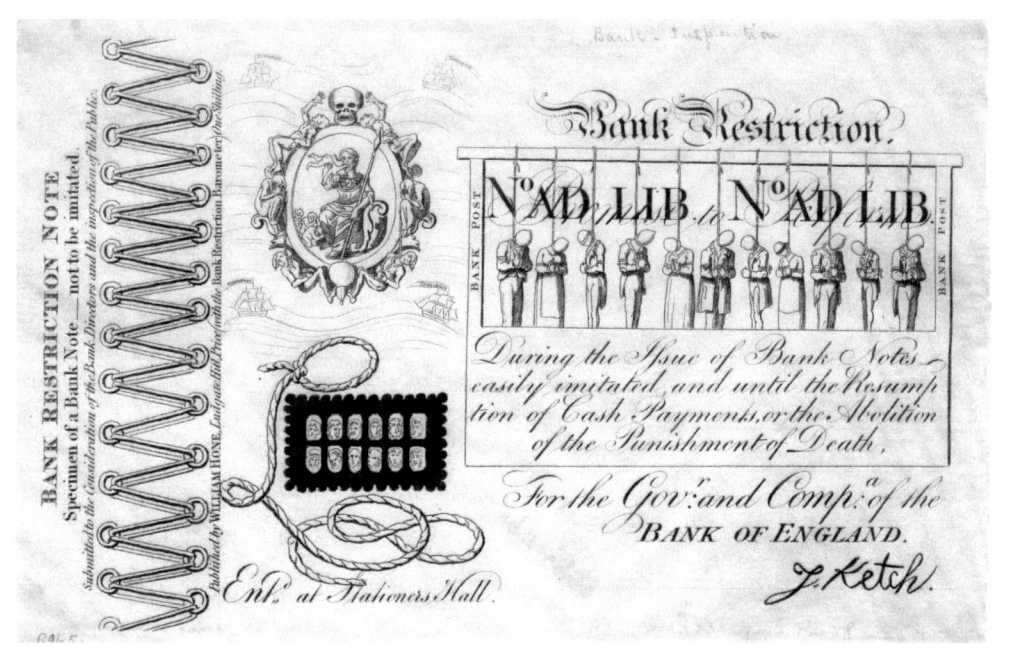

Satirical prints highlighted the death toll resulting from the Bank's prosecutions for forgery. Above: 'The Bank Restriction Note', created in 1819 by George Cruickshank and William Hone.

In 'A Panorama of the Times' (1821) the panels of a fairground booth open out to show, on the right, four people hanging from a gallows labelled 'Bank Restriction'.

As Home Secretary the Tory Robert Peel started a process of repealing and revising the law on many felony crimes.

Below: Millbank Penitentiary, London opened in 1816. Reformers supported incarceration, which offered the opportunity for remorse, as an alternative to the death penalty and transportation.

Execution of Esther Hibner,

For the Murder of a Parish Apprentice Girl.

THOU SHALT DO NO MURDER.

ESTHER HIBNER the elder ESTHER HIBNER the younger, and ANN ROBINSON, the latter a young woman possessed of a most unfavourable countenance, were indicted for the wilful murder of Frances Colpitt, a child 10 years of age.

Mr. Bolland (with whom was Mr. Ailey) stated the case. He observed, that the facts he had to lay before the Jury must excite the greatest horror in the minds of those who heard the dreadful narration; but, he thanked God, that such a case as the present was of unfrequent occurrence in this country. The deceased, who was only ten years of age, was a pauper, and was apprenticed to the prisoner Esther Hibner, the elder, who resided at Platt Terrace, Pancras-road, by the overseers of St. Martin's parish, to learn the business of fabricating tambour work. She was apprenticed on the 7th April, 1828, and in the month of October following a system of the most cruel & unnatural treatment was commenced by the prisoners towards the unfortunate deceased and the other children who were placed under the prisoner's care by St. Martin's and other parishes. They were not allowed sufficient sustenance, were compelled to rise to begin work at three and four in the morning, & were kept at work till eleven at night, sometimes two in the morning, and sometimes all night. They had scarcely any bed to lie on, and frequently during the most inclement season their resting place was the flooring, and their only covering was an old rag. The prisoners and their family had good bedding & clothes & every comfort that they desired The children were not permitted to go out to obtain necessary air and exercise; and thus the cruel treatment they had experienced had terminated fatally with three of them. The child which was the subject of the present indictment had been reduced to such a deplorable condition that her feet mortified, & this, combined with the bursting of an abscess on the lungs, brought on by the ill treatment the child had by experienced, occasioned her death. The breakfast which was allowed the children was a slice of bread and a cup of milk; and if they were indulged with this luxury they had no more food all the day. Sometimes the elder Hibner said the deceased & the other children had not earned their breakfast, & then a few potatoes were given them in the middle of the day, & nothing more afterwards till the following morning; nine pounds of potatoes were divided amongst the whole family, which consisted of 12 persons; they were allowed meat only once a fortnight, & on Sundays they were locked in the kitchen, the windows of which were closed. It would be proved that the younger prisoner, Hibner, had taken the deceased from the frame, and knocked he down on the floor; she had then taken the deceased up, and knocked her down again; when the elder prisoner was informed that the deceased was lying in the room ill, instead of affording her that protection which she was bound to do, she replied—"let her lie there." The deceased, when in that state, that she could scarcely crawl about the house, was told by the younger Hibner to clean the stairs; she attempted to do it, but fell exhausted, and was unable to accomplish the task; the younger Hibner then took the deceased up stairs, and flogged her with a cane and a rod, and afterwards sent her down to finish the stairs; when she came down she was unable, from weakness, to go in the proper place for the calls of nature, and ---- she had into a pail of water; the prisoner Robinson, who was standing by, remonstrated with her to empty this ---, saying, "curse her, do it again, and that will finish her." The others cried for food, until to satisfy the cravings of nature had eaten the meat that was brought in for the day, and also some pieces of meat which had been picked out of the wash that was obtained for feeding the pig. It would be proved also that all the prisoners had beaten the deceased, sometimes with a cane, sometimes with a rod, and sometimes with a shoe. The Medical Gentleman who attended the deceased before death, and examined her body of ev---- wards, would prove that they found large sores on the feet of the deceased, and her toes were mortifying and falling off. After death they examined the body, and found it in the most dreadful state, produced by the ill treatment she had experienced from the prisoners, and for want of proper food and nourishment. The Coroner demanded the most serious attention of the Jury; and he felt satisfied that they would give the circumstances the most serious consideration, before they arrived at their decision.

Susan Whilley, one of the girls apprenticed to the elder prisoner, knew the deceased; she used to be compelled to get up to work between three and four o'clock in the morning and continued working till ten and eleven o'clock at night; the deceased was allowed a slice of bread and a cup of milk for breakfast, and got nothing more all day; sometimes the elder Hibner said the deceased had not earned her breakfast; and then she was allowed only a few potatoes in the middle of the day and nothing more afterwards till the following morning; nine pounds of potatoes were divided among the whole family, which consisted of twelve persons; the deceased slept on the floor of the workshop with seven other apprentices; they had no bed, but had a sheet under and over them, and no other covering was allowed during the winter; they were allowed meat only once a fortnight, and on Sundays they were locked in the kitchen, the window of which was closed; they had a regular supply of victuals up to October, when it was discontinued, and the deceased looked sick soon afterwards; all the prisoners beat the deceased, sometimes with a rod, sometimes with a cane, and sometimes with a slipper; the younger Hibner had taken the deceased from the frame, and knocked her upon the floor and she pulled her up and knocked her down again. The younger Hibner, had also taken the deceased by the heels & plunged her into a pail of water which was intended for washing the stairs, and the prisoner Robinson said, "Curse her, dip her again, and finish her." The deceased used to cry for food; and the elder Hibner said she might cry on, for she should not have any. The elder Hibner's son kept a pig. and wash was brought to the house for it; and the deceased would take peices of dirty meat out of the wash and eat them. Half a pint of milk was taken daily for the family.

Several of the unfortunate children were next examined, and gave corroborating evidence. One of them stated t at on the Saturday morning, when the deceas ed was knocked down stairs by one of the unnatural women, she became senseless; that she (witness) assisted her into the kitchen, where she lay down; soon afterwards she became speechless, and died with a portion of her half slice of bread in her mouth; on her telling Mrs. Hibner that the deceased could not speak, her reply was—"Oh, let her lay and die, it will be a good riddance." When she died in the evening. she went to her mistress and daugh- who appeared glad at the intelligence, and desired her to wash the body and lay her out, which she did, assisted by an other little girl.

The Learned Judge summed up at great length, and the Jury returned a Verdict of Guilty. She was then taken back to the condemned cell, where she wrung her hands, and wept bitterly. This morning, April 13, she was brought out upon the fatal platform at Newgate, where, after a few moments spent in prayer, she was launched into eternity.

Copy of a Letter written by the Prisoner the night before her execution.

Dear S—Now are my eyes opened to the full extent of my cruelty to the poor children Committed to my charge, when no reparation can be made, and the moments are number'd which I have to live —Oh! most unhappy, & lost woman that I am wretched and undone, what infamy and disgrace have I heaped upon my own head. Where were the feelings of a Woman, and a Mother when I could inflict such barbarous and inhuman tortures upon poor helpless infants who had every claim to my compassion and tenderness. But the vengeance, of Heaven, which sleepeth not, has found me out and now I must prepare to render up an awful account to the righteous Judge of mankind—Have mercy, O Lord, & pardon my sins, my cruel sins, for Christ his sake.—Farewell, dear S— my hour is close at hand, a long, long fare- well.
E H

Attend ye tender mothers dear, and listen unto me, Your feeling hearts will bleed to hear this barbarous cruelty;
(and more,
Since Mother Brownrigg's awful doom, now sixty years
Such treatment to poor infants was never heard before.
Esther Hibner, and her daughter, Oh 'tis horrid for to tell,
(dwell.
Those cruel barbarous wretches, at Battle Bridge did Eight female apprentices they had as we can learn;
Who by their own industry, did them a living earn.
One meal a day to them she gave, and that consisting slight,
(day and night,
Two potatoes, not a bit of bread, made them work near In agony and misery they lay upon the floor, (sure.
With scarce a rag to cover them & pinched with hunger For 20 hours each day they toil'd and slav'd most shamefully,
And if a murmur scap'd their lips sare punish'd they would be;
Thus hanger, cold, and toil, and stripes, was all their And if they for one moment pray'd, she heeded not their pray'r,
One Frances Colpitt, ag'd 13, she being sick & sore,
The monster no compassion shew'd, but us'd her as before The child knock'd her down the stairs, in rain she wept and cried
(and died
They hooted and her piercing moans, and there she lay This horrid deed to Providence, at last was brought to light. When the Overseer did them behold, it did him much affright. An they were then committed, their trial to await.
Now when at Newgate they were tried, the court was shock d to hear.
The poor child's dreadful sufferings, which plainly did appear. The Mother instantly was sent ned by the law's decree. This morn she answer'd for her crimes upon the gallows tree.

Printed by J. Catnach, 2, Monmouth Court, 7 Dials.

An execution broadside sold for the hanging at Newgate of Esther Hibner at Newgate in 1829. These cheap newsheets often included lyrics for songs about the hanged.

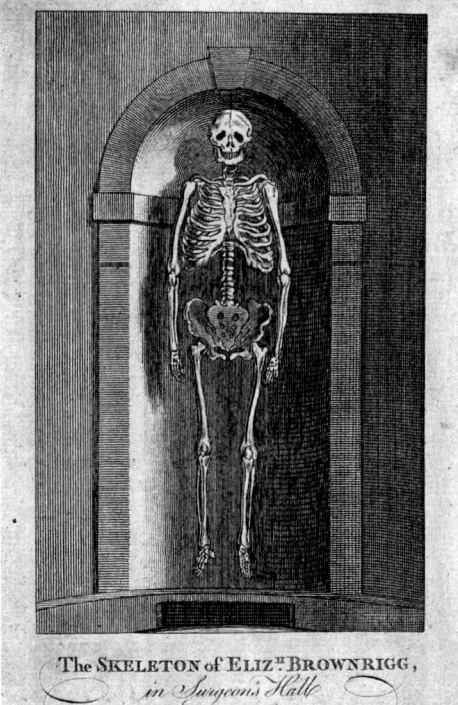

William Hey, who dissected the body of the so-called 'Yorkshire witch' Mary Bateman at Leeds General Infirmary after her execution in 1809 and raised over £80 in ticket sales. Parts of Bateman's body were later distributed as macabre keepsakes.

Left: In London, after anatomisation, skeletons of murderers were put on public display at Surgeon's Hall.

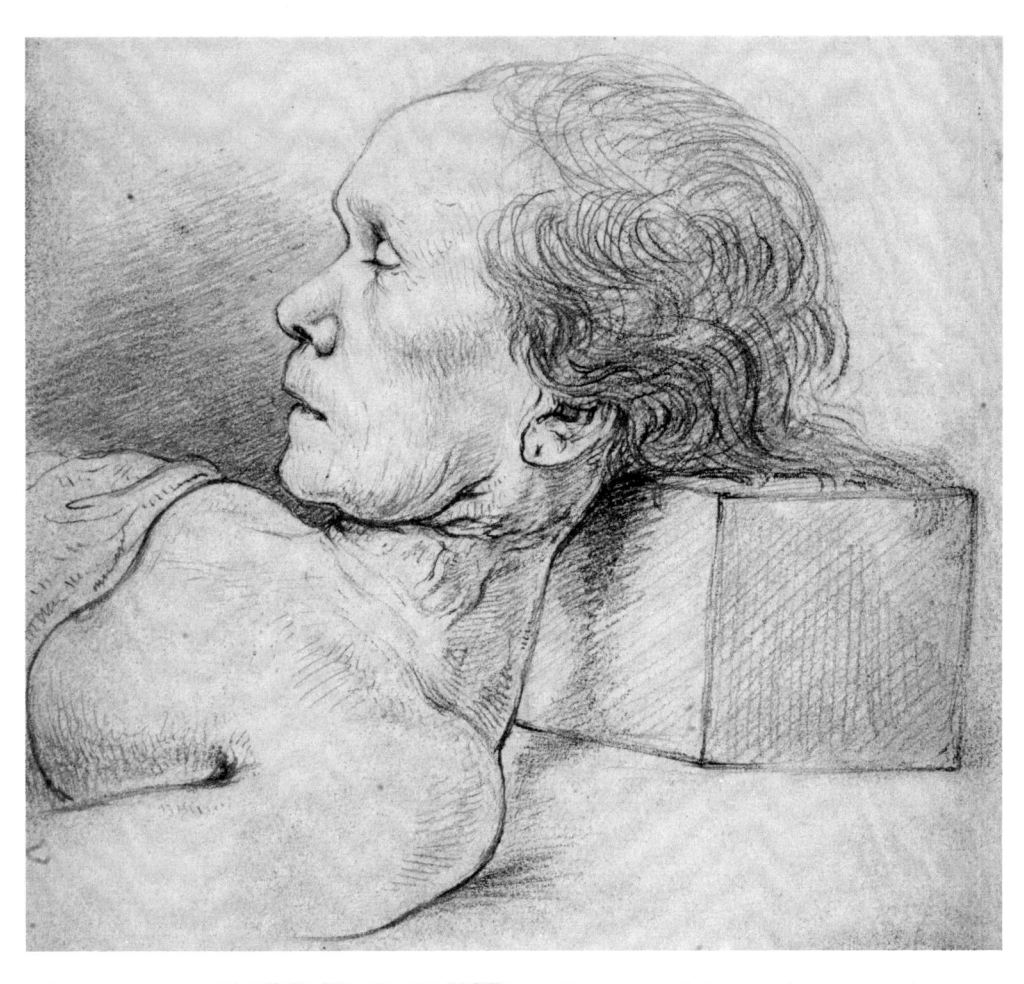

Eliza Ross (left) was known as the 'female burker' when she was convicted in 1832 of the murder of an old woman in order to sell her body to anatomists. Above: William Clift drew her body on the dissecting slab at the Royal College of Surgeons.

The rotunda of the Bank of England, where in late 1803 Ann Hurle attempted an audacious deception involving share certificates.

SARAH LLOYD, MELINDA MAPSON, ELIZABETH FRICKER

Lofft also hinted that Sarah may not have been of average intelligence. She was, he wrote,

a very young and wholly uneducated woman, naturally of a very tender disposition, and, from her mild and amiable temper, accustomed to be treated as their child in the families in which she had lived, and who consequently had not learned fortitude from experience either of danger or hardship.

On the morning of the execution, according to Lofft, Sarah 'took an affectionate, but composed and even cheerful, leave of her fellow-prisoners, and rather gave them comfort than needed to receive it'. She gave him her few possessions, to be passed on to family members and inmates. She dressed in white with a black ribbon on her bonnet and arms and a black sash around her waist. Lofft sat beside her in the cart as she was conveyed from Bury St Edmunds Gaol to the place of execution, Tay Fen fields, about a mile out of town. The day was windy and it poured with rain, and he held an umbrella over her. Then he mounted the scaffold with her and for fifteen minutes addressed the crowd, denouncing the Home Secretary, justifying his intervention and praising Sarah, who was now weeping beside him. As her time approached, Sarah was asked if she had anything to say. She replied that she had spoken her mind, and what she said 'was true respecting Clarke'.

Lofft later wrote that, 'She dignified, by her deportment, every humiliating circumstance of this otherwise most degrading of deaths, and maintained an unaltered equanimity and recollectedness, herself assisting in putting back her hair and adjusting the instrument of death to her neck.' A prayer was said and she was 'launched into eternity, amidst the tears of a number of her sex.' For Lofft, Sarah was a paragon of feminine submission even as she died:

After she had been suspended more than a minute, her hands were twice evenly and gently raised, and gradually let to fall without the least appearance of convulsive or involuntary motion, in a manner which could hardly be mistaken, when interpreted, as designed to signify content and resignation.

Lofft organized the burial, which was to be at eight that evening in the grounds of Bury St Edmunds Abbey. When he arrived with the body, a thousand people had already gathered there. He told them that Sarah's mother had attempted suicide when the appeal for mercy failed and he reminded them of Sarah's respectability ('for respectability was not to be confined to rank or riches, but is applicable to every person who gains his livelihood by honest industry'). There was a commotion when he alleged that the authorities had denied Sarah a burial service and the event became an opportunity to voice suppressed class anger, with shouts of 'The rich have everything, the poor have nothing.'

Lofft's view of Sarah Lloyd was not the prevailing opinion. 'Had this unhappy girl been instructed in the rudiments only of Christianity, of which she was utterly ignorant, this crime probably would never have been committed,' intoned the author of the trial report, bewailing the fact that she 'lost her virtue, her sense of rectitude, and her life' as if there was an inevitable progression from one failure to the next.

A stone, erected in the graveyard at the abbey, reflected this more conventional view of Sarah's transgressions.

Reader,
Pause at this Humble Stone.
It Records
The fall of unguarded youth
By the allurements of vice
And the treacherous snares of Seduction
SARAH LLOYD
on 23rd April 1800
in the 22 year of her Age
Suffer'd a just but ignominious Death
for admitting her abandoned Seducer
into the dwelling House of her Mistress
in the night of 3 Oct 1799

SARAH LLOYD, MELINDA MAPSON, ELIZABETH FRICKER

and becoming the instrument in his hands
of the Crimes of Robbery and House burning
These were her last words
May my example be a
warning to Thousands

The communities in Suffolk, as in other rural areas, were close-knit. Mrs Syer probably knew or was at least acquainted with Sarah Lloyd's family. She certainly had no known reason to distrust Sarah, who appears to have been in the thrall of Joseph Clarke, and she must have been utterly surprised when the crime occurred. Life operated differently in the cities. In London, a middle-class householder might be forced to employ someone knowing almost nothing about them, taking a written character reference on trust. We don't know the circumstances of 30-year-old Melinda Mapson's hiring by Mr and Mrs Dignam in 1809. Perhaps she presented them with a genuine letter of introduction; perhaps she had someone counterfeit it for her; perhaps she turned up without one and proved highly persuasive. It is not unreasonable to assume that the Dignams were desperate to fill the situation and Melinda arrived at just the right time: their previous servant, Margaret Garey, had left their employ earlier that day.

Melinda reported for duty to 5 New Street, Covent Garden at nine o'clock on the evening of 10 February. Ann Dignam showed her the house and explained her responsibilities and, before retiring to bed, asked her to open the door to her husband William, a grocer with premises in York Street, who would be returning from his club. She was also to put out the kitchen fire and wake her new mistress the next morning at quarter to seven. Mr Dignam duly came home some time after eleven, greeted his new servant, said he hoped she liked her place and went up to bed. Melinda did not go to bed. Instead, she spent the whole night gathering up the Dignams' most portable and valuable belongings, including a large counterpane which she may have used to bundle the goods in. Before dawn she decamped via the front door, possibly with the help of an accomplice – her booty was large and heavy.

The following morning, after waiting in vain for Melinda to come upstairs to wake her, Mrs Dignam got up to investigate. The servant's bedroom was empty, the bed stripped of sheets. The rest of house had been ransacked. In all, the Dignams had lost two pairs of boots, tea, sugar, soap and candles from a locked drawer, tablecloths, silk handkerchiefs, bed linen, curtains, a timepiece, gowns and many items of silverware: a punch ladle, tablespoons, teaspoons, a tea caddy shell and sugar tongs. Margaret Garey's locking box, which had been left with the Dignams for collection the next day, had been broken into and her gowns, petticoats, stockings and shifts were missing. As they went from room to room assessing the damage, the Dignams tracked the evidence of Melinda's misdoings: drawers cut open, drips from the tallow candle on the floor, disarray everywhere. Down in the kitchen, the fire was still burning and the front door was open.

Using a false name, Melinda pawned the goods at dealers in Whitechapel, the City and High Holborn, after which she was absorbed back into the anonymity of the metropolis. It was not until ten months later that her whereabouts was discovered: she was arrested by Joseph Snow, a Newington constable, at the Waggon and Horses near Elephant and Castle in Southwark in connection with another crime. Snow realized that she was wanted for the raid in New Street and asked Mr Dignam to come and identify her. Duplicates (pawnbrokers' receipts) were found on her and more were discovered at her brother's place at an old clothes shop in Rosemary Lane, Whitechapel, in the East End.

Melinda appeared at the Old Bailey on 11 April 1810, where the Dignams, Margaret Garey, the pawnbrokers and Joseph Snow gave evidence against her. As soon as the prosecution case had finished, the judge was careful to establish the value of the goods taken, so that there could be no mistake.

Judge to Mrs Dignam: All these things that are found, what value do you put upon them?

Mrs Dignam: I think they are worth more than forty shillings.

Judge to Mrs Dignam: Whereabouts was the value of all the property that you lost?

SARAH LLOYD, MELINDA MAPSON, ELIZABETH FRICKER

Mrs Dignam: I value them at thirty pounds.

Theft of forty shillings (£2) and over automatically qualified for a capital sentence (the level rose in 1827 to £5). Juries sometimes returned a 'partial verdict', where the defendant was found guilty but the goods stolen were valued at, say, thirty-nine shillings. On the Home Circuit during the eighteenth and early nineteenth centuries not only were female defendants in property crimes forty per cent more likely than their male equivalents to secure an outright acquittal but they were also fifty per cent more likely to have the value of goods stolen downgraded.

Juries might also choose a less serious offence from an array of charges presented by the prosecution. In October 1809, 23-year-old silk worker Ann Cooper took a watch, clothes, shoes and an umbrella from the east London home of her employer, James Chapman. At her trial for feloniously breaking out of the house with her booty, the jury found her guilty only of stealing and she was transported for seven years.

In cases where there was clear evidence of mental illness, juries might deliver a not guilty verdict. In 1819 Elizabeth Dunham was caught stealing keys from a gatehouse at the Bank of England and was discovered to have amassed a collection of over 4,000 others at her lodgings. When she made incoherent statements at her Old Bailey trial, the jury thought she was insane and acquitted her.

A married woman could plead that she had been forced by her husband to commit a crime (wives owed a duty of obedience to their husbands) but that pressure had to be clear and unequivocal, and the man had to be present during the crime. The trial record does not explicitly state that Melinda attempted the 'married defence', as it was known. It would not have done her much good if she had. Georgian law was muddled and uneven when it came to married women and their legal status and ordinary people were often mistaken on how a plea of marital coercion could be used. Leniency was generally only shown to women where there was a man available to convict.

At the time she was hired, Melinda told the Dignams that her husband was away at sea and that he sent her four shillings a week, but the identity, and indeed the existence, of this man was never proved. Nevertheless, she blamed him for forcing her into the robbery:

> *The door was never fastened. Mr Dignam went to bed and left me in the kitchen. There was someone knocked at the door. I opened the door. It was my husband. He swore if I resisted in letting him come in he would take my life. Accordingly he came in and my fright was so great that I went out of the house and went to my lodgings near Temple Bar. He brought the property in question home, and made away with it as he thought proper.*

The jury rejected Melinda's explanation and found her guilty, and the judge pronounced sentence of death. On 13 June, she was hanged outside Newgate, alongside Richard Jones, who had been convicted of fraud. 'The man appeared a wretched squallid [sic] figure, in the dress of a sailor, stupidly insensible to the horror of his situation; while the woman [Melinda] was shook almost to premature dissolution by her feelings. A very great concourse of idle spectators attended,' reported *The Public Ledger and Daily Advertiser*.

Eight years after Melinda Mapson was hanged, the Quaker prison reformer Elizabeth Fry gave evidence to the Committee on the Police of the Metropolis on the effects of capital punishment on prisoners in Newgate. She quoted from her notes on a visit to the prison in 1817 just after the execution of Elizabeth Fricker for robbery:

> *Instead of finding, as I expected, the whole of the criminals awfully affected by what had passed, I found a spirit of pity and lamentation over the sufferers, with such an impression that the punishment exceeded the crime, that it excited a feeling of great displeasure and even bitterness, not only towards our laws but to those who put them into execution, and so far from softening the heart, or leading it from evil, it appeared to harden them, and make them endeavour to justify their own criminal conduct.*

SARAH LLOYD, MELINDA MAPSON, ELIZABETH FRICKER

Fry was among a group of religiously inspired reformers who felt that capital punishment had a morally deleterious effect on the lower orders. In her opinion, it was a failure. It did not deter criminality, as it was intended to do, but did the complete opposite. She and her fellow reformers were also alarmed at the public scenes on execution days, when people in the crowd showed either indifference to the fate of those hanged or an inappropriate enjoyment of the spectacle:

Does capital punishment tend to the security of the people? By no means. It hardens the hearts of men, and makes the loss of life appear light to them; and it renders life insecure, inasmuch as the law holds out, that property is of greater value than life. The wicked are consequently more often disposed to sacrifice life to obtain property.

Supporters of the status quo believed that the gallows was an unpleasant but necessary way to induce conformity in the criminal classes and anyone else tempted to commit crime. The solemn authority with which executions were performed, and the terror they induced, played a crucial part in maintaining order. The serendipitous nature of justice, where felons could not be sure they would be hanged or reprieved, gave everyone a fear of pain and death and made society safer.

Fry, initially drawn to Newgate as an arena where she could do God's work by bringing women to religion, was horrified not only by the barbarity of capital punishment but also by conditions in the female wards. On her first visit in 1813 she was reduced to tears. The prison was a place of total misery. Three hundred women lived in two rooms, sleeping in three tiers. They had few clothes, hardly any food, and many were caring for babies and children. Although busy with her own large family (she had eleven children), by 1816 she had managed to persuade prison officials to allow her to set up a school inside Newgate. A small space was cordoned off and she started classes there, attracting inmates by providing food, and using educated, trusted prisoners to assist. She achieved a transformation of morale, discipline and conditions and within a year she had set up the Ladies' Association for the Reformation of Female Prisoners in Newgate, which led to the establishment of the British Ladies' Society for Promoting the Reformation of Female Prisoners, the first nationwide women's association.

Elizabeth Fry ministered to and comforted the condemned women in Newgate, including Elizabeth Fricker.

> *I have just returned from a most melancholy visit to Newgate, where I have been at the request of Elizabeth Fricker, previous to her execution tomorrow morning, at eight o'clock. I found her much hurried, distressed and tormented in mind. Her hands cold and covered with something like the perspiration preceding death and in a universal tremor. The women with her said she had been so outrageous before our going that they thought a man must be sent for to manage her. However, after a serious time with her, her troubled soul became calmed.*

The previous October at the Old Bailey Elizabeth Fricker, a 30-year-old widow, had been found guilty of a robbery at the house of her employer, Ann Ashworth, who lived in Berners Street in the Marylebone area of London. During the night of Sunday, 28 July 1816 she and her lover William Kelly had stolen over £400 worth of silver and linen.

That evening Elizabeth's fellow servant Hannah Holloway noticed that she was behaving oddly: she declared that she needed to go out (it was after dark) and, after Hannah had persuaded her to go to bed, suddenly remembered that she had left her book downstairs (she was not a regular reader). The next morning, she was up early and woke Hannah, who discovered the burglary and alerted Mrs Ashworth. Large parts of the house were in disarray: the sideboard had been forced open and all of the silver plate taken.

When Bow Street constable Samuel Plank inspected the premises he found that there had been no forced entry and that the door lock could not have been picked as there was no keyhole on the outside. Elizabeth tried to convince him that the burglars had got in through a

SARAH LLOYD, MELINDA MAPSON, ELIZABETH FRICKER

window, but the potted plants there had not been disturbed. He began to have suspicions that she was involved. The following day, she was seen talking to a man she later claimed was a 'tally man' to whom she owed money. By Tuesday she had been arrested and soon afterwards a trunk containing the stolen goods was found at the home of Hannah Compton, who had been asked to store it for safekeeping. William Kelly (the 'tally man') and James Hitchen were arrested and charged with burglariously breaking and entering a dwelling house. Kelly's father Peter was charged with receiving stolen goods.

At the trial at the Old Bailey Elizabeth declared that she was 'thoroughly innocent of the charge laid against me' and William Kelly tried to save his co-accused by assuming guilt for the entire operation. He and Elizabeth were found guilty and sentenced to death, while Peter Kelly was ordered to be transported for fourteen years and Hitchen was acquitted.

Elizabeth Fricker and William Kelly were scheduled to die with five other felons. On the day of their execution, *The Morning Post* reported that 'there were more spectators assembled than on any former occasion', probably attracted by the prospect of seeing seven people, including a woman, executed. There was an hour's delay – Thomas Cann, a forger, had been 'nearly in a state of insanity' during the night and had had to be straitjacketed before he could emerge from Debtors' Door on the side of Newgate – which caused some of the crowd to drift away. The first 'unfortunate creature' to appear was Elizabeth. According to *The Observer*, she 'displayed great despondency and wept most bitterly'. She was followed by William Kelly and the others. As she was conducted to the scaffold, Elizabeth stopped crying and looked wildly at the crowd. She asked the hangman not to hurt her and requested that she might be allowed to take her leave of Kelly. He was brought forward and they embraced, after which he shouted out to the crowd, 'She is innocent, innocent! Murdered! Murdered!' but was prevented from speaking further. All seven died 'apparently without much struggle'. Their bodies were left for the usual hour and, as none of them were murderers, were afterwards handed over to their family or friends.

WOMEN AND THE GALLOWS 1797–1837

Only two other women were executed for theft crimes after Elizabeth Fricker, the last being Amelia Roberts in 1827, who with her co-defendant Patrick Riley robbed her employer of goods worth over £400. Their execution at Newgate was a hideous spectacle, with Riley refusing to be hooded, somehow clinging to the rope and eventually being killed by someone pulling on his legs.

By the 1830s there was an acceptance that prison was a more appropriate form of punishment for property crimes. Prison regimes were rigorous and they offered the chance for moral regeneration, repentance, rehabilitation and religious instruction. In 1832 the Punishment of Death Act removed the death penalty from shoplifting and stealing horses, cattle and sheep; in 1834-5 letter stealing and in 1837 burglary and theft from a dwelling house became non-capital crimes.

CHAPTER 9

Ann Hurle
London, 8 February 1804

*

Mary Ann James
London, 17 February 1818

*

Fraud

In 1805 19-year-old Esther-Jane Jenner appeared at the Old Bailey charged with falsely obtaining a cruet stand valued at just over £1 from a glass and china seller by saying that she was sent to collect it by a regular customer. Found guilty, she was sentenced to a month in Newgate and fined a shilling. Her crime, like many of the frauds prosecuted at the Old Bailey, involved goods of low value or small sums of money. Esther-Jane herself was not typical. Fraud was overwhelmingly a male crime. Between 1797 and 1837 at the Old Bailey just over a thousand men were prosecuted for fraud, ten times as many as women.

The crimes themselves divide into misdemeanours and felonies, and here it was the value of the offence that was the deciding factor. In 1798 Mary Welchford, who was accused of obtaining three guineas under false pretences after she pretended to a publican that she was borrowing on behalf of one of his regular customers, was sentenced to be whipped at Newgate but in 1809 Mary Grimes, who tried to obtain a seaman's pension she was not entitled to, was hanged.

Perhaps the most notorious fraudster of the age was the banker

WOMEN AND THE GALLOWS 1797–1837

Henry Fauntleroy who appropriated £250,000 from the investors in Marsh, Sibbald & Co, which his father had co-founded. Some of the money was spent on debauchery, the rest, Fauntleroy claimed, filled a massive hole in the bank's finances. Despite his obvious guilt, a number of respectable bankers testified at his trial to his character, two sets of judges assessed the trial on points of law and a committee of the bank's creditors petitioned for his sentence to be remitted. None of them could save him and he was hanged at Newgate in 1824. It goes almost without saying that none of the four women who were executed for crimes of fraud and deception attracted attention of this kind or on this scale.

In 1792 Jane Hurle took a job as housekeeper to Benjamin Allin, an elderly gentleman who lived in Greenwich on the south side of the Thames. Over the years, as Mr Allin grew increasingly frail, rarely leaving the house and receiving no visitors, Jane took over more and more of his personal management. She helped him with his stocks and shares and showed him where to sign when he received dividends from his stockbroker. Jane's niece Ann occasionally visited the house and, although Mr Allin was acquainted with her, he did not know her well. Ann, on the other hand, regarded Mr Allin with a great deal of interest. She was a clever and resourceful young woman and gradually a plan that would make her fortune formed in her head. Ann knew that the owner of stocks could transfer them to another by making out a deed or power of attorney authorizing another person to transact the business. The deeds were issued by the Bank of England directors and filled in by the owner of the stocks in the presence of two witnesses.

On Saturday, 10 December 1803 Ann crossed the river to the City and enquired at the Bank of England coffee shop for a stockbroker called George Francillon. Francillon had first met Ann the previous year when she sold £50 of her own stocks on coming of age. She now told him that she wanted him to take out a power of attorney for Benjamin Allin. She explained that she had been brought up in Mr Allin's household and that he wanted to give her £500 in stocks as a 'reward or recompense for her services to him for some years'.

ANN HURLE, MARY ANN JAMES

Ann was back at the Bank of England at eleven o'clock on Monday morning with the power of attorney, which was now somewhat tattered but bore Benjamin Allin's signature as well as that of Peter Verney, a cheesemonger, and Thomas Nowland, a carpenter, both living in Greenwich. Before the document could be executed, however, it had to be examined, so Francillon left it with a clerk. Meanwhile, Ann went off to sell the stock (she would not be able to transfer the cash to herself until the power of attorney was approved). When she and Francillon returned to the Bank the inspector of letters of attorney, Thomas Bateman, told them that there was a problem: the signature was given as 'Benjamin Allin' whereas in the examples of Allin's signature in the Bank's files the word Benjamin was abbreviated. That was because Mr Allin is not accustomed to writing much, said Ann, but if there was a doubt, she would get a fresh power of attorney and a new signature. Mr Bateman, unwilling to put her to extra expense, preferred that she get Mr Verney, with whom he was slightly acquainted, to sign a second endorsement. He asked Ann how the paper became so mutilated and she told him that the dog had got hold of it.

Francillon was becoming concerned. While they waited in Bateman's office, he asked Ann about herself. She mentioned that she had recently married a James Innes. That will cause another problem, said Francillon, as the power of attorney should be in your married name. Seeing her mistake, Ann backtracked furiously. Her new husband was 'a person of bad character', she said. He had persuaded her to go to Bristol, where they had gone through a ceremony in a private house. Within two hours he had stolen her money and some of her clothes, boarded a ship and abandoned her. Furthermore, he was already married. Why did Ann embark on this seemingly irrelevant fiction? She may have felt that her plan was not going well and marriage would give her additional credibility in the eyes of Francillon and the clerks at the Bank, or she may have anticipated that she would have to explain her actions to a court and was, if need be, planning to blame a husband.

Ann left with the power of attorney in her hand, saying she would be back at noon the next day, while Francillon went to Holborn to call on Owen and Hicks, attorneys to the Hurle family, who had recommended Ann to him the previous year, presumably in the matter of selling her own stocks. They told him that they knew nothing about her marriage. By now, he was having serious doubts.

The next morning, Tuesday, Ann was back with the document, now endorsed by Peter Verney, or apparently so, which she left with Francillon. His suspicions had not abated but he was still not completely sure that it was a forgery, so he asked her to return on Wednesday. In the meantime, he called on Ann's father James, a carver and gilder, and asked him to accompany him to see Mr Allin. That interview confirmed his fears.

The following morning, as he walked through the rotunda at the Bank, Francillon saw Ann standing near the door, in the company of a man. 'Miss Hurle, you are come very early this morning. I will be with you in a minute,' he said, and hurried to speak to the clerk. Within minutes he was called in to see the directors of the Bank, to whom he handed the power of attorney. At some point during the day, the Bank authorities identified Ann as the person who had at the beginning of December sold £100 of stock by impersonating Elizabeth Hurle, another of her aunts. Downstairs, while waiting in the Bank for Francillon's return, Ann must have realized that her plan had failed and decided to flee.

Soon afterwards, Ann's putative husband, James Innes, was tracked down and arrested. He admitted accompanying her while she impersonated her aunt Elizabeth, but claimed that he had also been deceived by Ann, who had told him that she was an heiress. He said that she had asked him and a man called James Robinson to go with her to Bristol to search for the will of a recently dead relation who had left her a 'considerable fortune'. Robinson later corroborated this account.

Ann was arrested in Bermondsey, and along with Innes and Robinson, taken before magistrates at Mansion House. She did not appear to appreciate the serious situation she was in, possibly hoping that an air of insouciance would help. Innes and Robinson were discharged – they were judged not part of a conspiracy – but Ann was committed and remanded at the Poultry Compter, a small prison in Cheapside notorious for its poor conditions, to await trial. On 11 January 1804, having been transferred to Newgate, she appeared at the Old Bailey, the charges relating only to her attempt to obtain the fraudulent power of attorney for Benjamin Allin and not to the impersonation of her aunt Elizabeth. It was an easy case to prove. Ann finally fully understood the danger she faced and fainted twice while the witnesses, Francillon, Bateman, Verney and Nowland, as well as her aunt Jane and a somewhat confused Benjamin Allin, gave evidence against her. She offered no defence, was found guilty and sentenced to death.

The following Tuesday she and other condemned prisoners were brought up before John Silvester, the notoriously hard-line Recorder of London (see Chapter 1). As *The Times* reported:

He particularly took notice of the case of forgery by Anne [sic] Hurle, and said, that her crime was particularly aggravated, by the selection of an infirm and imbecile old man, incapable of management of his own concerns, in order to defraud him, by her artfulness of his property in the funds. It was absolutely necessary, he observed, that the funded property of this Country, so universally diffused, should be guarded by the strictest law, and the infliction of the heaviest punishment.

The only way for Ann to delay her imminent death was to claim she was pregnant, and this she did but it was swiftly disproved by a jury of matrons and she was scheduled to die alongside Mathuselah Spalding, who had been convicted of 'an unnatural crime' (sodomy). A petition for mercy presented to the king failed. The magnitude of her offence 'admitted of no other alternative than the execution of the law'.

Ann stopped eating. At the condemned service in Newgate, she collapsed. A few days later, in the hours before her execution, her parents visited her for the last time. At eight in the morning of

WOMEN AND THE GALLOWS 1797–1837

Wednesday, 8 February, dressed in black and wearing a cap, pale and weak, she emerged through Debtors' Door into the street. Accompanied by the Ordinary of Newgate, she and Spalding were put in a cart and taken a few yards to the top of Old Bailey at its widest part near St Sepulchre's Church. They were to die, not on the so-called New Drop which used portable apparatus and included a platform allowing victims to fall a short distance vertically, but the old way, on the common gallows, strangled as the cart on which they stood was pulled away by horses.

Just before the noose was put around Ann's neck she seemed to be about to speak but was too weak to do so. The huge crowd, reportedly moved by compassion, became agitated and started shouting, only quietening when the sheriff told them that their behaviour was improper. Hoods were pulled over the faces of the condemned, the nooses adjusted and the horses moved off. Ann 'gave a little scream' and appeared to be 'in great agony, moving her hands up and down' for two or three minutes. An hour later her body was cut down and taken inside Newgate to be claimed by her family. 'An amazing concourse of spectators were collected on the occasion, all of whom commiserated the fate of Ann Hurle; while that of Mathuselah Spalding...excited sentiments of a very different description,' reported *Bell's Weekly Advertiser*.

The Times published a letter from 'Humanus' who alleged that the reason for not using the New Drop was that the staff at Newgate were too lazy to bring the apparatus out of storage and assemble it.

Ann was buried at St Alfege Church in Greenwich, where she had been christened and where other members of the Hurle family were interred.

Ann Hurle's opportunism found an echo thirteen years later when Elizabeth Thomas, an out-of-work servant on her way from London to Cornwall to see her mother, struck up a conversation with Miss Baker, a young woman travelling with her in the coach. Miss Baker told Elizabeth that she was soon to be married and was looking for a servant. She offered Elizabeth the job on the spot and arranged to meet her at Exeter in a few days' time. What would make more sense than for Elizabeth to give Miss Baker her clothes and papers for safekeeping until they met up again?

That was the last Elizabeth saw of her new acquaintance until they faced each other at the Old Bailey, where Miss Baker, whose real name was Mary Ann James, had been indicted on nine alternative charges, three of them capital. Twenty-year-old Mary Ann had found a certificate for £115 worth of stocks amongst Elizabeth's papers and cashed them in using a fraudulent power of attorney. The deception was only discovered when Elizabeth came up to London to collect her dividend and was told that the stocks were no longer hers. Six weeks later, while out walking, Mary Ann was arrested by Samuel Plank and John Foy, from Marlborough Street Police Office.

'I am apprehending you on suspicion of forging an instrument, and selling stock out of the funds,' Plank told her.

'I know what you mean,' she said, 'You mean Mrs Thomas. I did do it. I was persuaded to by a man named Goddard. After I received the money I took it down to Chard in Somersetshire, and gave him the whole of it, except a small sum.'

Mary Ann had applied to stockbroker Peter Woodward for a power of attorney. She told him that Elizabeth Thomas was her relation and was financing her new business. Unlike Ann Hurle, she succeeded in the transaction and was paid the cash.

Mary Ann appeared at the Old Bailey on 3 December 1817. Her defence was that she was 'in great distress' but had then taken a situation in Chard, where Philip Goddard pressurized her into going to London to commit the crime for a payment of £25. There seems to have been only a half-hearted attempt to identify Goddard and assess his role in the affair. The case was hopeless and a guilty verdict inevitable.

In Newgate, in the weeks before she was executed, Mary Ann accepted the spiritual advice of Elizabeth Fry and became friends with convicted utterer Charlotte Newman with whom she died, alongside two men, William Hatchman, convicted of forgery, and John Attel, of burglary on 17 February 1818 (see Chapter 10).

WOMEN AND THE GALLOWS 1797–1837

In this period, only one woman found guilty at the Old Bailey on a charge relating to the fraudulent cashing in of shares managed to escape the gallows. What made Mary Swain's case different?

In September 1814, Mary Maguire and Bridget Mulhern deposited £40 with stockbrokers Rumford and Ashby for the purchase of an annuity issued by the Bank of England. What they did next shows something of the difficulties the poor, who moved home frequently, faced in securing items of value. Back at their lodgings in the Borough, south London, Mary and Bridget sewed the receipt for the deposit into the lining of one of Bridget's gowns and placed it in her trunk. Six months later, they pawned the trunk, which now also contained £3 in cash and a duplicate (pawnbroker's receipt) for Mary's trunk, with Mr Barber in Borough High Street. They may have done this not because they particularly needed the money but in order to give the trunk a permanent and safe home before they both set off on long journeys.

Unfortunately, both women were soon in trouble with the law. Mary travelled to Stirling in Scotland to see her sister, where she was arrested the day after she arrived for associating with women who pretended to be soldiers' widows in order to fraudulently draw their pensions. Bridget likewise was incarcerated, for posing as a soldier's wife in Middlewich, Cheshire, although she was indeed the wife of Owen Mulhern, a soldier.

Attempting to draw pensions or claim prize money belonging to dead servicemen was a crime that led to the execution of two women in this period. In 1809 Mary Grimes presented herself to the clerk of the check office at Greenwich Hospital and claimed that she was the widow of Thomas Roughton, who had served on board HMS *Eurus* in 1796 and that she was owed his prize money of over £24. She was proved to be an impostor. Five years later Catherine Foster swore falsely that she was the sister of Charles Serjeant, who had died on the *Nassau* in 1808. Grimes and Foster both hanged.

After four months in gaol in Stirling, Mary Maguire was destitute, without money or sufficient clothing. Not realizing that Bridget was also in prison, she had a letter sent to her friend Mary Swain in the Borough, enclosing the duplicate for the trunk and asking her to get

Bridget to retrieve it, take the receipt for the annuity to the Bank of England and collect the interest, and to send it and the £3 and the clothes to Scotland for her relief.

Mary Swain, a 26-year-old mother of four young children and who had herself fallen into want, collected the trunk and then decided to pawn the clothes and help herself to some of the funds in the annuity. At the Bank of England she pretended to be Mary Maguire while her friend Hannah Morrison posed as Bridget Mulhern. She received £12 of stock but made the mistake of signing as Mary M'Guire. The difference in the spelling of Maguire's name meant that the stockbroker had to ask his clerk to draw up an affidavit to swear to the name change. That and Mary Swain's panicky and loud demands to hurry up with the payment ensured that he had a clear memory of the whole transaction. However, before long, encouraged by her earlier success, Mary went back and drew out the remaining £28.

In Stirling, Mary Maguire heard nothing back from Mary Swain or Bridget Mulhern and after a further four months' incarceration was acquitted and released, forced to make her way back to London as an indigent, receiving poor relief in the parishes she passed through. Meanwhile, Bridget Mulhern was also released. On her return to the Borough she went to Mr Barber to retrieve her trunk but was told that Mary Swain had it. She hurried off to see her. The trunk, of course, was empty.

'I might as well confess the truth,' said Mary Swain. 'Unfortunately I signed Maguire's name. Do not go to the Bank. I drew the money.'

Mary Swain, promising to pay back £10 immediately and the balance when her husband's quarterly pension came in, persuaded Bridget to share her lodgings, and as she had nowhere else to go she agreed. They even came to an arrangement where Mary would look after Bridget's son for five shillings a week while she went down to Hastings, presumably to be with her husband. Somewhere along the way, possibly when Mary Maguire arrived back from Scotland, whatever goodwill existed between these women disappeared and a constable was called in. In January 1817 Mary Swain was taken before a magistrate and was committed for trial at the Old Bailey on the capital charge of forgery, prosecuted by the injured party, which was the Bank of England. Mary Maguire, Bridget Mulhern, an array of Bank of England clerks and the stockbroker gave evidence at the trial the following month. Mary Swain interjected with questions to her former friends ('Did you not lodge with me till February, at different times?'; 'Did you not leave your son at my house?'; 'Have you not received £4 14s and 9d of the first payment?'), but at the end the jury found her guilty and Judge Holroyd passed the statutory sentence of death on her.

The press almost completely ignored Mary Swain's trial and published no details. Although Mary's name appears in newspapers' published lists of prisoners found guilty of capital crimes at the Old Bailey, and later amongst those whose sentences were to be considered by the Prince Regent for reprieve, no newspaper bothered to report that she had indeed been saved from the gallows, probably because the details of the case showed that it was a dispute between people of Irish origin, whose mundane infighting was of little interest.

Why was Mary Swain's sentence commuted? After all, the following year, in a widely reported case, Mary Ann James was hanged for her deception in creating a bogus power of attorney to cash in Elizabeth Thomas's annuity certificates. It may have been simply that the Bank was unwilling to make a martyr of Mary, the young mother of four children, or that her offer to pay back the money was seen as a sign of repentance.

Despite the Bank's relative lenience, eleven months after her trial, languishing in the women's ward in Newgate, Mary Swain paid a scribe to write to the directors of the Bank asking for further remission of her sentence. She expressed thanks to the Bank and to God for her reprieve, and contrition for the crime, but pleaded for compassion for her children 'who have been deprived of my protection for a long period'. We know nothing more of her life, only that the Bank rejected her request. However, a woman of about her age is recorded as having been buried in Spa Fields in 1822 but we have no way of knowing if this is 'our' Mary or merely another poor woman of the same name.

ANN HURLE, MARY ANN JAMES

As we shall see in the next chapter, public opinion about the capital punishment of property crimes, especially those relating to fraud and forgery, was changing. In 1818 the Society for the Diffusion of Knowledge upon the Punishment of Death, and the Improvement of Prison Discipline published *On the Effects of Capital Punishment*, a collection of journalism and essays exploring the pointlessness of the death penalty, in which the fate of Mary Ann James was described. It said: 'Her conduct was such that there is every reason to believe, that if her life had been spared...she would have lived to a good purpose, and have become a valuable member of society.'

CHAPTER 10

Sarah Bailey
York, 12 April 1800

*

Charlotte Newman
London, 17 February 1818

*

Harriet Skelton
London, 24 April 1818

*

Uttering Forged Bank Notes

The forgery of bank notes was made a capital crime in 1697 and in 1725 extended to uttering, the passing of a forged document with intent to defraud. After 1797 there was an exponential increase in the manufacture of counterfeit notes, and of uttering – a direct result of a measure to deal with a credit crisis that was, at the time, assumed to be temporary. This was the so-called Bank Restriction, which allowed banks to issue low denomination notes for the first time. Before this date, on request, banks were obliged to 'pay the bearer' of a banknote the appropriate value in gold, that is, in gold and silver coins. These were known as specie payments.

By 1795, gold bullion stocks at the Bank of England were running low, the result of the drain caused by the war with France and a series of bad harvests. On 25 February 1797, Prime Minister William

Pitt asked for an emergency meeting with King George III. News had just arrived of a French invasion at Fishguard. As it turned out, it was easily repelled but the event led to a loss of confidence and Pitt feared a run on the banks. He persuaded the king to announce the temporary suspension of specie payments with immediate effect; bankers and merchants supported this line and on 3 May the Bank Restriction Act passed into law. The Bank was now allowed to issue one and two pound notes, which it did in copious quantities. The notes were ludicrously easy to copy and for many that temptation was too great to resist.

The Bank was the implacable enemy of forgers and employed an in-house team of inspectors and lawyers to deal with them. The result of this sudden rise in currency crime was an obvious and, to some, disturbing spike in prosecutions. The penalties were severe: hanging, or transportation if you were lucky. The numbers of people going to the gallows were enormous. Between 1783 and 1797 there were four prosecutions for forgery, but from 1797 to 1821 there were over 2,000 – and more than 300 executions. By 1821, when the 'temporary' restriction ended, the clamour of public disapproval of the Bank's ruthless pursuit of forgers and utterers could not be ignored.

Fifteen of 'our' 131 women were hanged for forgery crimes (not including coining), most of them relating to uttering bank notes. More than twenty times as many men were hanged for forgery in the same timeframe. Women were more often prosecuted for uttering than for manufacturing notes (which was generally carried out by skilled male engravers) because they were consumers, the purchasers of clothes, food and cheap items, and so had more chance of offering false notes in payment and receiving change without attracting suspicion.

One notable feature of the forgery business was that while the primary centres of manufacture were in the north, particularly in Birmingham and Liverpool but also in Manchester and Leeds, utterers were most active in London, where they could more easily disappear into the anonymity of the metropolis.

WOMEN AND THE GALLOWS 1797–1837

In 1799 a spate of uttering in the area around Leeds, which was attributed to a 22-year-old itinerant hawker called Sarah Bailey and her unnamed male companion, drew the attention of the Bank of England, which commissioned its veteran inspector Thomas Bliss and Bow Street officer Thomas Carpmeal to travel north to track them down.

When they arrived in Otley, near Leeds on 26 October 1799 Bliss and Carpmeal discovered that Sarah was already in custody, her partner having previously decamped, and that it had been an effort to keep hold of her. She had first been arrested by innkeeper Thomas Pybus for stealing one of his silver mugs. Pybus called in a local constable who took her, and the mug, to Thomas Clifton, the local justice of the peace. After Clifton questioned her, she gave the constable the slip and managed to get herself a place on the mail coach to Sheffield, but was caught just before it departed. She then filched the silver mug from him and disposed of it. *The Leeds Intelligencer* was highly amused at the constable's incompetence:

> *The Constable, who had charge of the mug...was perfectly astounded when it was not to be found. He looked about, and began to consider whether there was not magic in the business. He searched in the crown of his hat, he even examined his inexpressibles; but was at last relieved from his embarrassment by a gentleman, who found the cup upon the road.*

Sarah was locked up at the inn in the care of the Otley Volunteers, one of the many local civil defence groups formed during the Napoleonic Wars. That night, she sang hymns, prayed fervently, protested her innocence, and persuaded one of the Volunteers to help her with another escape attempt. While the others slept, using sheets and blankets tied together with her garters, she managed to lower herself, 'although a very lusty woman', from the first floor window into the street and ran off. A passer-by noticed the blankets and alerted the officer in charge, who assembled his men and ordered drums to be beat. Sarah was found hiding in a hayloft three miles away.

SARAH BAILEY, CHARLOTTE NEWMAN, HARRIET SKELTON

The next we hear about Sarah is that she was hanged at York Castle on 12 April 1800, alongside John M'William, a forger. In the clichéd words of the newspaper reports, she 'appeared...to have a strict sense of [her] unfortunate situation, and conducted [herself] in [her] last moments, with becoming fortitude'.

The Bank usually pressed for the death penalty for persistent and unrepentant forgers and utterers, even if they were female. Mary Lloyd, a widow with children, was executed six months after Sarah Bailey. The Bank had offered her the chance to appear as a witness for the Crown but she refused it, changing her mind only at the last moment. Pleas for mercy from the Sheriff of Chester Castle himself were ignored.

The Bank's well-funded system for detection and prosecution operated almost entirely separately from the normal processes of the justice system. A force of ten inspectors travelled the country to deal with hotspots of crime and the Bank sometimes privately hired police officers from London or other cities to go incognito into areas where they would not be identified. The Bank only pursued cases they felt sure they would win but that did not mean forgers and utterers were 'let off'. Although many were not prosecuted, or even apprehended, at the time they were detected, they were often spied on and followed, arrested only when the Bank had accumulated enough evidence against them to proceed. Some were persuaded to provide information against others or to take part in elaborate entrapments in return for a reduction in their sentences or a pardon. These tactics, as well as the growing toll of blood at the gallows, provided grounds for criticism of the Bank of England.

By 1801, a year after Sarah Bailey had hanged, the Bank understood that the Restriction would last for some while and that the public would object if it perceived that too many people were being hanged. While the Bank was duty-bound to protect the currency, its policy of making large numbers of low value notes available and its failure to design them securely meant that, in the view of many people, it carried a responsibility for the high incidence of the crime.

WOMEN AND THE GALLOWS 1797–1837

In May a new law permitted prosecution for the lesser offence of possession of false bank notes, to be punished with an automatic sentence of fourteen years' transportation. It was offered to those on capital charges only on condition they pleaded guilty. Those who refused the offer (only about thirteen per cent did) and who were subsequently found guilty usually found themselves facing death at the gallows. Not everyone was offered the deal and the Bank tended to take a more lenient position with women who uttered, many of whom were dragged into the crime by their male partners. This leniency was not necessarily born of compassion: the women's evidence was useful in building the case against their confederates. The final decisions about the fate of the condemned were made at the highest level; they were discussed by the Bank's committee of law suits, which consisted of the governor or deputy governor, five directors, and a secretary, assisted by a solicitor.

Between 1804 and 1834 at the Old Bailey alone there were 126 death sentences and 565 sentences of transportation and, in contrast with other property crimes, most of the death sentences were carried out. As time went on, and the numbers going to the gallows increased, public disapproval gathered pace. The Bank of England was criticized for putting commercial considerations over human life and the campaign against capitally punishing forgery crimes became a focal point for the debate on capital punishment. The especially high rates of execution in 1818, when four women were executed for uttering, two at Newgate and the others in Lancaster and Warwick, and fourteen men were executed for the same crime with a further thirteen for forgery, caused deep unease.

On 1 November 1817 Charlotte Newman was arrested after passing off a forged one pound note when buying half-boots at John Bartlett's shop in Denmark Street in central London. She and her companion George Mansfield had for some days been under surveillance by Samuel Plank and Charles Jeffries from the Marlborough Street Police Office. George was arrested as he loitered outside the shop and Charlotte immediately after she had completed her transaction.

SARAH BAILEY, CHARLOTTE NEWMAN, HARRIET SKELTON

She quickly explained to the officers that she was an 'unfortunate woman' (a prostitute) and that a 'gentleman' had given her the note 'in a coach'. Unsurprisingly, the officers were sceptical. Charlotte also denied that she knew George Mansfield, but Plank and Jeffries discovered that they were both connected with a lodging house in Bunhill Row, where twenty-eight counterfeit one pound notes were found in the room Charlotte rented. She and Mansfield were committed to Newgate to await trial.

The Bank's committee for law suits discussed the case and decided that they should be capitally indicted, noting that Mansfield was a notorious housebreaker and that Charlotte's husband had already been transported for uttering. Charlotte and George appeared together at the Old Bailey on 3 December 1817 where they pleaded not guilty and Charlotte tried to deflect blame from Mansfield, stating at the end of proceedings that 'the other prisoner is perfectly innocent, and knows nothing of the transaction.' Indeed, the jury decided that the case against George had not been made – he was, after all, arrested outside the shop and although clearly an associate of Charlotte's he was not seen to handle the notes himself – and that Charlotte alone was guilty.

This meant an automatic death sentence. Now the only avenue left to Charlotte was to beg for mercy from the Bank of England. Although in law the Bank had no jurisdiction over pardons and reprieves, in reality its say was almost always decisive. The committee for law suits had the option to indicate that it would not oppose a reprieve and its disinclination to interfere meant that capital punishment would proceed.

In Newgate, Charlotte and Mary Ann James, who had been convicted of fraud (see Chapter 9), came to the attention of Elizabeth Fry, the Quaker reformer who had made Newgate and the women in it her personal project. At some point in their encounter, Charlotte told Mrs Fry that she had committed the crime in order to be caught and transported. She had wished to join her husband in Botany Bay.

Charlotte knew she had little chance of mercy but late one evening in the week before she was due to hang, she wrote a letter to the

Bank, possibly with the assistance of Fry. Her heart-rending plea is preserved in the Bank's archives:

> *I most humbly hope your humanity will excuse the liberty I take to intreat your consideration of my most afflicting situation. I sometimes felt some hopes hearing of your great mercy towards those who have been allowed to plead guilty the last Sessions. I trust I feel most sensible the awful situation I am now in and the justness of my sentence. When I was at the bar my life was then in your hands and I now feel it more acutely. Let Mercy be blended with Justice. It is yet in your power to save the life of an unhappy sufferer which I most earnestly implore of you. How sweet will be the hours of reflection when you can rest upon your pillow and commune with God & yourself that life which if taken from one of God's creatures you have not power to give. A few days, nay hours, will determine this awful event.*

Also in the archives is a copy of the note that was sent back by the Bank's solicitors:

> *Charlotte Newman, I received your letter but I cannot interfere in your behalf. The Governor & Directors of the Bank have considered your case & they also decline to interfere.*

Two days later, on the Sunday before their execution, Charlotte, Mary Ann James and two men, William Hatchman and John Attel, were obliged to attend Newgate Chapel for the condemned sermon. This event was open to the public and tickets sold well. 'We never saw so crowded a congregation on any occasion to hear the sermon,' reported *The Observer*. The condemned were seated in a pew around a coffin in the well of the chapel.

The Ordinary, the evangelical Reverend Horace Cotton (who had been so unhelpful to Eliza Fenning – see Chapter 1), called on the condemned to repent. He was known for his abrasive style and would often scream at prisoners, threatening that they would burn in hell for eternity. The presence of two women in the condemned pew may have restrained him, although he still felt it was a good idea to spell out what they faced in two days' time. He chose as his text, 'Have pity on me, have pity on me, oh ye, my friends, for the hand of God hath touched me' from the Book of Job and 'dilated with much effect upon the necessity of a severe application to the doctrines and ordinances of God, in order that consolation might be derived, and forgiveness obtained.' The prisoners were to suffer 'a dreadful and ignominious death – disgraceful to themselves, disgraceful to those they leave behind' and he referred to their parents' grey hairs 'brought down with sorrow to the grave' and to 'wives made widows before their time'. He took it upon himself to explain to the congregation the seriousness of their crimes. Forgery, he said, was:

> *too prevalent, a crime which appears to increase with every session! and in a commercial nation like this, where public and individual credit is the vital principle of its daily transactions, perhaps it is as mischievous as any that can be committed against the commonweal; for it rudely bursts asunder the links which unite such a society in the great chain of mutual credit and confidence, and is calculated to plunge the whole into distrust and confusion.*

Addressing the women directly, he spoke of the 'big round drops rolling down your pallid cheeks – full well I hear the agonising sighs which issue from your hearts' and also of their 'hearty contrition' and 'unfeigned repentance'. And he entreated Christ to number them amongst those whose 'unrighteousness is forgiven, and whose sin is covered'. At this point, when 'there was scarcely a dry face' among the gathered, Cotton finished by exhorting the congregation 'however they may abhor the offence, let them learn to pity the offenders.'

At six o'clock in the evening before her death, Charlotte wrote to Elizabeth Fry, telling her that she had achieved a state of calmness about her impending end. 'The mercies of God are boundless,' she said, 'and I trust through His grace this affliction is sanctified to me, and through the Saviour's blood my sins will be washed away. I have much to be thankful for. I feel such serenity of mind and fortitude.'

On the morning of 17 February, shortly after eight, the sheriff, under sheriffs and others went first to the cell where Hatchman and Attel were confined, attended by Cotton. He ushered them into the press yard, where their leg irons were removed, Hatchman showing signs of distress and saying in a 'tremulous' voice, 'I have seen a great deal of trouble in my time; thank God, however, it will soon be at an end; it must be an easy death.' It did not turn out to be so.

Executions were emotionally risky affairs. The authorities wanted them to be solemn and orderly ceremonies of high drama, from which the spectators took away a message that the pain of death was not worth the rewards of crime. But there was always a danger of disorder and protest in the crowd. It suited the authorities if the condemned expressed their guilt and went willingly and calmly to their death yet many failed to maintain the appearance of equanimity. On the morning of the execution, Mary Ann and Charlotte were engaged in 'devotions of a sincere and truly repentant character' but as their time approached they were 'in hysterics', which delayed their exit into the street. According to an account given by the sheriff later, they could not be brought out in this state as 'they would have died without knowing they were going into eternity.' Eventually, they were ready to leave the prison but they had to be physically supported as they emerged through Debtors' Door and climbed the scaffold.

Attel and Hatchman joined them on the platform, where all four knelt in 'fervent' prayer. Hatchman was said to have looked into the crowd to see if he could recognize his friends and appeared anxious to say something, but did not. He saluted Charlotte, evidently a prearranged sign of encouragement.

The condemned were prepared for the drop: the hoods were pulled over their faces, the ropes adjusted, and the women's skirts were tied; Cotton pronounced the words,'In the midst of life we are in death' and gave the signal, after which the four were 'launched into eternity'. It was a botched job. Some of the ropes had been badly positioned, 'especially that of Hatchman', and caused great agony. 'The women

SARAH BAILEY, CHARLOTTE NEWMAN, HARRIET SKELTON

were deeply affected,' reported the papers, meaning that Charlotte and Mary Ann were convulsed for longer than was usual. The crowd reacted by hissing and groaning.

An eyewitness later reported to the City of London's Court of Common Council on the executions, telling them that 'there was never anything more revolting to human nature' and that the sufferings of the executed were protracted and augmented. 'What added considerably to the horror,' he said, 'was that two of the sufferers were females, one of whom (Mary Ann James) exhibited symptoms of suffering which were almost too shocking to describe, and which drew from the surrounding multitude the most bitter execrations.'

Opponents of the death penalty were appalled. They pointed out that John Attel was the father of four young children and his wife was heavily pregnant with another. Mary Ann James had been brought up 'with much indulgence' but had 'afterwards had to pass through various afflictions and temptations'. She was said to have fallen into bad company but her conduct in prison had been exemplary. If she had been allowed to live, they argued she could have become a valuable member of society.

Charlotte Newman was one of two women executed in 1818 for uttering. The other was Harriet Skelton, born Harriet Goodluck, who was orphaned at three and then fostered by a respectable family until, at the age of 15, she entered domestic service. She married John Skelton in 1809 but the relationship was a disaster, destroyed by his alcoholism, and he abandoned her. Harriet was relieved when her brother Beamsley Goodluck offered to take her in but before long it became apparent that Beamsley was engaged in the passing of forged notes. He told Harriet that he was doing so only in order to clear a debt and asked her to help by passing a few herself. She refused but eventually, to keep him out of debtors' prison, or so she believed, she relented.

In 17 January 1818, Harriet walked into George Howard's confectioners shop at 36 Princes Street in the Soho district of London, and bought cakes. In payment she offered a one pound note. As was standard practice, Howard asked for her name and address.

'Mrs Jones. My address is Windmill Street,' she said.

Howard wrote the details on the back of the note. Shortly afterwards, at 6 Leigh Street, near Red Lion Square, Harriet was arrested. It is likely that officers or agents of the Bank of England had been following her for the past few weeks. By now her husband was back on the scene, and he too had become involved in Beamsley's forgery set-up.

In prison Harriet was counselled by Elizabeth Fry, who was struck by her demeanour. She was, she wrote, of 'particularly prepossessing appearance... A very child might have read her countenance, open, affectionate, and confiding; expressing strong feelings, but neither hardened in depravity, nor capable of cunning.'

Before the trial, Harriet wrote to the Bank of England to explain her role in the crime:

Guilty as I am, and deservedly involved in disgrace, I am not guilty to that extent which is supposed... Part of my time was employed at my business of doing upholstery work of the house which was furnished by my brother... I confess that my motive was not the good of the public but to gratify a desire of revenge on the part of my brother whose advice I sincerely regret that I followed. I hope these few remarks will convince you that I am not so abandoned a character as you suppose.

Whether encouraged by Fry or because she genuinely believed she had a chance of getting off the charges, she turned down the Bank's offer of a plea bargain. That decision was catastrophic. While she stood in the dock, a parade of shopkeepers from Piccadilly, Titchfield Street, High Holborn, Houndsditch, Aldgate and Soho gave incontrovertible evidence against her. The jury found her guilty of uttering, and judge John Burrough passed sentence of death on her.

Elizabeth Fry, deeply upset, called on the Home Secretary, Lord Sidmouth, to appeal for mercy. A heated argument ensued and Fry left Sidmouth's office disappointed. A few days later, Fry's friend Prince

SARAH BAILEY, CHARLOTTE NEWMAN, HARRIET SKELTON

William, the Duke of Gloucester (he was married to George III's daughter Princess Mary), accompanied her on a visit to Newgate where he talked to Harriet for nearly an hour. The prince then went with Fry to the Bank of England to plead Harriet's cause but the Bank officers remained unmoved.

In their memoir of their mother's life, Fry's daughters described Harriet's last days:

> *[Harriet] was ordered for execution...her deportment in the prison had been good, amenable to regulations, quiet and orderly; some of her companions in guilt were heard to say, that they supposed she was chosen for death, because she was better prepared than the rest of them.*

She wrote a last letter to her foster family in which she spoke of the shame of her terrible end and expressed repentance.

The Reverend Charles T. Mileham stated that Harriet's last words before approaching the scaffold at Newgate on the morning of 24 April were, 'God be merciful to me, a sinner.' As she and 28-year-old forger John Ward stood together in front of the small crowd, Ward embraced her. He was 'launched into eternity' first. Then it was Harriet's turn. She died without a struggle. After an hour their bodies were taken down and given to relatives.

The cases against Harriet's brother and husband were not pursued.

After Harriet's death, the satirical *New Bon Ton Magazine, or Telescope of the Times* noted the 'alarming increase in executions for forgery' and offered a number of remarks on the 'paltry and unfeeling conduct of Messieurs the Bank Directors'. It said: 'We have no doubt that very day [of Harriet Skelton and John Ward's executions], all the tribe of bloated brokers dined, or rather crammed, with their usual appetites.'

Writing in *The Examiner*, the Radical journalist and campaigner Leigh Hunt had many criticisms of the situation. He pointed out that because the Bank was legally the victim, retailers, who had no recourse to compensation when they were defrauded, suffered major losses. The genuine notes were 'clumsy, ill-invented and worse executed'. Hanging without mercy and transportation was doing nothing to deter forgers and utterers and he urged that another solution be found. He despaired of the Bank's policies. 'The Bank is rich and flourishing,' he wrote. 'Riches, we all know, harden the heart.'

The year 1818 was exceptionally bloody: twenty-seven people across England and Wales were executed for forgery or uttering compared to eighteen in 1817, but it ended with a watershed: two juries at the December sessions of the Old Bailey refused to convict any of those prosecuted by the Bank on forgery or uttering charges. The following month, the Radical bookseller William Hone (who had done so much to publicize the injustice done to Eliza Fenning) and the caricaturist George Cruikshank published a satirical print, the 'Bank Restriction Note'. Cruikshank claimed to have sketched it in ten minutes after seeing a woman hanged at the Old Bailey for passing a forged note (we can speculate that it may have been Harriet Skelton). The cartoon looked like a bank note but featured eleven hanged figures, three of them female. The pound sign is a curled rope, the signature is that of J. Ketch, the notorious seventeenth-century executioner, and Britannia is an old woman eating her children. *The Examiner* said it 'ought to make the hearts of the Bank Directors (if they have hearts) ache at the sight'.

The last woman in England or Wales to be executed on forgery charges was 43-year-old Sarah Price, found guilty of uttering a forged one pound note to a shoemaker. She appears to have rejected the Bank's offer of a plea bargain and was hanged at Newgate on 5 December 1820. Efforts were made to save her: Queen Caroline, the estranged wife of George IV, wrote to her husband asking for her life (which probably had an adverse effect). Sarah was executed with five others, including John Madden, aged 22, also convicted of forgery. His appearance on the scaffold prompted protests amongst the crowd, who shouted, 'No Bank!' but when Sarah Price emerged, a small figure dressed in black, the anger of the spectators escalated and they cried, 'Murder, murder!' and 'Down with the Bank!' In the moments before she dropped she was said to have shown 'a degree of fortitude beyond anything that can be expressed'. Her son was reported to have been transported for a similar offence some time previously.

While the Bank's directors were seemingly impervious to criticism, they were quite separately moving to end the 'paper system' as the economic conditions no longer required it. The Bank Restriction Act was rescinded in 1821. That was not the end of uttering, counterfeiting and coining, or the end of execution for those crimes, although it was greatly in decline. In 1822, seven people were hanged, all of them men, in 1823 only four. Thomas Maynard, hanged at Newgate on the last day of 1829, was the last person executed for forgery crimes.

The strengthening of feeling against the capital punishment of forgery crimes signalled the dismantling of the so-called Bloody Code, the collection of over 200 felonies that attracted the death penalty. In fact, it was during the 1820s that the phrase itself was coined, a way of characterizing these laws as archaic, belonging to a bygone era of irrationality and brutality. What was required now was a general overhaul of the law relating to felonies. That would not happen for another ten years, but change was coming.

CHAPTER 11

Charlotte Long
Gloucester, 31 August 1832

*

Arson

Arson was primarily a rural crime and usually involved setting fire to hayricks, often as revenge against a farmer by a former employee. It was viewed with great seriousness because hayricks were valuable and, unlike most property crimes, there was also a risk of injury or death to those who had to put out the flames. It was overwhelmingly a male crime. Between 1800 and 1837 around 100 men but only four women were hanged for it. In 1813, when Elizabeth Osborne was tried at Bodmin in Cornwall, felons sentenced for arson were capitally punished at a rate of one in two, high for a property crime. Twenty years later, when Charlotte Long was hanged, those odds had not changed.

Just after half past ten on the night of 25 July 1833, Jesse Organ, a 39-year-old farmer in North Nibley, Gloucestershire, left his house in a panic. A young weaver who had been passing his fields had just run to tell him that one of his haystacks was alight. Thankfully, Organ managed to extinguish the fire quickly and most of the hay was saved.

The weaver had seen a woman wearing a black bonnet, a dark gown and a shawl wrapped around her 'cloak ways' (that is with the corners tied round her neck in front) near the haystack. She seemed anxious not to be seen. Not long afterwards, he saw something 'like a firework' fly out of the haystack. That was when he rushed to the farmhouse to

144

CHARLOTTE LONG

alert Organ. A local labourer also saw a woman walking towards the rick. 'Good night,' he said, to which she mumbled a reply and turned her head away. Organ's was not the only haystack attacked that night. Two other North Nibley farmers, Mr Nichol and Mr Gillman, had their stacks set on fire. The stacks were all within a stone's throw of each other and the arsonist had lit them in quick succession.

The village was soon alive with gossip and rumour, and within days James Baylis, the tithing officer, and Henry Exell, the parish officer, arrested Betsey Burford and took her before the magistrate, where she accused another woman, Charlotte Long, of being responsible. There was known antagonism between Exell and Charlotte. Some months previously, he had accompanied her out of North Nibley to the parish of Alkington, nine miles away. She was pregnant. In order to avoid the additional burden on parishioners for the upkeep of bastard children it was standard practice to remove them to another parish if at all possible. Charlotte had some kind of family connection to Alkington, which encouraged the parish officers to push her out of North Nibley. While she was being removed, she was alleged to have said to Exell, 'You have bit off my finger, so I will bite your thumb.'

There was another reason the parish officers wanted Charlotte to leave: her sexual incontinence. Her husband, John Long, by whom she already had two children, had been transported to Australia for theft four years earlier, so the child she was carrying could not be his. She gave birth to a boy in Alkington but shortly afterwards the family returned to North Nibley.

Now, as Exell searched her house, he warned her that Betsey was alleging that she was responsible for the fires. 'Betsey Burford has dug a ditch for me, and I shall fall into it,' she replied. 'She is the beginning and the end, and the mother of the fact.' Charlotte was arrested and taken to Gloucester Gaol to await trial. Betsey, meanwhile, turned King's evidence. She admitted being an accomplice but blamed Charlotte.

Charlotte, her baby boy in her arms, appeared at the Gloucester Summer Assizes in front of Judge John Gurney, who had a reputation as a severe and unsympathetic judge (as a younger man he had prosecuted Eliza Fenning – see Chapter 1). Betsey claimed that Charlotte wanted revenge on Henry Exell because he had ejected her from the parish and that she had initially planned to set fire only to his ricks. But, she went on, Charlotte was worried that she would be suspected because she had publicly threatened Exell during her removal and, to cast attention away from herself, she decided first to light the stacks of three entirely blameless people. Betsey recounted what Charlotte had told her about what happened:

> *The prisoner told her that she first went to Mr Nichol's rick, and having put a quantity of powder in it, she struck a light with some tinder and set it on fire; she then proceeded to Mr Gillman's rick and fired that; after that she proceeded by Richard Hooper's shop, through Adam Porrit's wheat field, and from thence into the Moors. In going to Mr Organ's rick, she said she met William Philpott, who wished her good night; she turned her head from him so that he should not know her, but at the same time wished him good night, in a feigned voice. On reaching Mr Organ's rick, she put a quantity of powder into it, and having struck a light on the remaining portion of the tinder, she put it with the powder and left the rick.*

Betsey's account conveniently included a description of what Charlotte had worn that night: 'Her shawl was tied mantle-fashion.' Charlotte could not stop herself from speaking out in court: 'Betsey Burford, I hope God will have mercy on your soul. I forgive you. You often told me how to do it, but I never said I would do so.'

Finally, it was her turn to speak.

> *I never threatened anyone; but Betsey Burford said if she had the use of her limbs as I had of mine she would make Nibley smoke again; and she said with bitter oaths, not fit to mention, that if Mr Exell had served her as he had served me she would burn everything he had.*

CHARLOTTE LONG

The limbs Charlotte referred to were Betsey's legs: she suffered from rheumatism and sometimes walked with difficulty.

Then Judge Gurney recalled the witnesses who had seen 'a woman' that night and asked them whether she had been lame. They all answered in the negative and this was enough to satisfy him that the woman was Charlotte and not Betsey. The two character witnesses Charlotte called did not attend, although a member of the Organ family, John, 'gave her a character of goodness of disposition'.

Gurney summed up and told the jury to regard Betsey Burford's evidence as the testimony of an accomplice and to treat it with caution; if they nevertheless were convinced that Charlotte Long had committed the offence, whether at Betsey's instigation or not, they should find her guilty. This they did, although the foreman added, 'We beg leave most strongly to recommend the prisoner to mercy, because we think she must have been set on as a tool of some other person.'

Jesse Organ and another of the prosecutors were shocked to find that Charlotte now faced death. 'My Lord, I believe she was drawn into it by someone else, and I wish to recommend her to mercy,' pleaded Organ but Gurney refused to countenance a request for a reprieve. Like so many other women found guilty of a crime, she was not judged on the crime alone.

> *I cannot attend to these recommendations. I have considered this matter very much. There were three ricks fired, all on the same night. The prisoner is not a young girl, and I find that her husband has been transported. There was a case at York, which was tried before me, where a very young girl had been set on to commit an offence of this kind by a person much older than herself, and there she was examined as a witness against the person who had instigated the commission of the crime, but this is a very different case.*

Gurney was referring to Mary Hunter, a 47-year-old wife of a labourer, whom he had sentenced to hang at York Castle three months earlier. The case against her hinged on the word of Hannah Gray, who claimed

WOMEN AND THE GALLOWS 1797–1837

that Hunter had threatened to tear her liver out if she did not set fire to farmer John Marshall's wheat stacks and would give her a new frock if she did. Gray was described as 'of weak mind' and Mary Hunter and her husband had a longstanding dispute with Marshall. Hunter went to her death protesting her innocence.

While Gurney passed sentence, Charlotte was overcome, crying and begging for mercy. The scene was described in *The Gloucestershire Chronicle*:

> *Almost every person present was in tears, and the Learned Baron [Judge Gurney] himself was so overcome, that at the conclusion of his address to the prisoners his voice faltered, and as soon as the fatal sentence had been passed, the female prisoner dropped on the floor, and was carried out of court moaning most dreadfully.*

The Morning Herald was outraged that Charlotte Long had been convicted on the word of an accomplice, with no corroborating evidence:

> *Now, by the law of England, as understood at the present day, no person can be convicted on the unsupported testimony of an accomplice; because the presumption that an accomplice tells the truth is not so great as the presumption that the evidence of a person of that description is fabricated for the purpose of shifting the guilt from his or her own shoulders upon those of another.*

In the view of the newspaper, Long's conviction was not legal.

The Morning Herald objected also to the identification evidence. A woman seen near a hayrick just before it was seen in flames does not mean that that woman set fire to it. Further, no one had identified Charlotte as being the woman, as none of the witnesses had seen her face. The most they could say was that she was not lame. Indeed Betsey Burford herself could have been that woman, as she admitted that she was only sometimes lame. It was never proved in court that gunpowder had been found at Charlotte's dwelling.

CHARLOTTE LONG

In the opinion of *The Morning Herald* the law that condemned Charlotte was 'barbarous': it made no distinction between the guilt of a person who sets fire to a stack of hay in a field far away from a dwelling house and that of someone who sets fire to a habitation. And it was a disgrace for a Christian country to send a woman to the scaffold with an infant at her breast 'for an offence which is punished with death in no other civilized country.' One hundred and six inhabitants of North Nibley and vicinity signed a petition seeking mercy for Charlotte, citing as grounds that the crime was instigated by Betsey Burford, a 'bad character', and that the ricks were not near property.

The Gloucestershire Chronicle interviewed Ann Linton, the matron of Gloucester Gaol, about Charlotte's conduct in her final days. Charlotte had confessed that she had set fire to the ricks, she said, but told her that Betsey Burford had offered her money to do it.

> *Betsey Burford wished me to do it, and I said, if I take a fire stick in my hand I shall be detected; if I take a candle it will be seen, and I shall be caught; when Burford replied, 'I'll tell you how you must do [it]; take a piece of tinder, put it in a rag with some gunpowder and then blow it, and it will take fire; then come and give me the signal as my husband will be in bed. I did go and give the signal within two minutes after I had fired the ricks.*

Charlotte appears to have approached her fate in a state of serenity and resignation. The death of her infant son, who had been handed into the care of her sister, was a relief to her. On 31 August at about eleven o'clock, after making a confession to the chaplain of the gaol and in front of 'an immense crowd of spectators' she mounted the scaffold and suffered her fate. She died alongside Thomas Gaskins from Deerhurst who had been convicted, in a separate case, of setting fire to a rick belonging to his master.

Charlotte Long was the last woman in England to hang for arson. In 1837 arson was removed from the list of capital crimes.

CHAPTER 12

The End of the Bloody Code

The architect of change in the criminal code was not a Whig agitator for reform, a Quaker opposed to the death penalty or a Radical aiming to shake up the status quo. He was a Tory whose motivation was not compassion for condemned felons but a belief in the need for a stricter and more effective system of justice.

When Robert Peel was appointed Home Secretary in 1822, Britain had the largest collection of crimes meriting the death penalty in the world, encompassing hundreds of separate statutes. In a wide-ranging review of law, justice and policing Peel included measures to consolidate, regularize and tidy up the criminal law and aimed to head off growing criticism from Whigs and other reformers of the way the death penalty was applied. Peel fully supported capital sentences for property crimes (he adamantly refused to receive relatives pleading for the lives of middle-class forgers Henry Fauntleroy and Joseph Hunton) but he accepted that the deterrent power of capital punishment had been diluted by its erratic implementation and the disproportionate punishment of low value crimes.

The collection of capital crimes usually referred to as the Bloody Code included obsolete offences designed to deal with behaviours that were once seen by the genteel class as insupportable social evils perpetrated by the poor. In 1822 to steal from a rabbit warren, be in the company of gypsies for a month, cut down trees in an orchard and go about at night with a blackened face were all still capital offences. The statutes were a confusing mess, with an overabundance of laws covering the same subjects: ninety-two dealt with theft and 120 with forgery. Between 1825 and 1828 Peel repealed or revised nearly 280 statutes. The laws on theft were reduced to thirty pages and by 1830 forgery offences were consolidated into a single statute. The Waltham Black Act of 1723, which had brought in many of the more bizarre capital offences, was rescinded. Petty treason – and its special punishment for women – was abolished; all murders were now to be charged and tried in the same way. Many of the changes merely encapsulated what had become common practice. There was no point in keeping offences that were never laid against wrongdoers, or retaining the death penalty for crimes that were never capitally punished.

Peel knew that his changes required two developments: better prisons and better police. Every county was now obliged to run a common gaol or house of correction, to be financially supported by local rates, and to adhere to common standards in the provision of food. He overcame traditional resistance to the establishment of a police force and brought in the Metropolitan Police Act of 1829, which created a professional, civilian police force to replace the hotchpotch of paid and unpaid London constables, nightwatchmen, police and informers. It was a model later extended across the country.

On 15 November 1830 the Duke of Wellington's Tory government lost a vote of no confidence. Now, for the first time in forty-seven years, the Whigs were in power. Under the administrations of Lord Grey and Lord Melbourne, they embarked on a programme of rapid and radical reforms: the Great Reform Act of 1832 addressed electoral abuses and inconsistencies; in 1833 slavery was abolished; and various Factory Acts tackled the use of children in industry. There were also sweeping changes to the capital code. The Punishment of Death Act of 1832 removed from the list of hanging offences shoplifting, the theft of horses, cattle and sheep, and some types of forgery; in 1834–5 sacrilege, letter stealing and returning from transportation were removed, followed in 1836 by forgery and coining and in 1837 arson, burglary and theft from a dwelling house. The impact was immediate. Rates of execution dropped sharply. In 1836 the total number of executed fell below twenty (fourteen men and three women) for the first time. In the forty-one years between 1797 and 1837 over 2,000 men and

WOMEN AND THE GALLOWS 1797–1837

131 women were hanged; in the next forty-one years this was down to 442 and thirty-four.

After the 1833 hangings of Mary Hunter and Charlotte Long for arson no woman was executed for anything other than murder. (After 1836 the same was true for men, with the exception of five executed for attempted murder.) In 1868 Frances Kidder, who killed her 12-year-old stepdaughter, became the last woman executed in public. From the middle of that year all hangings took place inside prison, unseen by the public.

Overall, in the 147 years from 1837 until the end of hanging in 1965, sixty-four women were executed, an average of one woman every two years (the rate for men was twelve a year). Ruth Ellis, who shot her boyfriend in what was widely accepted as a crime of passion and was hanged in 1955, was famously the last of them.

A browse through the stories of the women listed in Part 3 shows that late Georgian justice was swift and severe. Those felons lucky enough to be reprieved from death and imprisoned or sent to Australia endured harsh regimes and difficult conditions, but at least had the opportunity to rebuild their lives. Those who climbed the steps of the gallows on their final journey had no such chances.

Part 3

Chronology:
Women Hanged in England and Wales 1797–1837

A list, in chronological order, of all the women executed, along with their ages and details of their crimes where known, as well as alternative spellings of their names.

A couple of cautions: contemporary newspapers provided a lot of this information, as did execution broadsides, the cheaply produced sheets sold at the event, but both sources can be unreliable. In general, women convicted of petty treason (for women, this meant the murder of a husband or employer) were taken to the gallows on a sledge or hurdle drawn behind a horse. I have only included this detail where I have found it in a contemporary source.

ELIZABETH BROCKLEBY or BROKESBY
Drawn to the gallows and hanged in Lincoln on 17 March 1797, for the poisoning murder of her husband (petty treason).

After she was sentenced to death, Elizabeth Brockleby was removed from the bar 'in a state of insensibility' which lasted until her execution. She was so distressed that she was supported on her journey to the hurdle. After being drawn to the gallows she was lifted on to the platform. She was the first woman in England and Wales not to be burnt for petty treason (from the mid-eighteenth century, as a mercy, women were generally strangled before they were tied to the stake).

WOMEN AND THE GALLOWS 1797–1837

ELIZABETH AMOS
Drawn to the gallows and hanged on Penenden Heath, Maidstone, Kent on 20 March 1797, for the poisoning murder of her husband Stephen (petty treason). Aged 19.

In her last moments, Elizabeth Amos expressed 'penitence, sorrow and contrition' and her words 'drew tears' from the assembled spectators.

DIANA or ELIZABETH DAVIES or DAVIS
Hanged in Presteigne, Radnorshire on 10 May 1797, for stealing sheep.

Diana Davies, a repeat offender, and her son James were prosecuted by three Shropshire farmers for stealing sheep later recovered at Presteigne in Radnorshire. She was capitally convicted by Judge George Hardinge (see Chapter 4). James was transported.

REBECCA HOWARD
Hanged in Norwich, Norfolk on 9 August 1797, for the murder of her illegitimate baby son.

After the body of a four-week-old baby was discovered near Bishopsgate Bridge in Norwich, Rebecca Howard, a field worker, was soon identified as the mother. She had left her lodgings with the baby in her arms and on her return told the landlady that she 'hoped it [the baby] was happy, and that better care would be taken of it than she could give it'. She showed no sign of distress and went to bed. Her defence counsel produced a witness to say that she had been 'deranged' on the day of the murder and that she was generally 'either very sullen or in great spirits'. However, the judge attributed her fluctuations in mood to conscience rather than mental illness. She was said to have 'swooned away' during her trial but thereafter 'conducted herself with the greatest propriety'. After she arrived at the gallows at Norwich Castle, she sang a psalm and addressed the crowd, exhorting them to observe the Sabbath and to place their faith in God, and warning women to 'avoid temptation' and to be on their guard against deceitful men. The crowd was estimated to be about 20,000.

CHRONOLOGY

REBECCA DUNN
Drawn to the gallows and hanged on Kennington Common, Surrey on 21 August 1797, for colouring copper coins with silver (high treason). Aged about 70.

After receiving the sacrament in a private chapel at the New Gaol in The Borough, Southwark, Rebecca Dunn was placed on a sledge and drawn two miles to Kennington Common.

MARIA THERESA PHIPOE or MARY BENSON
Hanged at Newgate, London on 11 December 1797, for the murder of Mary Cox. Aged 38.

A procuress from Dublin, Maria Theresa Phipoe was convicted at the Old Bailey in 1795 for a violent attack on John Courtois (or Curtoys), a rich French peruke-maker to the aristocracy, whom she had coerced into writing a promissory note for £2,000 (she later tried to sell it), and sentenced to death. The verdict was overturned on a technicality and she was later charged with dealing in stolen goods and imprisoned for a year in Newgate. Afterwards she took on a new identity, Mary Benson, a French *emigrée*, and in straitened circumstances, moved to the East End of London. Two years later, she was again arrested, this time for murdering Mary Cox, who was discovered bleeding 'like an ox' from a wound in her throat at Phipoe's lodgings. The two women had been trading stolen goods when Phipoe suddenly turned on her. The Old Bailey jury took just twelve minutes to return a guilty verdict and a sentence of death automatically followed. In prison awaiting execution, Maria attributed her crimes to the use of laudanum. On the day of her death, she was reported to have wept and shown penitence but just before she dropped, pulled herself together, 'her countenance not changing till the cap was drawing over her face'. An execution broadside reported her alleged last words: 'I warn you all not to give way to passion. It has been the destruction of Mrs Cox, and will plunge me headlong into eternity!' She left a guinea for the most deserving debtor in Newgate and gave the same to her executioner. After dissection at the College of Surgeons, her body was exhibited to the public in a courtyard near the gallows.

WOMEN AND THE GALLOWS 1797–1837

ELIZABETH BROWN
Hanged at Newgate, London on 30 May 1798, for uttering a forged bank note. Aged 44.

The first female hanged for uttering after the imposition of the bank note Restriction on 3 May 1797. Elizabeth Brown, a servant in a public house, tried to buy a pair of silver spoons from Samuel Phillips's shop in Shoreditch, London but the Bank of England two pound note she offered was immediately suspected. On arrest, she was held in a back parlour, where she threw a packet of papers, probably further forged notes, into the fire. Although she initially blamed others for passing the notes to her, she later admitted that she had been given blank notes and promised a share of the profits. She vehemently denied to the Bank's solicitor that her son, an apprentice to an engraver, had helped her 'fill them up', that is, to add the required serial numbers and signatures.

ANN WARNER
Hanged at Newgate, London on 28 November 1798, for coining (high treason). Aged 56.

Ann Warner was caught red-handed with her accomplice, 18-year-old Catherine Lahey, in the act of colouring base (copper) coins in their lodgings in King Street, Covent Garden. Damning evidence – aqua fortis, used to bring the silver colour out, and blacking, to take the shine off – was found in the room. Lahey was later respited and transported for life to New South Wales.

SARAH WILLIAMS
Hanged on Penenden Heath, Maidstone, Kent on 18 March 1799, for the murder of her illegitimate baby daughter.

A servant to a baker in Woolwich, Sarah Williams successfully concealed her pregnancy but came under suspicion when a baby's body was found in the privy. She was suspected of having killed two previous children.

CHRONOLOGY

MARY ANN MARTIN
Hanged at the New Gaol, Exeter, Devon on 23 March 1799, for the poisoning murder of Margaret Palmer.

On the gallows, insisting on her innocence to the last moment, Mary Ann Martin refused for an hour and a half to give 'the fatal signal', the indication to the hangman, usually a dropped handkerchief, that she was ready.

BETTY LIMPANY
Hanged at the New Gaol, Exeter, Devon on 5 April 1799, for arson. Aged 17.

Betty, a servant, set fire to the house of her master, William Leach, at Kentisbeare, Devon.

MARGARET HUGHES or HAYNES
Hanged in Canterbury, Kent on 4 July 1799, for the poisoning murder of her husband Thomas (petty treason).

Convicted in July 1798 of poisoning her husband, a private in the Hereford regiment of militia, Margaret Hughes was immediately reprieved because she was pregnant but warned that she should not entertain any hope of mercy after her child was born. A year later, on the scaffold, she thanked the sheriff and the clergyman who had attended her, declared that she was ready to meet her 'blessed redeemer', shook hands with the hangman and sang a psalm. 'She was neatly dressed, and conducted herself with the most becoming fortitude,' reported the *Kentish Chronicle*. Despite the rain, a large crowd watched her die.

ELIZABETH LAVENDER
Hanged in Horsham, Sussex on 22 July 1799, for the murder of her illegitimate baby son. Aged 17.

When the body of a newborn baby showing injuries made with a knife was discovered in a tub in a cellar at Fairlight, East Sussex, Elizabeth Lavender was soon suspected. A surgeon examined her and determined that she had recently given birth. Newspapers reported that she 'trembled and wept much' on the scaffold but expressed the hope that others would not copy her example.

MARY NICHOLSON
Hanged in Durham on 22 July 1799, for the poisoning murder of Elizabeth Atkinson, her employer's mother.

According to newspaper reports, when John Atkinson of Little Stainton, near Darlington suspected that his servant Mary Nicholson was stealing from him, he induced her to confess, promising on his part to drop the matter and not tell the young man who was courting her. After the lover became aware, Mary took revenge by putting poison in some 'pudding meat', which was eaten by five people including Elizabeth Atkinson, who died. The sentence of death passed in August 1798 was respited on a point of law and, while the twelve judges of the Common Law Courts in Westminster deliberated, Mary resided in the Durham Bridewell, working as servant to the gaoler. Her execution was notable because the rope used to hang her snapped as she dropped. She was forced to wait an hour while another was found.

MARY THORPE or THORP
Hanged at York Castle on 17 March 1800, for murdering her illegitimate child. Aged 22.

Mary Thorpe left her home in Ecclesfield and gave birth in lodgings near Sheffield. Some days afterwards she wound tape around her baby son's neck, attached a stone and put him in the river.

See also Chapter 4.

SARAH BAILEY
Hanged at York Castle on 12 April 1800, for uttering a forged bank note. Aged 22.

In 1799 the Bank of England sent an investigating officer and a Bow Street runner to look into a cluster of bad bank notes in Otley, near Leeds. They found Sarah Bailey already in custody. A travelling hawker and alleged thief, Sarah tried several times to escape but was executed the following year.

See also Chapter 10.

CHRONOLOGY

SARAH LLOYD
Hanged in Bury St Edmunds, Suffolk on 23 April 1800, for stealing in a dwelling house. Aged 22.
With her lover Joseph Clarke, Sarah Lloyd, a servant, stole valuable items from her employer. Her case attracted the support of a local magistrate.
See also Chapter 8.

ANN MEAD
Hanged in Hertford on 31 July 1800, for the murder of 18-month-old Charles Proctor. Aged 16.
Aged 15 when she poisoned her employers' young child with arsenic, Ann Mead offered few clues to her motivation.
See also Chapter 2.

ELIZABETH JOHNSON
Hanged at York Tyburn on 23 August 1800, for uttering a forged one pound bank note.
Elizabeth Johnson was also capitally charged with uttering two counterfeit half guineas and possessing further notes and coins. She was hanged at York Tyburn without Micklegate, a large open area outside the city walls, which now forms part of York Racecourse. She was said to have been 'totally insensible to her dreadful situation, and continued so up to the time of her execution'.

MARY LLOYD
Hanged in Boughton, Cheshire on 18 October 1800, for uttering a forged one pound bank note.
Mary Lloyd, a widow with a family to maintain, was charged with three others for uttering false one pound Bank of England notes at Altrincham and Stockport. The Bank rejected efforts to pardon her because she had earlier turned down the opportunity to appear as a prosecution witness. On the day of her execution she confessed to the crime but maintained that she had received the notes from George Mills, who was tried with her and acquitted. Before she died in front

of a large crowd of spectators, she appealed to God to look after her orphaned children.

HANNAH PALMER
Hanged with her brother John at Warwick on 1 April 1801, for the murder of Mary Palmer, her sister-in-law. Aged 19. John was hanged in chains.

The Palmers were from Snitterfield near Stratford-upon-Avon in Warwickshire. John was a day labourer, married to Mary, with whom he had a child. The marriage was unstable and the couple separated more than once. At harvest time in 1800, after an absence, John returned to his wife in order to live off her gleanings from the cornfield. He and his sister Hannah, encouraged by their mother Sarah, tried several times to poison Mary, and eventually, on 17 November, enticed her into a field under the pretence of gathering turnips and there attacked her. While Hannah held Mary's arms, John slit her throat and to stem the deluge of blood skewered the wound together. After this they sewed the body into a winnowing sheet and threw it in the River Avon, hoping that the waters, which were in flood, would take it away. John Palmer propagated a story that Mary had gone off with another man but that he had managed to retrieve her (blood-soaked) clothes, which as her husband were his property. He sold these to another sister, assuring her that Mary would not be returning to reclaim them. When Mary's body was discovered the next day at the weirbreak at Welford her brother became suspicious and managed to obtain some of the bloody clothes as evidence. John was arrested and taken to Warwick Gaol and Hannah and her mother followed ten days later. Sarah Palmer died in prison before she could be tried and her disgusted neighbours in Snitterfield demolished her house.

ALICE CLARKE
Hanged in Ruthin, Denbighshire on 13 April 1801, for the murder of her illegitimate baby daughter.

In 1800 Alice Clarke was convicted of murdering her child by burying her face down in a dungheap at Rhôs Nefs near Wrexham.

CHRONOLOGY

She 'pleaded her belly' but was found not to be pregnant and hanged at the next available assizes.

HANNAH EASTWOOD
Hanged at Lancaster Castle on 2 May 1801, for uttering forged bank notes.

Hannah Eastwood, executed alongside three men who were also convicted of forging notes, was the first woman to be hanged in Lancashire since 1772. Six years later, John Eastwood and Joseph Eastwood, who were probably members of her family, were convicted of forgery offences at Lancaster Assizes and transported for fourteen years.

SUSANNAH MOTTERSHALL or MOTTERSHED
Hanged in Lincoln on 23 July 1801, for the murder of Samuel Glew. Aged 23.

Samuel Glew, from Epworth in Lincolnshire, was robbed of £40 by 26-year-old Elizabeth Lamb and Susannah Mottershall, who beat him with an axe and threw him in a ditch. Lamb confessed and turned King's evidence. On the scaffold, Susannah Mottershall warned the spectators to avoid Lamb who 'had sworn falsely against her life.'

ANN BAKER
Hanged in Oakham, Rutland on 3 August 1801, for stealing and killing sheep.

Ann Baker was the last woman in Britain hanged for this crime.

SARAH CLARIDGE
Hanged in Warwick on 7 August 1801, for the drowning murder of her four-year-old son.

Sarah Claridge was accused of throwing her child into the canal at Ashted, near Birmingham.

MARY VOCE
Hanged in Nottingham on 16 March 1802, for the poisoning murder of her six-week-old daughter Elizabeth. Aged 24.

After an inquest following the sudden and agonized death of her baby daughter, Mary Voce was committed for trial at Nottingham Lent Assizes. She blamed neighbourhood children for mistakenly giving the baby arsenic, which she had intended to use to kill herself.

See also Chapter 4.

MARIA DAVIS or DAVIES and CHARLOTTE BOBBETT
Hanged in Bristol on 12 April 1802, for the murder of Davis's 15-month-old son Richard. Aged 20 and 23.

On 4 December 1801 Maria Davis, a widow, and her friend Charlotte Bobbett abandoned Davis's 15-month-old son Richard on Brandon Hill in Clifton, Bristol hoping that he would be found and cared for, but the child perished from exposure. Before their hanging on St Michael's Hill, they were reported to have attributed their 'present deplorable condition' to 'disobedience to their parents, idleness and dissolute company'. On the scaffold, 'after some time spent in exercises of penitential devotion, the wretched victims kissed each other, and then, clasping hands together, were launched into eternity.'

MARY LAPPIDGE or LAPPAGE
Hanged in Warwick on 15 April 1803, for uttering forged bank notes.

Mary was convicted with her partner William Grainger, who was respited and transported for life.

MARTHA CHAPPLE or CHAPEL
Hanged at York Castle on 1 August 1803, for the murder of her illegitimate baby daughter. Aged 19.

Chapple, a servant in the household of Colonel Surtees in Ackland, Yorkshire, gave birth to a daughter after an excruciating labour. The baby's body was found with dreadful injuries ('Its mouth was torn down to the throat, and its jawbone forced away'). In court she said she could not remember killing her child: 'God knows, I loved my child before I saw it... I never meant it any harm.'

CHRONOLOGY

SARAH JONES
Hanged in Shrewsbury, Shropshire on 11 August 1803, for the murder of her illegitimate baby. Aged 27.

Jones's three-month-old baby was found in a deep pit in a field in the village of Benthall in Shropshire.

ANN HURLE
Hanged at Newgate, London on 8 February 1804, for forgery of a financial instrument. Aged 22.

Emboldened by at least one previous fraud, when she impersonated an aunt in order to sell £100 worth of her shares, Ann Hurle attempted an even more audacious crime: submitting a power of attorney in the name of the old man for whom another of her aunts was housekeeper, so that she could transfer £500 of shares into her own name. She unsuccessfully pleaded her belly.

See also Chapter 9.

ELIZABETH CAESAR or CARTER
Hanged in Winchester, Hampshire on 12 March 1804, for the murder of her female illegitimate baby.

ELIZABETH LANGHAM or LAUGHAN or LARGHAM
Hanged in Moulsham, Chelmsford, Essex on 19 March 1804, for the murder of her illegitimate baby.

Elizabeth Langham murdered her child in her husband's absence with the 18th Light Dragoons. She was extremely distressed on the day of her execution and had to be assisted on to the scaffold.

ANN HEYWOOD or HAYWOOD
Hanged at York Castle on 18 March 1805, for the murder of her female illegitimate baby. Aged 23.

When Ann's labour started, she told her fellow servant she had a cold and asked her to fetch her some milk. When the girl returned she found Ann in an outhouse, covered in blood. Later, a bloody penknife was found in her room and the mutilated remains of the child were discovered amongst some ashes. Ann confessed that she had given birth but maintained that she had not murdered the baby.

ELIZABETH BARBER or DALY or DALEY
Hanged on Penenden Heath, Maidstone, Kent on 25 March 1805, for the stabbing murder of John Dennis Daly. Aged 53.

Witnesses at the trial of Elizabeth Barber spoke of her seated in a chair calmly smoking a pipe while her partner, a Greenwich military pensioner, lay dying of a deep stab wound to the chest. The couple had earlier had a drink-fuelled argument about money, and scuffles and cries for help were heard by the downstairs neighbour. Barber claimed that Daly had stabbed himself but a surgeon at her trial proved that this was an impossibility. Barber's sexual history told against her – she had left her husband and children – as did the fact that she had previously been imprisoned for a year in Maidstone for stabbing a man.

MARY MORGAN
Hanged in Presteigne, Radnorshire on 14 April 1805, for the murder of her illegitimate baby. Aged 17.

Abandoned by the father of her child and desperate to keep her situation as an undercook at Maesllwch Castle, Mary Morgan stabbed her newborn child, whose body was discovered hidden in her room. Judge Hardinge wept as he condemned her to death, which would be an example, he hoped, to other young women contemplating sex before marriage.

See also Chapter 4.

ANN DAVIS or GORDON
Hanged on Horsham Common, Sussex on 3 May 1805, for the murder of her illegitimate baby.

BETTY or BETSEY HULCE or HULSE or BARBER or ROGERS
Hanged in Exeter, Devon on 12 August 1805, for the stabbing murder of her partner John Rogers. Aged 32.

CHRONOLOGY

John Rogers died from internal bleeding after Betty Hulce stabbed him in the chest just above the heart during a violent altercation at their home in Plymouth. They had argued about what she would wear to her estranged husband's funeral (he had died the day before). Rogers and his partner's husband were buried side by side.

MARY PARNELL
Hanged at Newgate, London on 13 November 1805, for uttering a forged five pound bank note. Aged 23.

At the Old Bailey on 10 April 1805, a string of shopkeepers and innkeepers testified to Mary Parnell passing off counterfeit five pound notes, most remarking on her 'high colour' – the result either of 'paint' or drink – but none noticing that she had only one eye. She was hanged with two men seven months after her trial. During the proceedings, the platform collapsed, throwing Mr Ford, the Old Bailey Ordinary, to the ground. He was 'much bruised'.

SARAH HERRING or PAGE
Hanged at Horsemonger Lane Gaol, Surrey with her husband Benjamin Herring, on 8 April 1806, for coining.

The Herrings were convicted of manufacturing a 'vast quantity' of counterfeit coins at their home at 9 St George's Fields in Southwark, south London where numerous false coins and implements and materials used in their manufacture were found. Benjamin claimed these were required for his trade as a maker of birdcages.

MARY JACKSON
Hanged at Lancaster Castle on 19 April 1806, for stealing in a dwelling house. Aged 20.

In May 1805 Mary Jackson was tried for the murder of 30-year-old Ann Smith at Oak Street, Manchester and acquitted, but was subsequently charged with stealing Smith's property. She implicated a man called James Cheetham, and persisted in this until two hours before her execution, after which she retracted and died 'with great firmness'.

WOMEN AND THE GALLOWS 1797–1837

ELIZABETH GODFREY or GODFRY
Hanged at Newgate, London on 23 February 1807, for the stabbing murder of Richard Prince. Aged 34.

The hanging of Elizabeth Godfrey, who died with John Holloway and Owen Haggerty, was a catastrophe. The executions attracted a huge crowd (the two men vehemently asserted they were innocent of the murder of John Cole Steele in Feltham in 1802, and probably were). Elizabeth Godfrey admitted stabbing her neighbour, a coachman, in the eye. The two had quarrelled after Prince sent for the watchman because Elizabeth was arguing loudly in her room with a man about money. At the hanging, the crowd surged and in the crush thirty-one people were killed.

MARTHA ALDEN or ALDIN
Drawn on a hurdle and hanged at Norwich Castle on 31 July 1807, for the murder of her husband Samuel (petty treason).

Samuel Alden's body was found in a pond on the common at Attleborough in Norfolk. A neighbour saw 'the two hands of a man appear, with the arms of a shirt stained with blood... His face was dreadfully chopped and his head cut nearly off.' Martha had taken up a billhook and attacked her husband, who was comatose after an evening in the pub, because he had threatened to beat her during an argument earlier that evening. She offered no defence at her trial. Her house was destroyed by neighbours after her death.

SARAH or SUSANNAH PUGH
Hanged in Hereford on 28 March 1808, for the murder of her 12-year-old daughter, also called Sarah.

In 1807 Sarah Pugh and her daughter were lodging in a poor part of Hereford, near Gaol Lane, sharing a room with their landlady and eking out a small allowance from the parish of Clifford, twenty miles away. Unable to pay the rent and given notice to quit, Sarah was facing the loss of her daughter, who was about to enter the poorhouse or be farmed out as a parish apprentice. It is likely that this anticipated departure tipped Sarah over the edge. As she went to bed in the evening of 11 June, she told her landlady that she did not expect to live long. At five the next morning she took a razor and slit the throat of the child sleeping beside her. Young Sarah's gasps for breath woke the landlady, who saw her mother try to cover the girl with bedclothes and then attempt to cut her own throat. While the landlady tried to wrestle the razor from Sarah, the child, covered in blood and in shock, ran naked into the street, apparently trying to find her sister in nearby Bye Street. She soon returned to the lodging house and collapsed on the floor. *The Hereford Journal* described the murder as the result of 'frenzied despair' and reported that Sarah had calmly stepped over her daughter's prone form as she was led away to a place of confinement,

MARY CHANDLEY or CHANDLER
Hanged at Lancaster Castle on 9 April 1808, for stealing in a dwelling house. Aged 19.

After stealing 'wearing apparel' from her master, Mr W. Stokes of Church Street, Liverpool, Mary Chandley set fire to the house. Stokes's daughter was burnt to death and another child badly injured. Chandley was acquitted of the murder but convicted of stealing. A broadsheet published after her execution described her as a 'handsome-looking young woman' but with an 'ignorant and depraved character'. It bemoaned her lack of Christian education and blamed her upbringing: '[Her] case...will excite our pity and compassion, when her youth is taken into consideration.' As the executioner drew the hood over her face in preparation for the drop, she cried, 'O man, I never will forgive you!' Her shrieks before the drop caused many in the large crowd of spectators to weep.

MARY GRIMES or BARRINGTON or GRAHAM
Hanged at Newgate, London on 22 February 1809, for fraud. Aged 31.

The wars with France gave rise to a number of frauds relating to prize money, back pay and pensions owed to the relatives of deceased sailors, who would have to swear that they were entitled to sums due. Mary Grimes, who was illiterate and in debt, presented herself to the clerk of the check office at Greenwich Hospital and claimed that she was the widow of Thomas Roughton or Rotton, who had served on board HMS *Eurus* in 1796 and that she was owed his prize money of over £24. She was proved to be an impostor. At the end of her trial she 'pleaded her belly' but a jury of matrons rejected her claim to be pregnant. She left a young child.

See also Chapter 9.

MARY BATEMAN
Hanged at York Castle on 20 March 1809, for the murder of Rebecca Perigo. Aged 41.

The trial of Mary Bateman née Harker ('The Yorkshire Witch'), a con artist, was a sensation across the country. Bateman's method was to invent an alter ego with supernatural powers who demanded money and goods in return for magic spells. After dissection, Bateman's body was put on display at Leeds Royal Infirmary and strips of her skin were sold as souvenirs.

See also Chapter 5.

SUSAN or SUSANNAH GRANT
Hanged in Warwick on 18 August 1809, for coining (high treason). Aged 64.

Susan Grant was discovered in possession of an edger, an instrument for marking shilling pieces around the edges.

REBECCA BLUNDELL
Hanged in Winchester, Hampshire on 12 March 1810, for the murder of her female illegitimate baby. Aged 40.

Rebecca Blundell, 'a poor travelling woman', went into labour at Fordingbridge, Hampshire and gave birth in a stable, accompanied by her partner, William Johnson, 'a Black'. She alleged that he stabbed the baby but also confessed that she had beaten her and buried her in bricks. The grand jury could find no evidence against Johnson, who was discharged. Reports of the trial described Blundell as 'wretchedly ignorant' and 'not duly impressed with the consequences of the crime she had committed.' She was executed on the day of her trial.

CHRONOLOGY

JANE CURRAN
Hanged in Winchester, Hampshire on 24 March 1810, for uttering. Aged 30.

After being entrapped by an agent employed by the Deputy Chief Constable of Manchester, practised utterers Jane Curran, her half-brother Forgey (or Fergy) McGuffin, who were born in Ireland, and Richard Faulkner, fled south to Gosport in Hampshire, where they continued their crimes. Curran was arrested with more than £100 of gold in the lining of her petticoat. During her trial, she held her young daughter in her arms. A group of genteel ladies from Winchester urged the judges to recommend a pardon for the sake of her child, to no avail.

FRANCES THOMPSON
Hanged at York Castle on 7 April 1810, for uttering. Aged 31.

Frances Thompson, a widow living in Beverley, Yorkshire, was entrapped by a constable sent by magistrates in Hull acting on information. Thompson sold him a bundle of counterfeit shillings and sixpences as well as a two pound note, and was promptly arrested. She and four men convicted of forgery at the same assizes were executed together.

MELINDA MAPSON or MINTOR
Hanged at Newgate, London on 13 June 1810, for robbery in a dwelling house. Aged 30.

Ann and William Dignam had not had Melinda Mapson in their home in Covent Garden, London for twelve hours before she absconded with £30 worth of their silver, linen and other valuables, which she swiftly pawned at shops in the east of the city.

See also Chapter 8.

BETTY AMPHLETT or AMPLETT
Hanged in Gloucester on 13 August 1810, for the murder of her illegitimate child. Aged around 21.

Betty Amphlett, who was illegitimate herself, was born in Bredon's Norton, Worcestershire, abandoned by her parents, who had many other children, and dependent on the good will of poor relations. After the Peace of Amiens in 1802, she accompanied her uncle, a shoemaker, to France, intending to settle there, but when war resumed she was held at Verdun, where she had several babies by a fellow English prisoner, all of whom died. Pregnant once more, she returned to England in June 1809 and was sent to her home parish, where she became a 'wandering outcast without means of subsistence for herself and her helpless infant' whom she subsequently killed at Coombe Hill by striking it with the heel of a shoe and throwing it in a pond. 'The duties of religion had never been inculcated upon her mind, and she was hardly even aware of the existence of God!!!' expostulated *The Gloucester Journal*. She went to her death in front of the county gaol, showing 'great penitence and decorum'.

JANE COX
Hanged in Exeter, Devon on 12 August 1811, for the poisoning murder of John Trewman, aged 15 months.

At first Jane Cox claimed that Arthur Tucker, the father of the child, had given her a pound to murder his illegitimate offspring, to whose mother he paid a weekly allowance. Tucker, from Hatherleigh, Devon, a widowed farmer who already had eight legitimate children, was indicted as an accessory but subsequently acquitted. Cox later withdrew her accusation but did not explain why she fed the child arsenic after she offered to take him for a walk. On the scaffold she addressed the crowd, reiterating her original accusation of Tucker and providing more details of the way he pressurized her to commit the crime, for which she also acknowledged she deserved to die.

ELIZABETH SMITH
Hanged in Ipswich, Suffolk on 23 March 1812, for the starvation murder of her eight-year-old stepdaughter Mary Ann. Aged 27. Executed with her husband John, aged 39.

John and Elizabeth Smith starved and beat Mary Ann, the eldest of John's three children by his first wife, and left her to sleep for three nights in December in a freezing shed. When John's sister visited their home in Cookley, Suffolk, at his request, she found Mary Ann dying and the others in an appalling state ('reduced to skeletons'). John and Elizabeth were found guilty at a trial in Ipswich and ordered for execution. The judge spoke of their 'unparalleled cruelties and tortures'. Elizabeth Smith was labelled 'Brownrigg the Second' in reference to the notorious Elizabeth Brownrigg, who was executed forty-five years previously for the murder of her apprentice Mary Clifford.

HANNAH SMITH
Hanged at Lancaster Castle on 13 June 1812, for riot and highway robbery. Aged 54.

Butter-seller Charles Walker prosecuted Hannah Smith for her actions during food riots in Manchester. He alleged that on 21 April 1812 she had stopped his cart in Ardwick and forced him to sell his stock at a shilling per pound, a reduction of threepence, by threatening to steal all of it if he did not comply. Thereafter he was forced to sell at the same price to a mob of up to 300 people. Smith was said to have climbed on the cart in order to pass out the butter. She was also charged with stealing a basket of potatoes from James Radcliffe. A mob had insisted that he sell them at eightpence a pound or, again, they would steal them from him. Smith made no defence on either charge, except to deny having stolen the potatoes, and was hanged with seven men who had been convicted variously of rioting, arson, house-breaking and stealing food. A troop of the Blues was deployed at the execution in anticipation of further disturbances, but it passed off without incident. Hannah Smith was the only woman hanged for riot in the nineteenth century, and the first since Margaret Boulker in 1795.

CATHERINE FOSTER
Hanged at Newgate, London on 12 August 1812, for perjury. Aged 35.

Catherine Foster swore that she was the sister of Doncaster-born Charles Serjeant, who had died on the *Nassau* in 1808 and that she was entitled to his goods and chattels. Her deception was uncovered when Serjeant's half-brother made an application to the Deputy

Inspector of Seamen's Wills on behalf of his widow. She was said to have behaved with 'much fortitude' at her execution and wore 'decent mourning'.

ANN ARNOLD
Hanged in Ipswich, Suffolk on 29 March 1813, for drowning her illegitimate son, aged about four.

The body of Ann Arnold's oldest child, an unnamed boy, was discovered by a shepherd in a pond at Spexhall, Suffolk. He was estimated to have been in the water for about three weeks. Arnold was swiftly arrested at Hardley in Norfolk and appeared at the Suffolk Assizes at Bury St Edmunds, where she was accused of stripping the boy down to his shirt and throwing him in. It was alleged that the father of her second illegitimate child had promised marriage on condition that she return the first child to his father, who paid a weekly allowance for him. When the boy's father refused to take him, she decided on a drastic course. Her execution attracted a large crowd.

SARAH FLETCHER
Hanged at the New Prison, Horsemonger Lane, Southwark, London on 5 April 1813, for the murder of her newborn illegitimate baby. Aged 19.

Sarah Fletcher's baby was found in the privy with one of her garters around its neck. At her execution on the roof of the gaol, Sarah wore an 'elegant dress of black silk' and 'appeared perfectly resigned to her fate'. The event was witnessed by an 'immense crowd' of spectators.

EDITH MORREY
Hanged in Chester on 23 April 1813, for the murder of her husband George (accessory before the fact and petty treason). Aged 37.

George and Edith Morrey lived at Hankelow, a small farming community in east Cheshire. They had been married for fifteen years and had five surviving children, the eldest aged 13. To observers, they appeared to enjoy a harmonious relationship. Their servant Hannah Evans said that the night before the murder, 12 April 1812, George and his wife had been 'playful' and were laughing together. She had not noticed any flirtation or improper behaviour between her mistress and John Lomas, the 20-year-old farm servant. Later that night, Lomas killed George Morrey as he slept in bed, by striking his head with an axe; Edith held a candle and passed him a razor to finish the job. Edith and John Lomas tried to make George's death look like the work of robbers who had followed George home from a cock fight to rob him of his winnings but signs that it was an 'inside job' were soon apparent. A blood-spattered shirt belonging to Lomas was found, and he was arrested. His confession led to Edith's own arrest (she immediately tried to commit suicide by slitting her own throat). At their trial before Judge Dallas, they were both found guilty. Edith 'pleaded her belly' and was respited until after the birth. During the trial Edith insisted on keeping her face hidden from onlookers. Lomas was hanged on 24 August and on 21 December Edith gave birth to a son. She was hanged at the next great session, again hiding her face in a handkerchief, and on the scaffold turning her back on the 10,000-strong crowd while the prayers were said.

AZUBAH FOUNTAIN
Hanged in Lincoln on 6 August 1813, for the poisoning murder of her husband Robert. Aged 36. Executed with her lover, George Turner Rowell, aged 23.

Rowell, a cooper from Melton Mowbray, where he was known to be 'habitually vicious', arrived in the Fountain household as a lodger. He was on the point of marrying the Fountains' daughter when he and Azubah, who were lovers, killed Robert by putting laudanum in his drink. Azubah Fountain was described as 'more imbecile than wicked, more weak than criminal'.

ELIZABETH OSBORNE
Hanged in Bodmin, Cornwall on 6 September 1813, for setting fire to a wheat mow. Aged 20.

According to *The West Briton*, Elizabeth Osborne's behaviour after she set fire to her former employer's corn 'created serious doubts of her sanity'. This 'unfortunate girl' boasted of her crime, setting fire to corn belonging to John Lobb, against whom she bore a grudge of unknown origins (she merely told the arresting officer that 'Farmer Lobb should eat barley bread as well as myself') and asserting that she had done it in order to be transported. Despite this, at her trial, she was judged to be in her right mind and sentenced to death. Thereafter she became deeply penitent, displaying a 'calm serenity' and 'surprising fortitude' on the scaffold at Bodmin where she met her death 'in a manner that astonished and affected the spectators in an extraordinary degree'.

MARY GIBBS
Hanged in Ipswich, Suffolk on 28 March 1814, for drowning her illegitimate 14-month-old daughter.

Mary Gibbs, who was originally from Essex, abandoned her daughter on the banks of the River Alde, near Hollesley Bay, Suffolk in October 1813. The child's body was found two weeks later. On her arrest, Gibbs said, 'I would not have destroyed it [the baby], had it not been for its blackguard father, who belonged to the 12th Light Dragoons.' She 'wept bitterly' on the scaffold.

SARAH OWENS
Hanged at Ilchester Gaol, Somerset on 20 April 1814, for housebreaking.

Sarah Owens was convicted with George Long and Elizabeth Hill of robbing the house of Mrs Lamilliare, Owens's employer, at Brislington, near Bristol. Hill was reprieved.

MARY COOK
Hanged in Dorchester, Dorset on 1 August 1814, for the murder of her female illegitimate child. Aged 25.

Mary Cook, from Netherbury in west Dorset, became pregnant by a married farmer who had three children. *The Gloucester Journal* described her as a 'fine young woman [whose] fate made a great impression' and reported that on the scaffold, she lifted her hands 'as well as she could' (they were pinioned) and exclaimed, 'Good people take warning by my fate – take warning.'

SARAH WHITE
Hanged in Salisbury, Wiltshire on 28 March 1815, for arson. Aged 44.

Sarah and John White were charged together with setting fire to a house at Broad Hinton, Wiltshire. John was acquitted.

SARAH WOODWARD
Hanged in Ipswich, Suffolk on 3 April 1815, for the murder of her newborn illegitimate son. Aged 25.

Woodward's child's body was found in the parish of Frostenden.

ELIZABETH WOLLERTON
Hanged in Ipswich, Suffolk on 25 July 1815, for the poisoning murder of six-year-old Robert Sparkes. Aged 51.

A farmer's wife and mother of at least eight children, Elizabeth Wollerton, from Denton, Norfolk, laced a plum cake with arsenic and sent it as a present to her elderly uncle, Tifford Clarke, of Kirby Cane, to whom she was in debt for £200 (she also stood to gain £500 from his will). It was probably not her first attempt to poison him; he told the court at Wollerton's trial at Bury St Edmunds that a previous cake had made him ill and he had asked her not to send any more, which she ignored. Clarke's housekeeper unwittingly gave the cake to her son-in-law, who fed it to six children for breakfast; the youngest, six-year-old Robert Sparkes, died as a result. Some of Wollerton's daughters gave evidence against her. A large crowd attended her execution.

ELIZABETH or ELIZA FENNING
Hanged at Newgate, London on 26 July 1815, for the attempted murder of her employer and his family, by poisoning. Aged 22.

Widely believed (then and now) to be a miscarriage of justice, the conviction of Eliza Fenning for poisoning her employer's family by giving them dumplings laced with arsenic was taken up by Radicals and reformers. Fenning denied the charge to the end and deliberately dressed in white for her execution.

See also Chapter 1.

SARAH COCK or COOK
Hanged in Hertford on 11 March 1816, for the drowning murder of her illegitimate son.

Sarah Cock was convicted of throwing her child into the river at Aston in east Hertfordshire. During his condemnation speech, Judge Charles Abbott was said to have been so upset that he was unable to address the court. 'The impression on the Court was so great, that there was not a dry eye to be seen,' reported the *Lancaster Gazette*.

DINAH RIDDIFORD
Hanged in Gloucester on 7 September 1816, for housebreaking. Aged 69.

Riddiford, her 71-year-old husband Abraham and two of their sons, Luke and Aaron, were charged with breaking into the home of Daniel Reed at Thornbury and stealing two sides of bacon, two pigs' cheeks, a piece of tongue, two bones, 30 pounds of butter in a pan and a copper kettle, together amounting to a value of £4. Abraham was acquitted, as was Aaron, but Dinah and her son Luke were convicted, and both were condemned, although Luke was respited and transported for life.

SUSANNAH HOLROYD
Hanged at Lancaster Castle on 16 September 1816, for the poisoning murders of her husband Matthew Holroyd (petty treason), her eight-year-old son William and 15-week-old Ann Newton.

In April 1816, Susannah Holroyd of Ashton-under-Lyne near Manchester bought an ounce of arsenic 'to kill rats and mice'. The next morning, after drinking coffee, her husband Matthew, a weaver, became ill. Susannah suggested he would feel better with some watery gruel but Matthew detected an odd taste and refused to drink more of it, saying, 'Suzy, you have put pepper in this gruel.' At this point, Susannah became infuriated, so he drank it. 'That's the last gruel I will ever make for you!' she said, which proved to be the case. William, their only surviving child, became ill with remarkably similar symptoms at about the same time. After a brief rally midweek, Matthew's condition worsened and Susannah called in the doctor but then refused to give Matthew any of the medicines he prescribed, saying it was pointless because 'her husband would die'. Five days later he did just that. William Holroyd died six hours after his father. Ann Newton, the baby daughter of the lodger, died the following Tuesday. After fluid from Matthew's stomach was analyzed and declared to be arsenic, Susannah was charged with both murder and petty treason. In her defence, she claimed that Matthew had sent her for the arsenic and that she had delivered it to him: 'What he did with it, I cannot pretend to say.' She did not react when the guilty verdict was read. At the end of the process, however, she put her head on the front of the bar 'from which she was with difficulty removed'. There was considerable antipathy towards Susannah in the court because many believed that Ann Newton was not the first baby to die in her care. On the gallows at Hanging Corner at Lancaster Castle, Susannah would only confess to the murder of her husband and claimed that he had innocently given their son some of the poisoned gruel and the baby had died of natural causes. Newspaper reports published after Susannah's trial alleged that the couple had quarrelled a few days before Matthew fell ill and that Susannah attributed her downfall to a recent 'connexion with another man'.

SARAH PERRY
Hanged at Newgate, London on 24 February 1817, for the murder of her female illegitimate baby. Aged 33.

Before dawn on 20 January 1817, Sarah Perry, a cook in a household in Manchester Square in the West End of London, locked herself in the kitchen. She gave birth, suffocated her child by pressing a dishcloth down her throat, and put the body in the coal cellar, all the time keeping her fellow servants at bay with denials and false explanations. Perry was convicted despite the evidence of a surgeon who said he could not tell whether the baby was born dead or not.

See also Chapter 4.

WOMEN AND THE GALLOWS 1797–1837

ELIZABETH FRICKER
Hanged at Newgate, London on 5 March 1817, for burglary. Aged 30.

At bedtime on 28 July 1816, Elizabeth Fricker, a live-in cook in a house in Berners Street in the West End of London, surprised her fellow servant by telling her she had 'left her book below'. In fact, she went downstairs to open the door to her lover William Kelly, who stole over £300 worth of fine silverware and linen. Fricker and Kelly were among seven executed together at Newgate, an event that attracted a huge crowd.

See also Chapter 8.

ELIZABETH WHITING
Hanged at Lincoln Castle on 15 March 1817, for the murder of her infant child. Aged 28.

Separated from her husband, Elizabeth Whiting became pregnant by an 'illicit connexion' with a labourer. Although during her trial she was so distressed she could barely stand at the bar, she was composed going to the gallows, declaring that she had no desire to live. The day before the execution, the prison chaplain read a sermon citing Isaiah 49: 'Can a woman forget her sucking child, that she should not have compassion on the son of her womb?' which was reported to have affected her deeply. Whiting was the first to be executed using Lincoln's New Drop 'calculated to produce a much greater effect on the public mind than the former mode of executions'.

ANN STATHAM
Hanged in Stafford on 21 March 1817, for the drowning murder of William, her illegitimate baby. Aged 28.

Ann Statham may have been suffering from a mental illness when she dropped or threw her five-week-old baby into the canal near Wychnor in Staffordshire on 29 July 1816. She gave several versions of what happened on that day but could not explain exactly why she had done it and there was no obvious motive. She had been living in Birmingham with the father of the child, Thomas Webster, a mail coachman, who was happy to support her and the baby and she was

CHRONOLOGY

not stigmatized amongst her family and friends for being an unmarried mother. Statham was the only one of seventeen prisoners condemned at the Stafford Lent Assizes not to be reprieved.

ANN HAWLIN
Hanged in Warwick on 14 April 1817, for the murder of her child. Aged about 30.

Ann Hawlin, described as 'a single woman, and of a very morose and cruel disposition', was originally from Knightcote near Warwick. She was criticized in *The Staffordshire Advertiser* for resisting 'every exertion made to convince her of the enormity of her crime, and to direct her attention to that source whence alone mercy could proceed'.

ELIZABETH WARRINER
Hanged at Lincoln Castle on 26 July 1817, for the poisoning murder of her 11-year-old stepson John.

Elizabeth Warriner had often been heard to say that she would be the death of her stepson. After the child died in her presence, she was said to have dragged his body out to the stable and hoisted him up in a halter, to make it look as if he had hanged himself. At first, no suspicion attached to her but after witnesses began to have second thoughts, John's body was disinterred and examined: there were no marks around the neck but it was judged that arsenic was in his stomach. On the morning of her execution, for which she dressed in white, Elizabeth approached the scaffold with her baby sucking at her breast. The hangman removed it and its cries were described as 'shocking to the surrounding multitude'. Elizabeth cried, 'Oh my child! My child!' before dropping a handkerchief to signal that she was ready to die.

MARY ANN JAMES or JONES
Hanged at Newgate, London on 17 February 1818, for uttering a forged document. Aged 20.

Mary Ann James attempted to defraud the Bank of England by obtaining a false power of attorney in order to sell a receipt for annuities, the property of Elizabeth Thomas. She was executed with Charlotte Newman.

See also Chapter 9.

CHARLOTTE NEWMAN

Hanged at Newgate, London on 17 February 1818, for uttering a forged one pound note. Aged 33.

Charlotte Newman and her associate George Mansfield were arrested after passing off a forged one pound note when purchasing half-boots in Denmark Street in London. A stash of twenty-eight further notes was found in her lodgings. Mansfield was acquitted.

See also Chapter 10.

MARGARET DOWD

Hanged at Lancaster Castle on 18 April 1818, for uttering a forged bank note. Aged 33.

Having previously been acquitted of receiving stolen goods at Lancaster Assizes, Margaret Dowd, an Irish woman, was arrested after uttering five one pound notes in Liverpool. She was one of fifty people at the Lent Assizes to be condemned to death. *The Staffordshire Advertiser* reported the scenes in court when they were brought up in six batches to hear their fate: 'The progress of this painful ceremony was occasionally interrupted by the frantic shrieks of some wife, mother, daughter, or sister of the unhappy delinquents; one of whom, a respectable aged woman, was obliged to be carried out of the court.' All but five were reprieved. Dowd was executed with four men, three of whom were convicted of forgery offences.

HARRIET SKELTON

Hanged at Newgate, London on 24 April 1818, for uttering forged pound notes. Aged 35.

After her conviction Harriet Skelton twice appealed to the Bank of England for mercy, without success. In Newgate her plight attracted the sympathy of Elizabeth Fry, who enlisted support for her cause from

CHRONOLOGY

eminent men including the Duke of Gloucester, who made a personal visit to Skelton in prison.

See also Chapter 10.

ANN BAMFORD
Hanged in Warwick on 24 April 1818, for uttering forged bank notes. Aged 60.

In 1813 Ann, the matriarch of a well-known family of forgers and utterers, and two male members of her family were imprisoned for theft, the men for a year and Ann for six months. Her husband William was transported in 1817 after being respited from a death sentence for uttering. The final phase in Ann's career started in January 1818 when Birmingham police raided her house in the middle of the night. They found a treasure trove of illicit items: counterfeit sixpences and shillings worth £75 ('papered and packed up for sale'), numerous false bank notes ('the best executed of any yet discovered'), and beautiful French shawls and lace ('in part payment for forged notes'). Eight people were arrested, including Ann and three members of her family, and a recruiting sergeant for the 52nd Regiment. They appeared before magistrates and were sent to Warwick Castle to await trial. In the end twelve people were tried, ten on forgery chargers and two for uttering. Ten were reprieved, including Ann's daughters Elizabeth and Rebecca Bamford, but Ann and 22-year-old William Gray were not. Newspapers focused on the fate of this young man: his wife, the daughter of an army colonel, was heavily pregnant and he had only recently joined the forgery gang. Ann elicited little sympathy. Although she was praised for her calm demeanour before her death in front of a 'considerable' crowd who had braved the bad weather to attend, her fate was unremarked. She was a middle-aged woman and had profited hugely from the trade she had been in for at least fifteen years.

ANN TYE or TIGH
Hanged in Gloucester on 4 May 1818, for the murder of her illegitimate newborn daughter, Phebe. Aged 38.

WOMEN AND THE GALLOWS 1797–1837

In a field in Dowdeswell, Gloucestershire in the small hours of a mid-December morning, a man saw Ann Tye in distress. He also saw a baby on the ground and heard her cry. While he went to fetch help, Ann carried the baby into a nearby wood, pushed moss and dirt into her mouth, wrapped her in two aprons and her cloak, covered her with moss and left her. An hour later, Ann was found wandering in the wood. She denied having given birth but five hours later the child, by now close to death, was discovered. After the inquest Ann was committed to Northleach Gaol and at the next Gloucester Assizes found guilty of murder. Execution was temporarily respited on a point of law but Tye was warned that she should not expect to be reprieved. In prison she showed signs of mental illness and stopped eating. The newspapers reported that, 'After the arrival of the warrant for her death, all fortitude forsook her, and the application of religious consolation was unable to inspire her with firmness; she was supported to the scaffold, and suffered in a sullen stupor.'

SARAH HUNTINGFORD
Drawn on a hurdle and hanged in Winchester, Hampshire on 8 March 1819, for the murder of her husband Thomas (petty treason). Aged 62.

On the night of 23 October 1818 71-year-old Thomas Huntingford, a man of 'remarkably quiet and inoffensive disposition' who had worked for sixty years as a shipwright in the Royal dockyard at Portsmouth, and his wife Sarah, who ran a grocer's shop, went to bed in their garret in Orange Street, Portsea as normal. Neither appeared drunk. In the middle of the night another resident, Samuel Bately, saw Sarah Huntingford, visibly shaking, going up to her room with a lighted candle. 'I am murdered and robbed,' she told him. With the landlady, Bately and Sarah opened the door to the Huntingfords' room. Thomas Huntingford was on the bed 'covered in clotted blood'. Blood spatters were all over the floor and the wall above his head. His skull had been caved in. Sarah claimed that two men, their faces blackened with soot, had been there and demanded money but no residents had heard them and the doors had not been forced. It was obvious that Sarah was lying. A bloody billhook was found at the foot of the stairs, her pockets and petticoats were bloodstained, and Thomas's body showed signs of rigor mortis – he had died some hours before Bately heard the noise on the stairs. There was evidence that Sarah was an alcoholic and had pawned Thomas's best coats. Before her hanging she refused to speak of the crime, and although she was 'fully alive to the consolations of religion' she declined to confess, saying that 'she would confess to God alone – and the act of dying was only momentary'. She was reported to have displayed 'firmness' at her execution. A crowd of over 10,000 watched her die at Gallows Hill, where the horse and cart method was used. The unruliness of the spectators led to a decision to draw up plans for a New Drop next to the gaol. The couple had been married for forty years, and Sarah had borne sixteen children, only two of whom survived.

SARAH HURST
Hanged outside the Town Hall, Aylesbury, Buckinghamshire on 12 March 1819, for the poisoning murder of her husband William Hurst (petty treason). Aged about 50.

Sarah Hurst (formerly Grizzel or Grissel), of Little Horwood, Buckinghamshire, a mother of four, was locked in an unhappy and abusive marriage with cordwainer William Hurst (they had both been widowed). After her conviction, she admitted that she had begged arsenic from neighbours, saying that it was for killing rats, baked it into a cake and served it to William in revenge for his abusive behaviour when she returned from church on Christmas morning. She said nothing on the scaffold.

HANNAH BOCKING
Hanged in Derby on 22 March 1819, for the poisoning murder of Jane Grant. Aged 16.

In the summer of 1818 Hannah Bocking, a servant girl from Litton in Derbyshire, applied for a job in domestic service but was rejected because of her 'unamiable temper and disposition'. The position went to Jane Grant instead. As Hannah's resentment grew, she started to plan, all the while appearing to be friendly to Jane. Ten weeks before the murder, she persuaded a young man to accompany her to a chemist to buy arsenic, claiming that her grandfather wanted it for killing rats. She mixed it into a spice cake, which 'under the guise of civility' she offered to Jane while they were out walking at Wardlow Mires, ironically within sight of the remains of murderer Anthony Lingard, who had been hanged in chains on a gibbet four years previously. Before she died, in agony, Jane told her parents that she thought the cake was the cause. Hannah showed no emotion and even when arrested and imprisoned was strangely detached. She was said to have implicated several members of her family in the crime, including a sister who was 'of delicate health' and was 'suffering dreadfully under the imputation' although she later withdrew the accusations. *The Derby Mercury* noted that her family was not destitute and that she was literate, but theorized that an early separation from her family, for unspecified reasons, may offer an explanation for her lack of 'the tenderer charities of life [and a] sense of social obligation; she had been deprived of moral instruction and the example of religious observance.' A large crowd witnessed her death in front of the county gaol at Derby, where she ascended the platform 'with a steady step'. As she dropped 'an involuntary shuddering pervaded the assembled crowd, and although she had excited little sympathy, a general feeling of horror was expressed, that one so young should have been so guilty and so insensible.' A broadside published after the execution described 'this wretched creature' as having 'a mind greatly darkened and depraved'. Hannah Bocking's execution was the first Derby had seen for sixty years.

MARY WOODMAN
Drawn to the gallows and hanged in Exeter on 22 March 1819, for the poisoning murder of her husband Charles (petty treason). Aged 30.

According to the trial judge at Exeter Assizes, Mary Woodman tried three times to kill her mild-mannered husband Charles. He had begged her to come back to him after she ran off with Richard Smallacombe, an itinerant fiddler known as Smiler. She agreed to do so, but immediately started planning how to poison him. In the week or ten days before he died she dosed him with litharge of gold (lead oxide), laudanum and arsenic, which succeeded in the job on 12 December. At her trial, her sister defended her by claiming that Mary had asked her to get cream of tartar, a purgative, and it was she who had made a mistake and asked for arsenic, which Mary had then thrown away. However, it did not help Mary's cause that she had joined two burial clubs, societies that allowed people to pay a small weekly sum towards the cost of a funeral, which would have yielded £20 on Charles's death. After the jury delivered their verdict, she shook her fist at the witnesses and shouted, 'Every one of you that have come against me is perjured! I hope the Devil will drag you all back into hell! God will forgive me, and I will come back again to all of you!' before being removed. At her execution she was reported to have 'shown the same obduracy and impenitence as she exhibited at her trial'. She refused to confess but quietly recited the Lord's Prayer before the drop. Smiler was not amongst the spectators, having been arrested and imprisoned for coining offences.

MARY BISSAKER or HARRIS
Drawn to the gallows and hanged in Warwick on 23 April 1819, for colouring base coins (high treason). Aged 56.

The Bissakers, based in Birmingham, were a notorious family of coiners and forgers. John Bissaker, Mary's husband, was executed in 1800 at Whitley Common, Coventry, for forgery and in 1807 Mary herself had been capitally convicted for coining offences but her sentence was commuted to two years hard labour. Before her execution, she was said to have addressed her fellow prisoners: 'Take warning from all of us that are going to suffer, but particularly from myself, who, in my old age, have brought myself to so dismal an end by a long course of wickedness. Again, I say, Repent, and do not break through the laws of your country.' Her dies (the two metallic pieces that are used to strike a coin, one on each side), with which she stamped silvered blanks as shillings, were bought by Joseph Wilkes, who was capitally convicted of coining with two others at Staffordshire Assizes four months later.

WOMEN AND THE GALLOWS 1797–1837

ANN HEYTREY
Drawn on a hurdle and hanged in Warwick on 12 April 1820, for the murder of her employer, Sarah Dormer (petty treason). Aged 22.

The Dormers, of Ashow in Warwickshire, forgave their maid Ann Heytrey, when she was persuaded by her brother to steal money from them. However, one hot summer's day, when a traditional fair was taking place in the village, she murdered her mistress with a knife. She readily confessed and gave no explanation for her actions.

See also Chapter 2.

SARAH POLGREEN or POLGREAN
Drawn on a hurdle and hanged in Bodmin, Cornwall on 12 August 1820, for the poisoning murder of her husband Henry (petty treason). Aged 32.

Sarah Polgreen (born Treman) was born into poverty, abandoned by her mother as a baby and sexually abused as a parish apprentice. She was said to have worked as a prostitute before she married Henry Polgreen bigamously. She poisoned him by lacing butter with arsenic. After her trial she confessed and said that her husband's 'well-founded jealousy and her aversion to him' were her motives. At her execution in front of a large crowd, she was reported to have forgiven witnesses who spoke against her at her trial, warned others tempted to commit similar crimes to learn from her fate, sung a hymn and shaken hands with her executioner. Her body was taken to a nearby farm building, where it was dissected and her heart removed and preserved.

REBECCA WORLOCK
Hanged in Gloucester on 16 August 1820, for murdering her husband Thomas with arsenic. Aged 36.

In her confession Rebecca Worlock explained that she had killed her husband Thomas, a butcher at Bitton in Gloucestershire, because of his 'jealousy' – he had 'repeatedly called her the most opprobrious epithets'. Indeed, she had told Mary Jenkins, a stranger she had persuaded to accompany her to buy arsenic, that the poison was not to kill rats but 'she had a hell of a fellow at home, whom she meant to do

CHRONOLOGY

for.' On 17 April Thomas Worlock came home tired and thirsty and sent his 13-year-old daughter across to the pub to get him some beer in a jug. Rebecca waylaid her on her return, sent her out to collect her younger siblings and tipped arsenic into the jug. Thomas knew something was not right almost immediately after he started drinking and spat out some of the crude powder. There was more in the bottom of his tankard but Rebecca whisked that away and hastily washed it out in a bucket. By now Thomas had begun to feel very ill, with a burning sensation in his mouth and the pit of his stomach. While Rebecca and Thomas were out trying to find a doctor, George Hook, the publican, and local man William Short came by and saw a glistening white powder in the bottom of the bucket. Short tasted it and said it had a roughish feel and a distinct aftertaste. Four days later, Thomas died. His body was autopsied and although the three doctors in attendance could not agree on the cause of death, Rebecca was arrested and indicted for murder. After an eight-hour trial the jury deliberated for seven minutes. Rebecca remained impassive until the sentence, when she wept and cried out, 'Oh my poor children!' Before her execution she gave her parish minister presents to be passed on to them.

SARAH PRICE
Hanged at Newgate, London on 5 December 1820, for uttering a forged one pound note. Aged 43.

The last woman in England to be executed on forgery charges. Sarah Price was found guilty of uttering a forged one pound note to a shoemaker in Castle Street, Leicester Fields (now Leicester Square) after turning down a plea bargain offered by the Bank of England. Her execution, alongside 22-year-old John Madden, led to protests in the crowd.

See also Chapter 10.

MARY CLARKE
Hanged in Northampton on 10 March 1821, for the murder of her husband John (accessory before the fact), with Philip Haynes or Haines, her lover.

WOMEN AND THE GALLOWS 1797–1837

John Clarke was cutting hay from a rick on his farm at Charwelton, Northamptonshire when he was shot in the arm by his former servant Philip Haynes, with whom Mary had been having an affair for the past two years. A surgeon amputated Clarke's arm but he died two days later. Haynes was later found hiding under barley straw in the barn, a letter from Mary Clarke in his possession. Further letters provided evidence of planning between the lovers.

ESTHER WATERS
Hanged in Leicester on 31 March 1821, for the murder of five-year-old Elizabeth Clarke.

Esther Waters strangled the child, the daughter of Matthew Clarke, her employer and lover. He helped dispose of the body in a well and was charged as an accessory after the fact. Waters gave birth while in prison. Newspaper reports of her execution described her as 'a tall masculine woman, of most disgusting appearance, and from her countenance seemed capable of any crime'. After execution, Leicester Infirmary displayed Esther's body for three days, charging visitors two pennies to view it. Matthew Clarke was sentenced to twelve months in the house of correction.

ANN BARBER
Drawn on a hurdle and hanged at York Castle on 13 August 1821, for the poisoning murder of her husband James (petty treason). Aged 45.

The Barber family fell into chaos when Ann, a mother of three, living in Rothwell, near Leeds, started a liaison with her young lodger, William Thompson, and left home to live with him. The couple were thrown out after a week when the landlord discovered the nature of their relationship. James Barber subsequently allowed them back in the house but the neighbours were so disgusted by this that they forced Thompson to leave. Ann put arsenic in her husband's beer (some reports say she gave him a baked apple) and, when he became ill, refused to call in a doctor, saying that it was of no use as he would 'surely be dead in the morning'. At her trial her defence was that her husband had killed himself in misery at her actions. The jury took ten minutes to convict her, and the judge made much of the 'dissolute inclinations' that had brought her to a 'miserable and ignominious situation'. Two days later, her shrieks during the journey to the scaffold were 'piercing beyond anything that it is possible to imagine'. On the scaffold, she was highly agitated and cried, 'O Lord, save me' and 'O God, bless my bairns.' The crowd of spectators was 'greater than ever seen on a similar occasion in York'.

ANN NORRIS
Hanged at Newgate, London on 27 November 1821, for robbery in a brothel (stealing from the person under aggravated circumstances). Aged 21.

James Thompson, a printer visiting his brother in London, claimed that on the evening of 9 October he had been assaulted and robbed in Whitechapel while on his way to a hairdresser's (it was more likely that he was looking for paid sexual services). He said that Mary Palmer, who was 16, approached him pleading for help ('For God's sake, come and help me, there is a person in distress'), but when he followed her into a courtyard and up some stairs to the first floor, he found himself locked in. Ann Norris stood against the door and demanded money, and Thompson ended up giving her two shillings. She demanded more and when he pushed her to one side and rushed downstairs he was surrounded by five other women, who took a further three shillings, beat him and tore his breeches. He alleged in court that Norris had told them to murder him but they desisted. Despite Norris claiming she and Palmer had never seen Thompson before, both women, who worked as prostitutes, were found guilty. Palmer was transported for life but Norris was condemned. Described by *The Morning Post* as 'of interesting appearance', she dressed in white for her execution and behaved with 'unexpected fortitude'. After the drop 'another scene of senseless ignorance transpired. Several men rubbed their necks and faces with the hand of the unfortunate female Norris.' The hands of executed criminals were thought to have magical healing powers. Her funeral at Whitechapel Church attracted many mourners.

WOMEN AND THE GALLOWS 1797–1837

HANNAH HALLEY
Hanged in Derby on 25 March 1822, for the murder of her newborn son. Aged 31.

A native of Mayfield, Staffordshire Hannah Halley worked in the Cotton Mill at Darley and lodged at Brook Street in Derby. Her baby was discovered, badly scalded, in a glass vessel under her bed and died four days later. Hannah's previous lies about having dropsy, failure to provide evidence of preparation for the birth and claims that 'the devil caused me to do it' combined with a 'depraved disposition' counted against her. It did not help that seven weeks before the birth, she had persuaded a man (not the father) to marry her.

RACHAEL EDWARDS
Drawn on a hurdle and hanged in Monmouth, Wales on 16 August 1822, for the poisoning murder of her husband William (petty treason). Aged about 26.

The Edwards ran the Cross Keys public house in Pontypool but their relationship was turbulent and Rachael was said to have 'formed an illicit attachment towards another man'. After persuading two women to buy arsenic for her, she poisoned her husband's milk. The trial lasted until eleven o'clock at night and the jury deliberated for two hours before finding her guilty.

GRACE GRIFFIN
Hanged in Berwick upon Tweed, Northumberland on 26 July 1823, for murdering her husband John.

Grace and John Griffin kept an unlicensed house in Berwick selling small beer and spirits. Their marriage was known to be unhappy and Grace had previously threatened to kill her husband. John died after a drunken night during which Grace had described him to her neighbours as a 'beast'. The next morning he was found groaning and retching, but managed to say that his wife had murdered him. He died a short time later. An autopsy found no visible external injuries but his bladder was ruptured and there was a black mark near the sacrum. Grace was accused of assaulting him with a fire poker. After a trial lasting into the

CHRONOLOGY

early hours, Grace was cleared of petty treason but found guilty of murder. She greeted the death sentence with no display of emotion.

HANNAH READ
Drawn on a hurdle and hanged in Leicester on 5 August 1825, for the drowning murder of her husband James (petty treason). Aged 36.

In the absence of her husband James, who had left home to avoid payment of a debt, Hannah, a mother of five, moved in with John Waterfield, a young widower whose wife she had nursed in childbirth, and later gave birth to John's child. When her husband returned, looking to resume their relationship, she persuaded him to meet her at Foxton, Leicestershire, where she pushed him into the canal, having first told him he looked 'such a figure in that smock-frock'. It was a ploy to get him to begin taking it off so that when it was over his head she could push him into the canal. She held him under the water with a long stick. Her execution was described in a broadside published after her death:

> *This unhappy woman was conveyed to the county Bridewell, the place of execution, upon a sledge, instead of being taken in the gaol waggon. Although the time of her removal was so early as between 5 and 6 o'clock, there were numbers of persons collected about the County gaol, and along the streets through which she passed anxious to get a sight of her before the fatal hour. A bed or mattress was placed upon the sledge, which was drawn by a horse, and upon which the prisoner was secured by a rope. On reaching the Bridewell, she was carried into the gaoler's house, where she was soon after attended by the Chaplain, and joined in devotion. About 11 o'clock she was again placed upon the sledge and drawn along the gaol yard to the foot of the steps leading to the scaffold.*

MARY CAIN
Hanged at Newgate, London on 16 January 1826, for the stabbing murder of Maurice Fitzgerald. Aged 44.

Mary Cain stabbed Maurice Fitzgerald through the heart with a kitchen knife when he interposed himself between her and her husband Jeremiah during a drunken quarrel at their lodgings in Horns Alley, Liquorpond Street, Clerkenwell. She told the Old Bailey she did not remember doing it and that 'when I drink I always lose my reason.' Her eldest child (she had given birth to fourteen, with five surviving) gave evidence against her.

AMELIA ROBERTS
Hanged at Newgate, London on 2 January 1827, for stealing from her employer. Aged 32.

Amelia Roberts, a servant, and her co-defendant Patrick Riley, a bricklayer's labourer, were found guilty of stealing numerous valuable items including candlesticks, jewellery, nutcrackers and a teapot, to the value of over £400, from Roberts's employer Morgan Fuller Austin's house in Red Lion Street, Clerkenwell. While Austin, a surgeon, was away at his country home, they loaded up a coach with boxes of stolen items and decamped. Austin caught up with them in Newport, Monmouthshire, where he found Amelia wearing his wife's dress and brooch and Riley his own silk trousers. Riley vigorously denied the charge and was backed up by Roberts who 'constantly asserted the innocence of her companion'. He was reprieved but Roberts was hanged, in part as a deterrent to other servants. Her demeanour on the morning of her death was described as 'extremely penitent and calm' in contrast to the distress of Thomas White, who was executed with her. He begged for mercy on the scaffold, refused to be hooded and, just after the drop, managed to cling to the rope. Someone underneath grabbed his legs and pulled. As he had nothing to cover his face 'the spectacle was most disgusting'. In contrast, Amelia Roberts's sufferings were 'over in an instant'.

RACHAEL or RACHEL BRADLEY
Hanged at Lancaster Castle on 26 March 1827, for drowning her illegitimate six-week-old daughter Mary. Aged 27.

On 18 January 1827, Rachael Bradley left her lodgings in Ashton-under-Lyne near Manchester with the baby she appeared to dote on. She returned later in the day, telling the landlady that she had given her child to the wife of the overseer at Thurlstone workhouse, twenty-two miles away. However, earlier that day Henry Hilton, a neighbour, had encountered her walking by the canal at Ashton. The baby was screaming and when he suggested she give the child the breast she said she had nothing for her and that she would 'either kill it or drown it.' She told him the father had refused to maintain her and had threatened violence if she did not dispose of her child. This was her third illegitimate child – two previous children had not survived. When Hilton discovered that she no longer had the baby, he called in a constable, who arrested her. At first she insisted that a high wind had swept the baby into the canal where she had drowned but soon confessed to throwing her in. The canal was dragged and the child's body recovered. Rachael was reported to have been half-starved when she arrived at Lancaster Castle to await trial. Her defence was that she was too poor to keep the baby, having pawned her clothes. She collapsed when sentenced and had to be carried out of the court in a chair. Two female convicts assisted her to her execution. A large and rowdy crowd attended.

SARAH JONES
Hanged in Monmouth on 11 April 1827, for the murder of her newborn illegitimate female child. Aged 26.

When Peter Potter, a gamekeeper working on Sir Charles Morgan's estate at Bassaleg near Newport in south Wales, found a bundle tied up with a handkerchief in the cart house, he opened it and was shocked to find the bloody body of a baby. He knew immediately who the father was – John Flook, a labourer on the estate – who told him that the child had been stillborn. Together they took the body to the mother, Sarah Jones, who lived with her parents in a cottage on the edge of the estate. Flook laid the body down and said, 'Do take it and let it be buried like a Christian, and not like a dog' and later Sarah's brother and father buried the child themselves in the churchyard. The local coroner heard about this, had the body disinterred and discovered that the child had two deep cuts across the throat. By now, Sarah had confessed that she had killed the child and claimed that Flook had known about it. Her motive for the killing may have been revenge on Flook, who had married another woman when Sarah was six months pregnant. She, her parents and Flook were arrested, although charges against the men were dropped. Despite strenuous efforts by her defence counsel, Sarah was found guilty at Usk on 9 April; her mother was acquitted. The court was in tears when the judge, Mr Serjeant Bosanquet, passed sentence. He pointedly referred to the behaviour of Flook (who had failed to appear as a witness): 'This is an awful scene and an awful lesson to all who have brought young women into the same situation as you were brought into, but more awful to the individual to whom your destruction is owing. He will have to answer it to his God.' *The Cambrian* described Sarah's appearance and demeanour:

> *The unfortunate woman was of short stature, stout made, with nothing in her countenance indicative of ferociousness, she stood during her trial without any perceptible emotion, but on receiving sentence was obliged to be supported by one of the officers in attendance, and was carried from the bar to the chaise which conducted her to the gaol.*

Two days later she went to the gallows in Monmouth in front of a large crowd, most of them female. She calmly asked the executioner not to make the rope too tight and to secure her skirts closely around her ankles before she dropped. *The Morning Post* reported: 'Her tale excited much commiseration...her resignation was praiseworthy, her repentance contrite, and her conduct firm and decided beyond precedent under such circumstances.' The judge had remitted the dissection of her body so her body was returned to her family to be buried in Bassaleg churchyard.

MARY WITTENBACK
Drawn on a hurdle and hanged at Newgate, London on 17 September

1827, for the poisoning murder of her husband Frederick (petty treason). Aged 40.

On 21 July 1827 at Brill Place, Somers Town in north London, Frederick Wittenback, a builder's labourer, ate most of the suet pudding Mary, his wife of twenty years, had prepared for lunch and soon became very ill. Mary showed the remainder of the pudding to a neighbour and asked if she thought it had been poisoned. Despite this, shortly afterwards, she ate some of it herself and also became ill. A doctor pumped Frederick and Mary's stomachs but Frederick was in a severe condition and died a short time later. His symptoms – sickness, pain in his legs and blindness – were consistent with arsenic but a postmortem examination did not conclusively identify this as the cause. Nevertheless, after the inquest, Mary was taken to Newgate to await trial. The Wittenbacks' marriage had been unhappy and erratic. Frederick had often 'misconducted' himself and the couple had split several times, with Frederick going off to live with other women. After a period of relative stability, they had been once more on the verge of parting. When sentenced, Mary fainted and her 'violent, hysterical screams' could be heard throughout the sessions building after she was removed from court. The couple had had seven children, three surviving, all girls in their teens and twenties. They visited her the day before her hanging: 'the scene of parting was affecting in the extreme.' On 17 September she was tied into a 'machine' (the equivalent of a hurdle) in a passage leading to the vestibule outside which the scaffold had been erected. This was then dragged outside, where she was transferred to the gallows. A huge crowd, mainly of women, had gathered. At that moment, a temporary stand collapsed and eleven spectators fell on to the people below, although no one was seriously injured. After she dropped, Mary's 'convulsive struggles' lasted for two minutes.

JANE SCOTT
Hanged at Lancaster Castle on 22 March 1828, for the murder of her mother. Aged 22.

Tried and acquitted of the murder of her father, Jane Scott, who lived in Marsh Lane, Preston, was then tried for the murder of her mother. Jane had been a prostitute since the age of 15 and regularly stole from her remarkably forgiving parents, who were left practically destitute. On 14 May 1827, she prepared porridge for them and they instantly became ill, both dying the next day. A coroner's inquest concluded that the Scotts had been poisoned and Jane was arrested and incarcerated in Lancaster Castle to await trial at the Summer Assizes. During Jane's trial for the murder of her mother, George Richardson told the court that she had wanted to marry him but when he said that he did not have the money for it, she had said that she would get it soon enough. In the condemned cell at Lancaster Castle she confessed to her sister not only to killing her two-year-old niece with a dose of laudanum in revenge for an argument the sisters had had earlier but also to poisoning her own illegitimate four-year-old son Tommy, the latter with arsenic mixed into treacle. When the time of execution approached, she was weak from lack of food (she had refused to eat) and paralyzed with fear, and was carried by two female prisoners to the drop, which was on a constructed balcony at the first floor level. A huge crowd had assembled, many of them from Preston, including some of her friends. The hanging, by Ned Barlow, himself a convicted felon who had been pardoned and allowed to continue his trade as executioner, was botched. According to the *Liverpool Mercury*, Barlow went below to operate the drop, leaving the two female assistants on the trap door above. They were only saved from falling through by the quick thinking of the chaplain who beckoned them away. Jane was left unsupported, fell back and swung round to face the crowd. The crowd reacted in horror. Newspapers used a variety of epithets to describe Jane Scott, including 'monster in human shape' and 'dreadful instance of human depravity'. She was the last woman to be hanged at Lancaster Castle. In 1875 *The Preston Herald* reported that her skeleton was sold at auction and could be viewed in a house in the back streets of Preston for a halfpenny.

CATHERINE WELCH
Hanged at Newgate, London on 14 April 1828, for the murder of her month-old baby boy. Aged 24.

CHRONOLOGY

On 1 March 1828 Catherine Welch, a seasonal worker in market gardens, was seen in Parsons Green, west of London, breastfeeding a child. The next morning the body of a baby boy was discovered in a watery ditch in a field. There was evidence that he had been strangled. Catherine was soon arrested. Although she eventually admitted that she had had a child, she claimed that he had died aged two weeks in Saffron Hill, a poor district of the city, and been buried in Marylebone, but could supply no details. Catherine confessed before her execution, explaining that she was friendless, destitute and starving and that her husband had deserted her when he found out that she was pregnant by another man. On the scaffold, she shrieked, wept and wrung her hands, crying out 'Oh my God, have mercy, mercy!' A huge crowd attended. Newspaper reports described her as a 'good-looking stout young woman'.

See also Chapters 4 and 6.

ELIZABETH COMMINS
Hanged in Bodmin, Cornwall on 8 August 1828, for the murder of her illegitimate child. Aged 22.

Before she was hanged, Elizabeth Commins confessed her crime and explained what had happened to her child. She was orphaned at 13, she said, and shortly afterwards went into service with a gentleman in Tywardreath, four miles from Fowey. There she became pregnant by a fellow servant and concealed her condition. When she went into labour, she pretended that she had stomach ache and went to the cow-house to give birth but when the baby cried, she struck its head against the side of a crib and covered it with chaff. After sentencing, Commins reportedly 'did not appear to be at all affected by her awful situation, and walked from the dock without assistance'.

ANN HARRIS
Hanged in Shrewsbury, Shropshire on 16 August 1828, for the murder of James Harrison (accessory before the fact). Aged 50.

When Ann Harris's son Thomas Ellson was charged with stealing sheep, a felony that could send him to the gallows, she and Thomas's father-in-law John Cox conspired to have James Harrison, the chief witness against him, murdered. They commissioned Cox's two sons John and Robert and another young man called Joseph Pugh to do the job and paid them fifty shillings. They enticed Harrison to a prearranged spot where they strangled and buried him. As there was now no witness against him, Ellson was acquitted but when he was rearrested for another crime, in order to reduce the charge against him, he told the authorities that Harrison had been murdered by his mother and the others. All five were found guilty, but Robert Cox and his father were reprieved. When it was clear that Ann's sentence would not be commuted, she fell into 'a deplorable situation'. Newspaper reports claimed that she had 'never heard of Jesus Christ till she came to the gaol, and the plainest doctrine of Christianity was to her unknown till she came within its walls'. She was executed in front of a crowd of 5,000, the first woman to be hanged in the county for twenty-five years. On the scaffold, her legs being bound together, she needed the help of Mrs Kitson, the matron of the gaol, and another woman, to reach the rope. After the drop, she 'struggled violently for a few minutes'. All the protagonists were active members of a large sheep-stealing gang operating in the neighbourhood of Market Drayton on the Shropshire-Staffordshire border. Newspapers noted that Ann was 'remarkably keen-looking, with a most malignant pair of sparkling black eyes'.

JANE JAMIESON or JAMESON
Hanged on Newcastle upon Tyne Town Moor on 7 March 1829, for the murder of her mother Margaret. Aged 30.

Twenty thousand people assembled to see Jane Jamieson, a 'fishwoman', hanged for killing her 60-year-old mother in a drunken row at Keelmen's Hospital, which housed sick and aged former fishermen and their families. There had not been an execution in Newcastle for twelve years and it was over seventy since a woman had been hanged. Margaret Jamieson lingered for several days after Jane attacked her with a poker and, although she had initially blamed her daughter, she later claimed that she had fainted and fallen. Jane was unrepresented at her trial in front of Judge John Bayley, who when pronouncing sentence, was reported to have said, 'You have lifted up your hands against your own mother, inflicting on her a most dreadful wound, and sent her to an untimely grave. You see the desperate consequences of immoderately taking liquor. I do not wish to aggravate your feelings or to add to what you already do feel.' Jane, who had remained calm throughout the trial up to this point, began to weep. As the court emptied, she sat in the dock, her hands covering her face 'in an agony of grief and despair' and was carried back to prison in a chaise, accompanied by a large and hostile crowd. Jane was executed using the old horse and cart method. Jane shut her eyes during the journey to the town moor, as she had been advised, so that she would not be overwhelmed by the sight of the crowd. After prayers and psalms, a hood was placed over her face. Supported by the turnkey and one of the officers, she got up on a stool on the platform in the cart, and the executioner adjusted the noose. She announced, 'I am ready' and the cart moved away. Her body was afterwards taken to the Newcastle Surgeon's Hall for dissection, where it was used for several days by the surgeon John Fife in his anatomical lectures. Newspaper reports described her as a 'notorious character', a 'woman of the lowest class' with coarse features (although her face did not 'present any peculiar indication of ferocity').

ESTHER HIBNER
Hanged at Newgate, London on 13 April 1829, for the murder of 10-year-old parish apprentice Frances Colpitts. Aged 61.

Frances Colpitts and six other female apprentices were discovered in a neglected and emaciated state in the care of Esther Hibner and her daughter who ran an embroidering business in north London. She died in hospital soon afterwards and an investigation revealed that the Hibners had buried another apprentice, 13-year-old Margaret Hawse, in secret the previous year.

See also Chapter 3.

ANN CHAPMAN
Hanged at Newgate, London on 22 July 1829, for the attempted murder of her three-week-old daughter Elizabeth. Aged 28.

The jury recommended mercy for Ann Chapman, who strangled her youngest child and left her for dead amongst brambles and stinging nettles in a ditch at Turnham Green, near Acton to the west of London. The baby was rescued by a farm worker who heard her cries and summoned the local police constable, John Williamson, who gave the child into the care of a wet-nurse. A few days later Williamson recognized Ann Chapman in nearby Hammersmith and, despite her protestations that her baby had died and was buried, took her into custody. She had had eight children and was separated from her husband, who was described in court as 'a very bad man, who had used her very ill', and she had lately taken up with Matthew Varney. They were both seasonal workers in the market gardens of the area. While awaiting trial, Ann confessed to leaving her baby in the ditch, but denied trying to strangle her, blaming Varney for rejecting the child as not his own. The trial jury delivered their verdict after conferring for three minutes but felt that she deserved mercy because the baby had survived and on account of her previous sufferings. Ann, described in some newspaper reports as 'a good-looking woman' appeared 'quite firm' on the scaffold but had to be supported by one of the sheriff's men before the drop. A broadside published after her death reprinted a letter to her mother in which she said that she had expected to be reprieved.

KEZIA WESTCOMBE
Hanged in Exeter, Devon on 17 August 1829, for the poisoning murder of her husband, Samuel. Aged 32. Hanged with her lover, Richard Quaintance.

Kezia Westcombe and Richard Quaintance put arsenic in Samuel Westcombe's broth at Whipton in Heavitree, Devon. Quaintance took two witnesses with him to buy sixpence worth of arsenic, claiming later that the victim had asked him to buy it to deal with an infestation of rats. The lovers halved the arsenic so that each could murder their partner, but Quaintance's wife survived after discarding her poisoned tea because it made her nauseous. At their trial, Kezia denied any knowledge of the crime but confessed shortly before her execution. *The Western Time*s was highly critical of Kezia's behaviour and her appearance: 'she had extraordinary high cheek bones, a sharp-pointed, indented nose, dark hazel eyes, and large black eye-brows... Her general appearance partook of what she really was, a strong, robust, vicious, cruel woman.' Before their execution, Quaintance, weeping as he was being pinioned, and Kezia, barefoot and dressed in a black serge gown with long pantaloons, were allowed to shake hands and have a final conversation, in which they blamed each other but also accepted their own guilt. On the scaffold, Kezia was in a state of collapse and had to be supported to the gallows. The deaths were witnessed by a crowd of 12,000, who watched in near silence.

See also Chapter 7.

MARY ANN HIGGINS
Hanged on Whitley Common, Coventry on 11 August 1831 for the poisoning murder of her uncle, William Moore Higgins. Aged 19.

After his brother died, William Higgins assumed the role of father to his niece Mary Ann and told her that he had left his savings to her in his will. At the beginning of 1831 Mary Ann met Edward Clarke, a watchmaker's apprentice, who encouraged her to fleece her uncle. Clarke boasted that 'I have only to go to the old man's house whenever I want money.' On 22 March 1831, Mary Ann bought arsenic and put it in her uncle's pea soup; he died the following day. When a neighbour noticed a white substance in the remains of the soup, Mary Ann was immediately under suspicion. At the inquest she admitted that she had poisoned her uncle but told the coroner that Clarke had goaded her to do it, and that he had frequently beaten and abused her. Both were committed for trial and appeared at the next Warwick Assizes, where Clarke was acquitted for lack of evidence and Mary Ann convicted. After a two-mile journey from Coventry Gaol by cart, accompanied by her coffin and a procession of officials, she arrived at Whitley Common where a crowd of 15,000 people had gathered to watch her die. Her head, severed during her postmortem dissection, was retained probably by the police surgeon, and in 1919 was on display as a curiosity in Coventry. At present it is in the possession of The Herbert Museum in Coventry. The skull retains some skin and cartilage and the waxy substance that was injected into the veins around her scalp remains.

ELIZA or ELIZABETH ROSS or COOK or REARDEN
Hanged at Newgate, London on 9 January 1832, for the murder of Caroline Walsh. Aged 38.

Eliza Ross was the only woman executed for 'burking' – committing a murder in order to sell the body to anatomists – and she was also the last person to be hanged for this crime.

See also Chapter 6.

MARY KELLAWAY
Hanged in Exeter, Devon on 26 March 1832, for the murder of her newborn female illegitimate child. Aged 28.

Mary Kellaway, a former farm servant from Stowford, gave birth in silence at her lodgings in Devonport and killed the child by tying tape tightly around her neck. Her roommate, who slept throughout the birth despite sharing a bed with Mary, discovered the body but neither she nor the landlady were at first suspicious. It was only when Mary was seen surreptitiously trying to cut the tape off (it was hidden in the folds of the baby's neck) that a constable was called. Mary sobbed throughout the trial, at which she was unrepresented. She could not use the 'linen defence' as she had no baby clothes to prove she was anticipating a live birth; and the local surgeon was of the opinion the baby was born alive (among other procedures he used the long discredited 'floating lung' test). The jury consulted for fifteen minutes and although they returned a verdict of guilty they pleaded unsuccessfully that 'if there was any power in the world to save life, that mercy would be extended to the prisoner.' Mary 'conducted herself with a due sense of her awful situation' at her execution, walked with a 'firm step' and, as she was being pinioned, asked God to forgive her.

CHRONOLOGY

SARAH SMITH
Hanged in Leicester on 26 March 1832 for the poisoning murder of Elizabeth Wood. Aged 28.

When her brother-in-law's fiancée Elizabeth Wood showed her money she received in wages for her work as a servant in Rothley, Sarah Smith decided to murder her with arsenic. The fact that the brother-in-law was having second thoughts about the impending marriage may have encouraged her. Sarah called in local surgeon Hamlet Vernon to treat the ailing Elizabeth and on one of his visits told him she was about to lay out arsenic to kill rats, asking him to mix the poison with breadcrumbs for her, probably so that she could later argue that Wood's death was a terrible mistake and that it was Vernon's fault. Smith may have also given Wood laudanum to disguise the pain from the arsenic. Smith's appearance at her day-long trial at Leicester, during which she was described as having 'bloodless features' and 'half-closed eyes' was judged to indicate her guilt. On the day of her hanging, in front of a crowd of 25,000 spectators, she had to be supported to the gallows. 'Being a light, diminutive woman (about five feet in height), her struggles continued longer than is often witnessed with culprits of greater size and strength,' observed *The Leicester Chronicle*, before noting that the sight of Smith's body 'suspended by the neck like a worthless dog...her limbs quivering in the mortal conflict' gave rise to sympathy for the sufferer rather than for her victim and called for the revision of the criminal code. 'We are more and more convinced,' opined the paper 'of the utter inefficacy of capital punishments as preventatives of crime.'

MARY HUNTER
Hanged at York Castle on 30 March 1833, for counselling and abetting Hannah Gray to commit arson. Aged 47.

After two haystacks were set alight on separate nights in January 1833 in Aberford, Yorkshire, 18-year-old Hannah Gray, 'a person of weak intellect', immediately confessed, but later claimed that Mary Hunter had threatened to tear her liver out if she did not set fire to farmer John Marshall's wheat stacks and would give her a new frock if she did. Mary Hunter and her husband Thomas, an agricultural labourer, had a long-standing dispute with the farmer over the pounding of some of Mr Marshall's foals in the pinfold (an enclosure held in common by the farmers of a parish, managed by the Hunters for a stipend). He refused to pay and blows were exchanged. The affair was settled by a magistrate but Mary Hunter was left dissatisfied. Thomas Hunter was arrested first and then discharged but after the second incident Hannah Gray confessed. The jury took five minutes to decide Mary Hunter's guilt and when pronouncing sentence of death Judge John Gurney stated that arson was 'a crime [which] has, to the disgrace of our national character, of late become alarmingly prevalent.' Hunter, he said, had 'aggravated a mind weaker than your own, and made her the instrument to serve your own most guilty purpose.' The mother of fourteen children, Hunter vehemently protested her innocence. Newspaper reports said that her last words were 'I am inn—' before the drop fell. Over 4,000 spectators attended. Hers was the first execution of a female at York since Ann Barber in 1821.

See also Chapter 11.

CHARLOTTE LONG
Hanged in Gloucester on 31 August 1833, for arson. Aged 33.

The jury recommended mercy for Charlotte, who was hanged for setting fire to haystacks, largely on uncorroborated testimony.

See also Chapter 11.

MARY HOLDEN
Hanged in Lancaster on 19 March 1834, for the poisoning murder of her husband Rodger. Aged 27.

Trapped in an unhappy marriage to Rodger Holden, a weaver, and possibly involved in an affair, Mary Holden took a reckless course. She ordered sixpence worth of 'flea powder' from a local shopkeeper and put it in the teapot. When Rodger came home from work and said he was thirsty, she pointed at the teapot. She may have thought that the fact that she had not *given* him tea or told him to drink it was a defence. At least one witness gave evidence that Rodger had treated Mary badly but the judge did not accept that as an excuse and admonished her for sending her husband 'out of the world unprepared to meet his maker, with all his sins upon him'. After sentencing, Mary said, 'My Lord, have mercy on me' but walked out of court 'with a firm step'; she later broke down and was 'overcome with grief'. Mary, a Roman Catholic, was attended by a priest and while awaiting her hanging 'behaved herself in a very becoming manner'. On the morning of the execution she was taken in a sedan chair to chapel to 'prevent the rude gaze of the debtors, as she had to pass through their yard' and then became 'suffocated with grief, and was dreadfully agitated'. On the scaffold she was 'calm and collected'. After the rope had been fastened to the chain around the beam, she said, 'Lord relieve me out of my misery!' She was praying aloud with the priest when the drop fell and thereafter 'struggled violently for some minutes'. *The Liverpool Mercury* described her as a 'decent-looking person of middle stature, rather of muscular frame, and though not of prepossessing appearance, yet there was nothing in her countenance indicating a ferocious disposition'. Mary's body was removed for interment within the precincts of the prison. The hanging did not attract a large crowd but it was observed that many spectators were women and that there were a 'great number of children'.

MARY SMITH
Hanged in Stafford on 19 March 1834, for the murder of her illegitimate 12-day-old daughter Mary Ann. Aged 24.

Pregnant by her master, James Harrison of Walsall, Mary Smith, described variously as 'a tolerably good-looking girl' and as having 'nothing prepossessing in her countenance', went to give birth at a house two miles away. After twelve days, she told her landlady she was taking the child to Harrison's house but instead went to the Wyrley and Essenington Canal near Bloxwich and threw the baby in. She instantly regretted her action but could not reach the child, who drowned. Then she went to see Mr Harrison and told him that the child was well and 'at nurse'. After the baby's body was discovered three days later, identified by her harelip, she and Harrison were both arrested but Mary quickly exonerated him. The trial was held in July 1833 but a legal issue over the name of the baby – both parents were Baptists and had not had her christened – meant that sentencing was delayed until the following assizes. 'The cries of the wretched woman, whilst the Judge was addressing her [for sentencing], were truly distressing; and many females in court were so much affected as to weep aloud,' observed *The Staffordshire Advertiser*.

URSULA LOFTHOUSE
Hanged at York Castle on 6 April 1835, for the poisoning murder of her husband Robert. Aged 26.

Robert Lofthouse, a clog and pattern maker of Kirby Malzeard, suddenly became ill, complaining of pain in the stomach and bowels, and died the next day. The doctor who attended him diagnosed cholera. However, Robert's siblings were suspicious. It became known that Ursula had bought arsenic from the chemist at Kirby, telling him that it was for a neighbour. Robert's body was disinterred and an autopsy revealed inflammation of the organs, thought to be caused by arsenic; the stomach was removed for analysis. Ursula told the constable who arrested her that Robert had 'very disagreeable breath', was mean with money and was in love with his sister-in-law. After the guilty verdict she 'wept profusely and when removed from the bar was quite insensible'; she refused to eat or drink. She confessed to having bought the arsenic but said her husband had taken it voluntarily and then sworn her to secrecy. The Lofthouses had been married for two years and had a child.

MARY ANN BURDOCK
Hanged in Bristol on 15 April 1835, for the poisoning murder of Clara Ann Smith. Aged 34.

After the death in October 1833 at 17 Trinity Street in Bristol of their 54-year-old lodger, Clara Ann Smith, Mary Ann (neé Williams) and her partner, Charles Wade, a married man separated from his wife, paid for the funeral. They told anyone who was interested that Smith had died in poverty and had no relations. Their fortunes noticeably improved immediately afterwards: Wade was able to pay off his debts and bought £400 worth of stock to start a business. He died in April 1834 and within weeks Mary Ann married a Mr Burdock. Some months later, Mrs Smith's relatives, who had been living abroad, arrived in Bristol and started inquiring about her estate (she was known to hoard large quantities of cash) and suspicions were aroused. Smith's body was exhumed and the contents of the stomach sent to the analytical chemist William Herapath of Bristol Medical School, who identified arsenic. Newspaper reporters deplored Mary Ann's ignorance (she could not read), failure to fully confess (she put the blame on the deceased Wade) and refusal to take part in the pre-execution service (she sat in chapel 'sullenly silent, never once rising or kneeling') but rather admired her appearance. She had a handsome face 'with a clear skin, dark hair, large dark eyes, aquiline nose, and altogether of a pleasing description'. For her execution she wore a black gown and bonnet and a coloured shawl. She was stout, so her weight caused 'almost instant death'. A crowd of about 50,000 filled Cumberland Road and Coronation Road for the first execution of a female in Bristol since 1802. Burdock left a teenage son and daughter.

CATHERINE FRAREY and FRANCES BILLING
Hanged at Norwich Castle, Norfolk, on 10 August 1835 for the poisoning murder of Mary Taylor and Robert Frarey. Aged 40 and 46.

Best friends Catherine Frarey and Frances Billing lived in a row of three cottages in the small village of Burnham Westgate in north Norfolk. They were charged with the murders of Frarey's husband Robert and of Mary Taylor, who was married to Billing's lover. They may also have been responsible for the death of an infant and for an attempt to poison Billing's husband James.

See also Chapter 7.

HARRIET TARVER
Hanged in Gloucester on 9 April 1836, for the poisoning murder of her husband Thomas. Aged 21.

WOMEN AND THE GALLOWS 1797–1837

Harriet and her 24-year-old husband Thomas Tarver lived together on bad terms in Chipping Campden, Gloucestershire; Thomas had deserted his wife at least once, forcing her to apply to the parish for relief. On 11 December 1835, after a breakfast of cold rice pudding, he went to work in the stables of the Noel Arms in 'perfect health' but he was soon complaining of acute stomach pain and a raging thirst with cold sweats. He went home and died the next day. A coroner's jury decided that he had been murdered and Harriet Tarver was to blame. She was known to have bought arsenic on two separate occasions. Her trial was a foregone conclusion and she was sentenced to death. Awaiting execution, she was penitent, 'attentive to her religious duties' and owned up to the crime. A large crowd gathered to watch her die (it was market day). On the scaffold she appeared to be faint and was seen moving her lips as if in silent prayer. The noose was not aligned correctly so 'her struggles were excessively violent for several minutes'. The couple left a baby daughter, aged about 12 months.

BETTY ROWLAND
Hanged in Liverpool on 9 April 1836, for the poisoning murder of her husband William. Aged 46.

William Rowland, a 50-year-old weaver, who lived with his wife Betty in a cellar in Butler Street, Oldham Road, Manchester, was taken ill on 18 December 1835 and died the next day. Betty set about arranging his funeral. Meanwhile, a neighbour, Jeremiah Cawley, suspecting foul play, had a word with the local beadle, James Sawley, who made it his business to look in at the cellar on the afternoon of the funeral. There he encountered a crowd of intoxicated guests who did not appreciate his efforts to halt proceedings in order to allow the coroner to view the corpse. Eventually, by claiming that he only wanted to ask Betty some questions, he managed to arrest her and take her to a lockup. She told him during the journey: 'Oh dear. I never gave him anything but a drop of brandy, and that I borrowed money to pay for. I am as innocent as a child, whether I suffer for it or not.' The coroner and the deputy constable were informed but as there was

CHRONOLOGY

no direct evidence against Betty, she was released and the funeral went ahead. Within days, however, William's body was dug up and the stomach sent for analysis by Mr Ollier, a surgeon; arsenic was found. Betty left the neighbourhood and did not attend the coroner's inquest held on 30 December. Soon it became known that she had recently bought arsenic, but when she was apprehended she claimed that her husband's death had been an accident: 'I put it into his gruel and thought it was sugar,' she said. She told a magistrate that her husband had been violent from the start (they had been married less than three years, and he was her third husband). Newspaper reports described her as 'a woman of low stature and very forbidding appearance'. She was found guilty at the next assizes in March and sentenced to death. Her execution, in front of the house of correction at Kirkdale was a riotous scene. Spectators started arriving from five in the morning to get a good view, although the event was not due to take place until three in the afternoon. They became bored and started pelting each other with missiles. Police attended but after they left, gangs of thieves started stealing tippets, bonnets and shawls from women, who were forced to take refuge in the gaol and to escape through the court house. Betty eventually appeared, attended by the chaplain, the Reverend Mr Horner, wearing a 'Lancashire bedgown, a linsey-woolsey petticoat and a frilled cap'. Her arms were pinioned and her clothes wrapped around her. She stood without assistance on the platform and after a portion of the burial service was read, the signal was given, the bolt withdrawn, and she dropped.

SOPHIA EDNEY

Hanged in Ilchester, Somerset on 14 April 1836, for the poisoning murder of her husband John. Aged 23.

Sophia Edney poisoned her much older husband by putting arsenic in fried potatoes and then adding it to the medicines prescribed by the doctor. She was buried within the confines of the prison.

See also Chapter 7.

Acknowledgements

The framework for this book was a list of names produced by Richard Clark and published on capitalpunishmentuk.org. I owe to him a substantial debt of gratitude for doing this amazing legwork and for making public all of his thorough research.

This project would not have been possible without Hedda Archbold, of HLA Agency, whose encouragement and support were invaluable, and my family, especially my partner Tim Clifford, whose wise words and editing skills are as golddust.

Most of the research was done in the National Archives, British Museum and the Wellcome Library, and online at The British Newspaper Archive (britishnewspaperarchive.co.uk), Old Bailey Proceedings Online (oldbaileyonline.org), Harvard Law School's Studies in Scarlet (http://online-learning.harvard.edu/course/studies-scarlet) and Broadside Collection (broadsides.law.harvard.edu), as well as the Bodleian's John Johnson Collection (johnjohnson.chadwyck.co.uk), and, increasingly, Google Books and archive.org. To all, my heartfelt appreciation for your work.

I would also like to thank the wonderful team at Pen & Sword, for guidance through the publication process.

Finally, to Twitter mates @sarahmurden @joanneharris3 @18thC and19thC, @helenrogers19c @AnnaMThane and @madamegilflurt, salutations and heartfelt thanks for your kindness and encouragement. Special acknowledgement to Louise Allen (@louiseregency) who gave me details of Sarah Hurst's background and crime and to David John Eason (@petticoatshang5) for pointers on Ann Heytrey.

Bibliography

ARCHIVES
Bank of England Archive
Bodleian Library: John Johnson Collection
British Library
British Newspaper Archive (BNA)
Harvard Law School Library special collection: Dying Speeches and Bloody Murders
Harvard Law School Library special collection: Studies in Scarlet
National Archives
National Library of Wales
Old Bailey Proceedings Online
Wellcome Library

GENERAL
Adams, S., Adams, S. (1825). *The Complete Servant*. London: Knight and Lacey.
Arnold, C. (2010). *City of Sin: London and its Vices*. London: Simon & Schuster.
Barrell, H. (2016). *Poison Panic: Arsenic Deaths in 1840s Essex*. Barnsley: Pen & Sword.
Beattie, J. M. (1986). *Crime and the Courts in England 1600-1800*. Princeton University Press.
Chesney, K. (1972). *The Victorian Underworld*. London: Penguin.
Crane, D. (2015). *Went the Day Well? Witnessing Waterloo*. London: HarperCollins.
Cruickshank, D. (2009). *The Secret History of Georgian London: How the Wages of Sin Shaped the Capital*. London: Random House.
Dickens, C. (1836). *Sketches by Boz*. 1. London: John McCrone.

Durston, G. (2007). *Victims and Viragos: Metropolitan Women, Crime and the Eighteenth-Century Justice System*. Arima Publishing.

Durston, G. (2013). *Wicked Ladies: Provincial Women, Crime and the Eighteenth-Century English Justice System*. Newcastle upon Tyne: Cambridge Scholars.

Eigen, J. P. (1995). *Witnessing Insanity: Madness and Mad-Doctors in the English Court*. New Haven and London: Yale University Press.

Emsley, C. (1996). *Crime and Society in England 1750-1900*. Harlow: Longman.

Evans, E. J. (1996). *The Forging of the Modern State: Early Industrial Britain 1783-1870*. Harlow: Longman.

Evans, J. (2011). *Hanged at Gloucester*. Stroud: The History Press.

Flanders, J. (2011). *The Invention of Murder: How the Victorians Revelled in Death and Detection and Created Modern Crime*. London: Harper.

Gattrell, V. A. C. (1994). *The Hanging Tree: Execution and the English People 1770-1863*. Oxford: OUP.

Gray, D. D. (2016). *Crime, Policing and Punishment in England, 1660-1914*. London: Bloomsbury Academic.

Gregory, J. (2012). *Against the Gallows: Capital Punishment and the Abolitionist Movement in Nineteenth Century Britain*. London: I. B. Tauris.

Griffin, E. (2014). *Liberty's Dawn: A People's History of the Industrial Revolution*. Yale: Yale University Press.

Griffiths. A. (1883). *The Chronicles of Newgate*. London: Bracken Books (1987 edition).

Grovier, K. (2008). *The Gaol*. London: John Murray.

Harvey, A. D. (1994). *Sex in Georgian England: Attitudes and Prejudices from the 1720s to the 1820s*. London: Phoenix Press.

Hay, D., et al (1975). *Albion's Fatal Tree*. London: Peregrine.

Hempel, S. (2013). *The Inheritor's Powder: A Cautionary Tale of Poison, Betrayal and Greed*. London: Weidenfeld & Nicolson.

Hibbert, C. (1963). *The Roots of Evil: A Social History of Crime and Punishment*. London: Weidenfeld & Nicolson.

BIBLIOGRAPHY

Hitchcock, T., Shoemaker, R. (2006). *Tales from the Hanging Court*. London: Hodder Arnold.

Hoffer, P. C., Hull, N. E. H. (1984). *Murdering Mothers: Infanticide in England and New England*. New York University.

Hufton, O. (1995). *The Prospect Before Her: A History of Women in Western Europe 1500-1800*. London: HarperCollins.

Inglis, B. (1971). *Poverty and the Industrial Revolution*. London: Granada.

Inglis, L. (2013). *Georgian London: Into the Streets*. London: Viking.

King, P. (2006). *Crime and Law in England, 1750-1840: Remaking Justice from the Margins*. Cambridge: CUP.

King, P. (2000). *Crime, Justice and Discretion in England, 1740-1820*. Oxford: OUP.

Knelman, J. (1998). *Twisting in the Wind: The Murderess and the English Press*. Toronto: University of Toronto Press.

Lennox, S. (2016). *Bodysnatchers: Digging Up the Untold Story of Britain's Resurrection Men*. Barnsley: Pen & Sword.

Linebaugh, P. (2003). *The London Hanged: Crime and Society in the Eighteenth Century*. London: Verso.

Linnane, F. (2003). *London's Underworld: Three Centuries of Vice and Crime*. London: Robson Books.

Linnane, F. (2009). *Madams: Bawds and Brothel-Keepers of London*. Stroud: The History Press.

MacDonald, H. (2006). *Human Remains: Dissection and Its Histories*. Yale University Press.

McLynn, F. (1991). *Crime and Punishment in Eighteenth-Century England*. Oxford: OUP.

May, A. N. (2003). *The Bar and the Old Bailey 1750-1850*. University of North Carolina Press.

Moore, L. (2000). *Con Men and Cutpurses: Scenes from the Hogarthian Underworld*. London: Penguin.

Moore, W. (2006). *The Knife Man*. London: Bantam.

Naish, C. (1991). *Death Comes to the Maiden: Sex and Execution 1431-1933*. London: Routledge.

Palk, D. (2007). *Prisoners' Letters to the Bank of England 1781-1827*. London: London Record Society.

Parascandola, J. (2012). *King of Poisons*. Dulles, Virginia: Potomac Books.

Parolin, C. (2010). *Radical Spaces: Venues of Popular Politics in London, 1790-c1845*. ANU Press.

Pearsall, R. (1983). *The Worm in the Bud*. London: Penguin.

Pinchbeck, I. (1930). *Women Workers and the Industrial Revolution 1750-1850*. London: Routledge.

Porter, R. (1982). *English Society in the Eighteenth Century*. London: Penguin.

Potter, H. (1993). *Hanging in Judgment: Religion and the Death Penalty in England from the Bloody Code to Abolition*. London: SCM Press.

Potter, H. (2015). *Law, Liberty and the Constitution: A Brief History of the Common Law*. Woodbridge, Suffolk: Boydell & Brewer.

Rose, L. (1986). *The Massacre of the Innocents: Infanticide in Britain 1800-1939*. London: Routledge & Kegan Paul.

Rudé, G. (1985). *Criminal and Victim: Crime and Society in Early Nineteenth-Century England*. Oxford: Clarendon Press.

Rule, J. (1992). *Albion's People: English Society 1714-1815*. Harlow: Longman.

Rule, J. (1986). *The Labouring Classes in Early Industrial England 1750-1850*. Harlow: Longman.

Steedman, C. (2009). *Labours Lost: Domestic Service and the Making of Modern England*. Cambridge: CUP.

Strevens, S. (2017). *The Yorkshire Witch: The Life & Trial of Mary Bateman*. Barnsley: Pen & Sword.

Thompson, F. M.L. (1988). *The Rise of Respectable Society: A Social History of Victorian Britain 1830-1900*. London: Fontana Press.

Uglow, J. (2014). *In These Times: Living in Britain through Napoleon's Wars, 1793-1815*. London: Faber & Faber.

Vickery, A. (1998). *The Gentleman's Daughter: Women's Lives in Georgian England*. New Haven, CT and London: Yale University Press.

BIBLIOGRAPHY

Wakefield, E. G. (1831). *Facts Relating to the Punishment of Death in the Metropolis*. London: James Ridgway.
Ward, R. (2015). *A Global History of Execution and the Criminal Corps*e. London: Palgrave.
Watson, K. (2004). *Poisoned Lives: English Poisoners and Their Victims*. London: Hambledon Continuum.
Whorton, J. C. (2010). *The Arsenic Century*. Oxford, New York: OUP.
Wilson, B. (2005). *The Laughter of Triumph*. London: Faber & Faber.
Wise, S. (2013). *Inconvenient People: Lunacy, Liberty and the Mad-Doctors in Victorian England*. London: Vintage.
Wise, S. (2004). *The Italian Boy: Murder and Grave-Robbery in 1830s London*. London: Jonathan Cape.
Yetter, L. (2010). *Public Execution in England 1573-1868*, Vols 5, 6. London: Pickering & Chatto.

PERIODICALS
Beattie, J. M. (1975). The Criminality of Women in Eighteenth-Century England. *Journal of Social History*, 8 (4), pp. 80–116.
Beattie, J. M. (1991). Scales of Justice: Defense Counsel and the English Criminal Trial in the Eighteenth and Nineteenth Centuries. *Law and History Review*, 9 (2), pp. 221–267.
Beattie, J. M. (2007). Garrow and the Detectives: lawyers and policemen at the Old Bailey in the late eighteenth century. *Crime, Histoire & Sociétés / Crime, History & Societies*, 11 (2), pp. 5–23.
Bynum, W. F. (1981). Rationales for Therapy in British Psychiatry, 1780–1835. In: Scull, A., *Madhouses, Mad-Doctors, and Madmen Book: The Social History of Psychiatry in the Victorian Era*. University of Pennsylvania Press.
Callahan, K. (2013). Women Who Kill: An Analysis of Cases in Late Eighteenth- and Early Nineteenth-Century London. *Journal of Social History*, 46 (4), pp 1–16.
Chassaigne, P. (1999). Popular Representations of Crime: The crime broadside – a subculture of violence in Victorian Britain? *Crime, Histoire & Sociétés / Crime, History & Societies*, 3 (2), pp. 23–55.

Cockburn, J. S. (1994). Punishment and Brutalization in the English Enlightenment. *Law and History Review*, 12 (1), pp. 155–179.

Cooper, R. A. (1981). Jeremy Bentham, Elizabeth Fry, and English Prison Reform. *Journal of the History of Ideas*, 42 (4), pp. 675–690.

Crosby, M. The Bank Restriction Act (1797) and Banknote Forgery. BRANCH: Britain, Representation and Nineteenth-Century History. Ed. Dino Franco Felluga. Extension of Romanticism and Victorianism on the Net. [Accessed 2016-04-30].

Davies, O., Matteoni, F. (2015). 'A virtue beyond all medicine': The Hanged Man's Hand, Gallows Tradition and Healing in Eighteenth- and Nineteenth-century England. *Social History of Medicine*, 28 (4), pp. 686–705.

Devereaux, S. (2004). Peel, Pardon and Punishment: The Recorder's Report Revisited. In: *Penal Practice and Culture*, ed. Devereaux, S. and Griffiths, Palgrave Macmillan.

Devereaux, S. (2005). The Abolition of the Burning of Women in England Reconsidered. *Crime, Histoire & Sociétés / Crime, History & Societies*, 9 (2), pp. 73–98.

Devereaux, S. (2009). Recasting the Theatre of Execution: The Abolition of the Tyburn Ritual. *Past & Present,* 202 (Feb), pp. 127–174.

Devereaux, S. (2013). England's 'Bloody Code' in Crisis and Transition: Executions at the Old Bailey, 1760–1837. *Journal of the Canadian Historical Association / Revue de la Société historique du Canada*, 24 (2), pp. 71–113.

Dick, A. J. (2007). 'The Ghost of Gold': Forgery Trials and the Standard of Value in Shelley's The Mask of Anarchy. *European Romantic Review*, 18 (3), pp. 381–400.

Downing, L. (2009). Murder in the Feminine: Marie Lafarge and the Sexualization of the Nineteenth-Century Criminal Woman. *Journal of the History of Sexuality*, 18, (1), pp. 121–137.

Feeley, M.M., and Little, D.L. (1991). The Vanishing Female: The Decline of Women in the Criminal Process, 1687-1912. *Law & Society Review*, 25 (4), pp. 719–758.

BIBLIOGRAPHY

Forbes, T.R. (1988). A Jury of Matrons. *Medical History*, 32, pp. 23–33.

Gavigan, S. (1989). Petit Treason in Eighteenth Century England: Women's Inequality Before the Law. *Canadian Journal of Women and the Law*, 3, pp. 335–374.

Gillis, J. R. (1979). Servants, Sexual Relations, and the Risks of Illegitimacy in London, 1801-1900. *Feminist Studies*, 5 (1), pp. 142–173.

Goodman, N. (1944). The Supply of Bodies for Dissection: A Historical Review. *BMJ*, 1944 (2), pp. 807–811.

Handler, P. (2005). Forgery and the End of the 'Bloody Code' in Early Nineteenth-Century England. *The Historical Journal*, 48 (3), pp. 683–702.

Houston, R.A. (2002). Madness and Gender in the Long Eighteenth Century. *Social History*, 27 (3), pp. 309–326.

Hurren, E. (2013). The dangerous dead: dissecting the criminal corpse. *Lancet*, 382, pp. 302–303.

King, P. (1984). Decision-Makers and Decision-Making in the English Criminal Law, 1750-1800. *Historical Journal*, 27 (1), pp. 25–58.

King, P. (2007). Newspaper reporting and attitudes to crime and justice in late eighteenth- and early-nineteenth-century London. *Continuity and Change*, 22 (1), pp. 73–112.

King, P. (2009). Making Crime News: Newspapers, Violent Crime and the Selective Reporting of Old Bailey Trials in the late Eighteenth Century. *Crime, Histoire & Sociétés / Crime, History & Societies*, 13 (1), pp. 91–116.

Knott, J. (1985). Popular Attitudes to Death and Dissection in Early Nineteenth Century Britain: The Anatomy Act and the Poor. *Labour History*, 49, pp. 1–18.

Lyon Cross, A. (1917). The English Criminal Law and Benefit of Clergy During the Eighteenth and Early Nineteenth Centuries. *American Historical Review*, 22 (3), pp. 544–565.

McDonagh, J. (2001). Child-Murder Narratives in George Eliot's '*Adam Bede*': Embedded Histories and Fictional Representation. *Nineteenth-Century Literature*, 56 (2), pp. 228–259.

McGowen, R. (1987). The Body and Punishment in Eighteenth-Century England. *Journal of Modern History*, 59 (4), pp. 651–679.

McGowen, R. (1999). From Pillory to Gallows: The Punishment of Forgery in the Age of the Financial Revolution, *Past & Present*, 165, pp. 107–140.

McGowen, R. (2007). Managing the Gallows: The Bank of England and the Death Penalty, 1797-1821. *Law and History Review*, 25 (2), pp. 241–282.

Nutt, T. (2010). Illegitimacy, Paternal Financial Responsibility, and the 1834 Poor Law Commission Report: The Myth of the Old Poor Law and the Making of the New. *The Economic History Review,* 63 (2), pp. 335–361.

Philips, D. (2003). Three 'moral entrepreneurs' and the creation of a 'criminal class' in England, c. 1790s-1840s. *Crime, Histoire & Sociétés / Crime, History & Societies*, 7 (1), pp. 79–107.

Phillips, N. (2013). A Case Study of the Impact of Wealth on the Criminal Justice System in Early Nineteenth-Century England. *Crime, Histoire & Sociétés / Crime, History & Societies*, 17 (1), pp. 29–52.

Rabin, D. (2002). Bodies of evidence, states of mind: infanticide, emotion and sensibility in eighteenth-century England. In: R. Jackson, ed., *Infanticide: Historical Perspectives on Child Murder and Concealment*, 1550-2000. Farnham: Ashgate, pp. 73–92.

Reay, B. (1991). The Context and Meaning of Popular Literacy: Some Evidence from Nineteenth-Century Rural England. *Past & Present*, 131 (May), pp. 89–129.

Rogers, N. (1989). Carnal Knowledge: Illegitimacy in Eighteenth-Century Westminster. *Journal of Social History*, 23 (2), pp. 355–75.

Sauer, R. (1978). Infanticide and Abortion in Nineteenth-Century Britain. *Population Studies*, 32 (1), pp. 81–93.

Sherwin, O. (1946). Crime and Punishment in England of the Eighteenth Century. *American Journal of Economics and Sociology*, 5 (2), pp. 169–199.

Shoemaker, R. B. (2008). The Old Bailey Proceedings and the Representation of Crime and Criminal Justice in Eighteenth-

BIBLIOGRAPHY

Century London. *Journal of British Studies*, 47 (3), pp. 559–580.

Shoemaker, R. S. (2004). Streets of Shame? The Crowd and Public Punishments in London, 1700-1820. In: S. Devereaux, P. Griffiths, eds., *Penal Practice and Culture, 1500-1900: Punishing the English*. Basingstoke: Palgrave Macmillan, pp. 232–257.

Steedman, C. (2007). A Boiling Copper and Some Arsenic: Servants, Childcare, and Class Consciousness in Late Eighteenth-Century England. *Critical Inquiry*, 34 (1), pp. 36–77.

Watson, K. D. (2013). Women, Violent Crime and Criminal Justice in Georgian Wales. *Continuity and Change*, 28 (2), pp. 245–272.

White, M. T. (2009). *Ordering the Mob: London's Public Punishments, c. 1783–1868*. PhD. University of Hertfordshire.

Wiener. M. J. (1999) Judges v. Jurors: Courtroom Tensions in Murder Trials and the Law of Criminal Responsibility in Nineteenth-Century England. *Law and History Review*, 17 (3), pp. 467–506.

Notes

Abbreviations

BC	*Bath Chronicle*
BG	*Bucks Gazette*
BM	*Bristol Mirror*
BNP	*Bury and Norfolk Post*
BOEA	Bank of England Archive
BWM	*Bell's Weekly Messenger*
CAM	*Cambrian*
CC	*Chester Courant*
CCJ	*Cambridge Chronicle and Journal*
CHC	*Cheltenham Chronicle*
CHO	*Coventry Herald and Observer*
CM	*Caledonian Mercury*
COU	*Courier*
CP	*Carlisle Patriot*
DM	*Derby Mercury*
EFP	*Exeter Flying Post*
EM	*Evening Mail*
EPG	*Exeter and Plymouth Gazette*
EX	*Examiner*
GC	*Gloucestershire Chronicle*
GJ	*Gloucester Journal*
GL	*Globe*
HAT	*Hampshire Telegraph*
HBPG	*Huntingdon, Bedford and Peterborough Gazette*
HC	*Hampshire Chronicle*
HJ	*Hereford Journal*
HO	Home Office
HP	*Hull Packet*
HT	*Hereford Times*
IJ	*Ipswich Journal*
IW	*Independent Whig*
KC	*Kentish Chronicle*
KG	*Kentish Gazette*

NOTES

KM	Kendal Mercury
KWP	Kentish Weekly Post
LC	Leicester Chronicle
LES	London Evening Standard
LG	Lancaster Gazette
LI	Leeds Intelligencer
LM	Leeds Mercury
LMG	London Medical Gazette
LPM	Liverpool Mercury
LS	London Standard
LT	Leeds Times
MA	Morning Advertiser
MAC	Manchester Courier
MC	Morning Chronicle
MH	Morning Herald
MM	Manchester Mercury
MP	Morning Post
NA	National Archives
NC	Norfolk Chronicle
NCC	Newcastle Chronicle
NCO	Newcastle Courant
NDJ	North Devon Journal
NM	Northampton Mercury
OB	Observer
OBPO	Old Bailey Proceedings Online
OUCH	Oxford University and City Herald
PC	Perthshire Courier
PLDA	Public Ledger and Daily Advertiser
RCG	Royal Cornwall Gazette
RM	Reading Mercury
RST	Radnorshire Society Transactions
SA	Sussex Advertiser
SC	Suffolk Chronicle
SI	Sheffield Independent
SM	Stamford Mercury
SNL	Saunders' News-Letter
STA	Staffordshire Advertiser
SWJ	Salisbury and Winchester Journal

TB	*True Briton*
TC	*Taunton Courier*
TM	*Tyne Mercury*
WALES	Archifau Cymru/Archives Wales
WB	*West Briton*
WJ	*Worcester Journal*
WK	*Warwick & Warwickshire General Advertiser*
WT	*Western Times*
YG	*Yorkshire Gazette*

Chapter 1: Eliza Fenning
Henry Wyatt: OBPO t18060416-63.
Eliza Fenning: *GL*, 25, 27 Mar 1815; *MC*, 18 May 1815; *SA*, 7 Feb 1825; *IW*, 22 Oct 1815; Fenning, E. (1815). *Eliza Fenning's own narrative of circumstances which occurred in the family of Mr Turner*. London: John Fairburn; Watkins, J. (1815). *The Important Results of an Elaborate Investigation into the Mysterious Case of Elizabeth Fenning*. London: William Hone. Anon. (1846) Mr Adolphus and His Contemporaries at the Old Bailey, *Law Magazine*, 35, pp. 54-67; Dickens, C. (1836). 1. *Sketches by Boz*. London: John McCrone; Hone, W. (1815). *La Pie Voleuse. The Narrative of the Magpie; or the Maid of Palaiseau. Being the History of the Maid and the Magpie. Founded upon the Circumstance of an Unfortunate Female having been Unjustly Sentenced to Death on Strong Presumptive Evidence*. London: J. Swan; Marshall, J. (1815). *Five Cases of Recovery from the Effects of Arsenic with the Methods so Successfully Employed for Detecting the White Metallic Oxide...relative to the guilt of Eliza Fenning*. London: C. Chapple; Thornbury, W., (1867). Old Stories Re-Told: Eliza Fenning (The Danger of Condemning to Death on Circumstantial Evidence Alone). *All the Year Round*, 18 (429), pp. 66-72. Seleski, P. (2001). Domesticity is in the Streets: Eliza Fenning, Public Opinion and the Politics of Private Life. In: T. Harris, ed., *The Politics of the Excluded c. 1500-1850*. Basingstoke: Palgrave Macmillan, pp. 265-290. Elizabeth Miller: *PLDA*, 8 Apr 1816; Hone, W. (1816). *The Important Trials at Kingston, 5th April 1816*. London: Printed for W. Hone.
Home Office (1819). *A Statement of the number of persons charged with criminal offence, who were committed...for trial...during the last seven years*. London.

NOTES

Chapter 2: Ann Heytrey
Ann Heytrey: *STA*, 11 Sep 1819, 22 Apr 1820, 3 Mar 1821; *CC*, 14 Sep 1819; *STA*, 3 Mar 1821; *Annual Register* (1822). London: Baldwin. *STA*, 3 Mar 1821. Anon. (1820). *The last dying speech and confession of Ann Heytrey, who was executed on the New Drop, Warwick, on Wednesday the 12th of April, 1820, for the murder of Mrs. Dormer, wife of Mr. Joseph Dormer, of the Dial House, Ashow, Warwickshire*. Leicester: Martin, Printer (broadside); Billingham, N. (2013). *Foul Deeds & Suspicious Deaths in Stratford and South Warwickshire*. Wharncliffe Books; *WK*, 15 April 1820.
Ann Mead: *NM*, 28 June 1800; *SA*, 4 Aug 1800.
Rebecca Hodges: *BNP*, 8 Mar 1809; Willis, W. (1838). *An Essay on the Rationale of Circumstantial Evidence*. London: Longman, Orme, Brown, Green and Longmans; Anon. (2 Jul 1831). On Insanity: Mr Amos's Lecture on Medical Jurisprudence. *London Medical Gazette*. In Australia, Rebecca was first placed in the factory at Parramatta, and later sent out to work as a domestic servant. Her propensity to go missing landed her in trouble in 1824 and she was punished with another spell at Parramatta. In 1827 she was described as 'incompetent to any kind of work'. In 1838 she was granted a conditional pardon. Her date of death is unknown.

Chapter 3: Esther Hibner
HO 17/118/7; *EM*, 13 Apr 1829; *MP*, 14 Apr 1829; *EPG*, 2 May 1829; *Lancet*, 1828–1829 (2), p. 158; Anon. (1829). *Particulars of the trial and execution of Esther Hibner, the elder: for the wilful murder of Frances Colpitt, a parish apprentice who was executed this morning at the Old Bailey* (broadside); Wakefield, E. G. (1834). *England and America: A Comparison of the Social and Political State of Both Nations*. New York: Harper and Brothers.

Chapter 4: Mary Morgan
WALES 4/533/3; *CAM*, 27 Apr 1805; *CC*, 4 May 1805; Kilday, A.-M. (2013). *A History of Infanticide in Britain, c. 1600 to the Present*. Palgrave Macmillan; Parris, P. (1983). Mary Morgan: Contemporary Sources. *RST* (53), pp. 57-64; Hardinge, G. (1818). *A Charge intended to have been delivered to the Grand Jury in April 1816. Illustrations of the Literary History of the Eighteenth Century* (3), p. 129; Hardinge, G. (1818). *The Miscellaneous Works, in Prose and Verse, of George Hardinge Esq.*

London: J. Nichols; Anon. (1943). A Gravestone at Presteigne and Its Story. *RST* (13), pp. 60-64.
Catherine Weeks: OBPO t18330704-33.
Elizabeth Harvey: OBPO t18011028-8.
Sarah Blacklock: OBPO t18370403-1112.
Jane Hale: OBPO t18361128-53a.
Mary Frances Jones: OBPO t18080406-35.
William Hunter: *Medical Observations and Inquiries*, 6 (1784), 271.
Rebecca Merrin: OBPO t18090920-114.
Catherine Welch: OBPO t18280410-17; *BWM*, 14 Apr 1828.
Mary Thorpe: ASSI 45/40/2; *LI*, 23 Dec 1799, 24 Mar 1800; Rede. T. L. (1831). *York Castle in the Nineteenth Century: Being an Account of All the Principal Offences Committed in Yorkshire from the Year 1800 to the Present Period.* London: John Bennett.
Ann Mountford: OBPO t18220522-45.
Mary Voce: *STA*, 20 Mar 1802; Taft, H. (1802). *An Account of the Experience and Happy Death of Mary Voce, who was executed on Nottingham Gallows...*; Sutton, C. (1802). *The Life, Character, Behaviour at the Place of Execution and Dying Speech of Mary Voce.* Burbage and Stretton; *A Full and Particular Account of the Life, Trial and Behaviour of Mary Voce*; Anon. (1802). *The last dying words and confession of Mary Vice [sic]...* Leicester: Pares, printer, High-street (broadside); Judge Graham: *PC*, 6 Oct 1836.

Chapter 5: Mary Bateman
TM, 13 Sep 1803; *LI*, 24, 31 Oct 1808, 27 Mar, 10 Apr 1809; *CC*, 11 Apr 1809; *BM*, 13 May 1809, 5 Sep 1812; *LM*, 27 Apr 1833; Anon. (1811). *Extraordinary Life and Character of Mary Bateman, the Yorkshire Witch.* Leeds: Davies and Co, Stanhope Press; *MP*, 28 Nov 1821; Elmhirst, E. (9 Sep 1954). Murderers' Leather. *Country Life.* Stevens, S. (2017)

Chapter 6: Eliza Ross
Eliza Ross: *NDJ*, 29 Dec 1831; *MA*, 9 Jan, 18 Feb 1832; *MP*, 10 Jan 1832; *NCC*, 14 Jan 1832; *BG*, 21 Jan 1832; *CM*, 23 Jan 1832.
Kezia Westcombe: *WT*, 22 Aug 1829.

Chapter 7: Frarey and Billing
Mary Wright: *NC*, 15 Dec 1832, 20 July 1833; *LES*, 6 Nov 1833; *HT*, 29 Dec 1832.

NOTES

Frarey and Billing: *NC*, 15 Dec 1832, 30 Mar, 20 Jul 1833, 15 Aug 1835; *HT*, 29 Dec 1832, quoting *Suffolk Chronicle*; *HBPG*, 10 Aug 1833; *LES*, 6 Nov 1833; Anon. (1832). The late jury of matrons at Norwich. *LMG* (12) pp. 22-26; Morson, M. (2008). *Norfolk Mayhem and Murder*. Barnsley: Pen & Sword; Marsh J. (1836); Marsh, J. (1836). Account of a method of separating small quantities of arsenic from substances with which it may be mixed. *Edinburgh New Philosophical Journal* (21), pp. 229–236.
Penelope Bickle: *WT*, 2 Aug 1834.
Sophia Edney: *TC*, 20 Apr 1836.

Chapter 8: Theft
Elizabeth Dunham: OBPO t18190915-72.
Sarah Lloyd: *IJ*, 26 Apr 1800; Notcutt, W. (1800). *Trial of Joseph Clarke, the Younger, and Sarah Lloyd, at the Assizes, held at Bury St Edmund's [sic], March 20, 1800, Before Sir Nash Grose, Knt.* Ipswich: S. Jackson.
Melinda Mapson: *MP*, 12 Apr 1810; *PLDA*, 14 Jun 1810; OBPO t18100411-3.
Ann Cooper: OBPO t18091101-28.
Elizabeth Fricker: *MP*, 6 Mar 1817; *OB*, 9 Mar 1817; Author (1847). Fry, K., Cresswell, Mrs. F. (1843). *Memoir of the Life of Elizabeth Fry, with Extracts from Her Journals and Letters*. Philadelphia: J. W. Moore; OBPO t18161030-31; Porter, G. R. (1843). *The Progress of the Nation in its Various Social and Economical Relations*. 5-8. London: Charles Knight and Co.

Chapter 9: Fraud
Ann Hurle: *MP*, 21 Dec 1803; *KWP*, 23 Dec 1803; *BWM*, 25 Dec 1803, 12 Feb 1804; I am indebted to http://bob-hammersley.co.uk/hurle/ann_hurle_times [accessed 2016-08-14] for transcripts of articles in *The Times*.
Mary Ann James: OBPO t18171203-67; *EX*, 22 Feb 1818; Society for the Diffusion of Knowledge upon the Punishment of Death, and the Improvement of Prison Discipline (1818). *On the Effects of Capital Punishment as Applied to Forgery and Theft*. London: John M'Creery.
Mary Grimes: OBPO t18090111-75; Anon. (1809). *The trials, dying speech and confession of Margaret Grimes alias Barrington, for taking a false oath, to obtain £24. 1s. 6d. supposed to be due to one Thomas Rotten*

as money; and John Nicholls, from Birmingham, for forgery, executed this morning before the debtor's door, Newgate. London: John Pitts (broadside).

Chapter 10: Forgery and Uttering
Forgery and uttering: Statistics quoted in McGowen, R. (2007). Managing the Gallows: The Bank of England and the Death Penalty, 1797-1821. *Law and History Review*, 25 (2), pp. 241-283.
Sarah Bailey: *LI*, 4 Nov 1799.
Bamfords: *LG*, 25 Apr 1818.
Baines: *HJ*, 8 Apr 1818; William, aka Kyle, was executed on 23 May.
Charlotte Newman: OBPO t18171203-55); *OB*, 1 Mar 1818.
Harriet Skelton: Carlyon, C. (1856), *Early and Late Reflections,* 3. London: Whittaker & Co.; OBPO t18180218-65; *Baptist Magazine*, Jul 1818; *New Bon Ton Magazine* (1818), 1.
Sarah Price: BOEA (M5/324); *SA, LI,* 11 Dec 1820; *SNL*, 20 Dec 1820.

Chapter 11: Arson
HO 17/47/146; *GC*, 24 Aug, 7 Sep 1833; *MH*, 30 Aug 1833, quoted in *The Punishment of Death: A Selection of Articles from the Morning Herald*, (1837), Vol 2. London: Hatchard & Son; Evans, J. *The last woman hanged for arson: Charlotte Long of North Nibley, 1833* gloscrimehistory.wordpress.com [accessed 2016-07-30]; Sergeant, T. (ed). (1835). *Reports of Cases Argued and Determined in the English Courts of Common Law*, 15. Philadelphia: P. H. Nicklin & T. Johnson.

Chapter 13: Chronology
1797-1806
Elizabeth Brockleby, Elizabeth Amos: *STA*, 1 Apr 1797. Diana Davies: WRO 4/531/7 www.llgc.org.uk [accessed 2016-04-28]. Rebecca Howard: *NC*, 12 Aug 1797. Rebecca Dunn: *HC*, 26 Aug 1797. Maria Theresa Phipoe: *New Monthly Magazine and Universal Register* (1819), 11; OBPO t17950520-27 and t17971206-7; Leach, T. (1815). *Cases in Crown Law, Determined by the Twelve Judges*. London: Butterworth & Son; *Sporting Magazine* (1798) 11; HO 26 and HO 27, and HO CR NAHOCR700020117; *HC*, 16 Dec 1797; Anon. (1797). *The last dying speech and confession, Birth, Parentage, and Behaviour, of Mary Benson, alias Maria Theresa Phipoe, who was executed this morning facing the*

NOTES

debtor's door, Newgate, and the extraordinary speech she made while she was standing under the gallows (broadside). Elizabeth Brown: OBPO t17980418-1. Ann Warner: OBPO t17980912-19. Sarah Williams: *KC,* 22 Mar 1799. Mary Ann Martin: *DM,* 4 Apr 1799. Betty Limpany: *SWJ,* 15 Apr 1799. Margaret Hughes: *KC,* 13 July 1798; 26 July 1799. Elizabeth Lavender: *BC,* 2 Feb 1799; *TB,* 2 Aug 1799. Mary Nicholson: *RM,* 20 Aug 1798; *CM,* 29 July 1799. Elizabeth Johnson: Anon. (1800). *The last dying words and confession of Elizabeth Johnson.* Nottingham: Samuel Tupman (broadside); *NCO,* 9 Aug 1800; Knipe, W. (1867). *Criminal Chronology of York Castle.* York: C. L. Burdekin. Mary Lloyd: *CC,* 15 Apr 1800; *DM,* 23 Oct 1800. Hannah Palmer: Anon. (1801). *Last dying speech and confession of John and Hannah Palmer: who were executed at Warwick, on Wednesday the 1st day of April, 1801 for the cruel and barbarous murder of Mary the wife of the said John Palmer.* Leicester: J. Throsby, Jun. (broadside). Alice Clarke: *CC,* 21 Apr 1801. Hannah Eastwood: *CM,* 11 May 1801; *MM,* 29 Mar 1808. Susannah Mottershall: *STA,* 9 May 1801. Sarah Claridge: *SM,* 21 Aug 1801. Maria Davis, Charlotte Bobbett: *GL,* 19 Apr 1802. Mary Lappidge: BOEA (M5/307); *NM,* 9 Apr 1803. Martha Chapple: Wade, S. (2007). *Yorkshire's Murderous Women.* Wharncliffe Books. Sarah Jones: *MP,* 24 Apr 1803. Elizabeth Caesar: *HC,* 19 Mar 1804. Elizabeth Langham: Storey, N. R. (2011). *A Grim Almanac of Essex.* The History Press. Ann Heywood: Anon. (1805). *A true and particular account of the three most horrid murders, that have lately been committed in the county of York – Ann Haywood, for the murder of her bastard child, John Wilkinson, for poisoning his wife, and Benjamin Oldroyd, for hanging his own father; with their condemnation, execution, &c.* London: Robert Lindsay (broadside). Elizabeth Barber: Knapp, A., Baldwin, B. (1810). *The New Newgate Calendar.* J. and J. Cunde. Betty Hulce: *STA,* 25 May 1805. Mary Parnell: OBPO t18050710-21.

1806-1815
Sarah Herring: Baggoley, M. (2013). *Surrey Executions: A Complete List of Those Hanged in the County During the Nineteenth Century.* Amberley Publishing. Mary Jackson: *LG,* 26 Apr 1806. Elizabeth Godfrey: Pelham, C. (1841). *The Chronicles of Crime, Or, The New Newgate Calendar.* T. Tegg. Martha Alden: Jay Smith, J. (1836). *Celebrated Trials of All Countries, and Remarkable Cases of Criminal Jurisprudence.* Philadelphia: L. A. Godey; *BNP,* 19 Aug 1807. Sarah Pugh: *HJ,* 19 Aug

WOMEN AND THE GALLOWS 1797–1837

1807. Mary Chandley: *HJ*, 19 Aug 1807; *MM*, 29 Mar 1808; Anon (1808). *A true and particular account of the crimes, trial, and behaviour of Mary Chandle...*(broadside). Rebecca Blundell: *HAT*, 31 July 1809; *HC*, 12 Mar 1810. Jane Curran: *HC*, 12 Mar 1810; *SWJ*, 2 Apr 1810. Frances Thompson: *LM*, 17 Mar 1810; Knipe, W. (1867). *Criminal Chronology of York Castle*. York: C. L. Burdekin. Betty Amphlett: *GJ*, 20 Aug 1810. Jane Cox: *BM*, 13 Aug 1811; *EX*, 18 Aug 1811. Elizabeth Smith: Anon. (1812). *The Suffolk Tragedy! The Trial and Execution of John and Eliz. Smith, for the Murder of Their Daughter* (broadside); Anon. (1812). *Brownrigg the Second; or the Cruel Stepmother: The Full Particulars of the Trial and Execution, of John and Elizabeth Smith...* London (broadside). Hannah Smith: *LG*, 20 June 1812. Catherine Foster: OBPO t18120513-44; *KG*, 14 Aug 1812; Anon. (1812). *Trials and Execution of Joseph Thompson, for forging a bill of exchange, for the payment of £118, 18s 4d, in the name of A. M'Dougall and Co. And Catherine Foster...* London: J. Pitts (broadside). Ann Arnold: *SM*, 2 Apr 1813. Sarah Fletcher: *SA*, 12 Apr 1813. Edith Morrey: Anon. (1812). *Trial & execution of John Lomas, and condemnation of Edith Morrey, for wilful murder* (broadside). Azubah Fountain: Knapp, A., Baldwin, W. (1828). *The Newgate Calendar* (4). London: J. Robins and Co. Elizabeth Osbourne: *WB*, in *EX*, 30 Aug 1813; *RCG*, 28 Aug 1813. Mary Gibbs: *PLDA*, 1 Apr 1814. Sarah Owens: *GJ*, 2 May 1814. Mary Cook: *GJ*, 15 Aug 1814. Sarah White: *OUCH*, 25 Mar 1815. Sarah Woodward: *CCJ*, 7 Apr 1815. Elizabeth Wollerton: *SC*, 29 July 1815. Sarah Cock: *LG*, 6 Apr 1816. Dinah Riddiford: www.thornburyroots.co.uk/crime/ dinah-and-luke-riddiford/ [accessed 2016-08-04].

1816-1825
Susannah Holroyd: *LG*, 21, 28 Sep 1816 ; *Annual Register...for the Year 1816 (*1817). London: Baldwin, Cradock and Joy; Anon. (dated 1821 but probably 1816). *Tiral [sic], execution, and confession of Susannah Holroyd for the barbarous murder of her husband, her own son, 8 years of age, and an infant 15 weeks old; having had connection with another man; who was executed at Lancaster, on Monday the 13th Aug. 1821 [sic], giving an account of her behaviour on the scaffold*. Elizabeth Whiting: *SM*, 21 Mar 1817. Ann Statham: *STA*, 22 Mar 1817. Ann Hawlin: *STA*, 26 Apr 1817. Elizabeth Warriner: Anon. (1817). *The Last Dying Words, Speech and Confession of Elizabeth Warriner*. Glasgow:

NOTES

John Muir; *LC*, 2 Aug 1817. Margaret Dowd: *MM*, 24 Mar 1818; *LG*, 6 Sep 1817; *STA*, 11 Apr 1818. Ann Bamford: *PLDA*, 29 Apr 1818. Ann Tye: Russell, W. O, Ryan, E. (1825). *Crown Cases Reserved for Consideration And Decided by the Twelve Judges of England from the Year 1799 to the Year 1824.* London: A. Strahan; *CHC*, 25 Dec 1817, 7 May 1818. Sarah Huntingford: *SWJ*, 9 Nov 1818, 15 Mar 1819. Sarah Hurst: *SM*, 26 Mar 1819. Hannah Bocking: *DM*, 25 Mar 1819; Anon. (1819). *The execution and confession of Hannah Bocking, aged 16, of Litton, near Bakewell, Derbyshire, who suffered on Monday the 22d of March, 1819, on the new drop, in front of the county gaol, Derby, for wilfully poisoning Jane Grant.* Leicester: Martin, printer (broadside). Mary Woodman: *EFP*, 25 Mar 1819. Mary Bissaker: *STA*, 17 Apr, 7 Aug 1819. Sarah Polgreen: *RCG*, 19 Aug 1820. Rebecca Worlock: Anon. (1820). *Trial of Rebecca Worlock, at the Gloucester Assizes.* Bath: W. Meyler and Son. Mary Clarke: Borrow, G. H. (1825). *Celebrated Trials and Remarkable Cases of Criminal Jurisprudence*, (6), pp. 464-468. London: Knight and Lacey. Esther Waters: *WJ*, 12 Apr 1821. Ann Barber: *LG*, 25 Aug 1821; *LC*, 18 Aug 1821; Drinkall, M. (2012). *Murder & Crime: Leeds.* The History Press. Anon. (1821). *A Particular Account of the Trial and Execution of Ann Barber, who was Executed at York, on Monday the 13th of August, 1821, Convicted of the Horrid Murder of James Barber, her own Husband* (broadside); Anon. (1821). *Dying Speech and Confession of Anne Barber, who was Executed at the Castle of York, on Tuesday last, Aug. 14, 1821, for the Wilful Murder of John Barber, her Husband...* Birmingham (broadside). Ann Norris: OBPO t18211024-4; *MP*, 28 Nov, 4 Dec 1821 ; Anon. (1821). *The Last Dying Speeches of the Unfortunate Criminals, who were Executed this Morning at the Old Bailey.* London: E. Thomas (Anon. (1822). Hannah Halley: *A full and particular account of Hannah Halley, a native of Newcastle, who was tried the 5th of April, 1822...* Stockton: Appleton (broadside). Rachael Edwards: *CAM*, 24 Aug 1822. Grace Griffin: Anon. (1823). *An account of the crime, trial, and execution of Grace Griffin, at Berwick upon Tweed, on Saturday last, 26th. July, 1823, for the murder of her husband* (broadside). Hannah Read: *CC*, 23 Aug 1825; Anon. (1825). *Particulars of the trial, execution, and confession of Hannah Read, who suffered at Leicester, on Friday last, for the wilful murder of her husband* London: Birt, printer (broadside)

1827-1836

Mary Cain: OBPO t18260112-16. Amelia Roberts: *MP*, 3 Jan 1827; OBPO t18261026-42. Rachael Bradley: *BWM*, 4 Feb 1827; *MP*, 28 Mar 1827; *MAC*, 31 Mar 1827; *SI*, 7 Apr 1827; 'Rachel Bradley's Downfall', Bodleian 2806 c.17 (356). Sarah Jones: *EM*, 11 Apr 1827, *CAM*, 21 Apr 1827; *MP*, 24 Apr 1827. Mary Wittenback: *LS*, 25 July 1827, 14 Sep 1827; *EX*, 16 Sep 1827; *MA*, 17 Sep 1827; *MC*, Courier, 18 Sep 1827. Jane Scott: *LPM*, 28 Mar 1828; *CC*, 1 Apr 1828; *LG*, 21 Aug 1875. Elizabeth Commins: *NDJ*, 14 Aug 1828; *BM*, 16 Aug 1828. Ann Harris: *CCJ*, 8, 29 Aug 1828; *YG*, 9 Aug 1828; *STA*, 16 Aug 1828; *MP*, 23 Aug 1828. Jane Jamieson: *NCO*, 7 Mar, 14 Mar 1829; Anon. (1829). *An account of the trial and execution of Jane Jameson, who was hanged on Newcastle Town Moor, March 7th, 1829, for the murder of her mother* (broadside); Hempel, S. (2006). *The Strange Case of the Broad Street Pump: John Snow and the Mystery of Cholera.* University of California Press. Ann Chapman: *LS*, 16 June 1829; *COU*, 22 July 1829; OBPO t18290611-62; Anon. (1829). *Particulars of the Trials and Execution of Charles Jones, Edward Turner, Thomas Crowther & Ann Chapman* (broadside); *BC*, 20 Aug 1829. Mary Ann Higgins: *CHO*, 1 Apr 1831; *HBPG*, 20 Aug 1831; www.criminalcorpses.com. Mary Kellaway: *MC*, 26 Mar 1832; *RCG*, 31 Mar 1832. Sarah Smith: *LC*, 31 Mar 1832; Anon. (1832). *Life trial and execution of Sarah Smith, who was executed this morning (Monday) for the wilful murder of Elizabeth Wood, at Mountsorrel.* Leicester: Smith (broadside). Mary Hunter: *LT*, 14 Mar 1833; *HP*, 5 Apr 1833; *CP*, 6 Apr 1833. Mary Holden: *LPM*, 21 Mar 1834. Mary Smith: *STA*, 3 Aug 1833; 22 Mar 1834. Ursula Lofthouse: *HP*, 10 Apr 1835; *YG*, 11 Apr 1835. Mary Ann Burdock: *BM*, 18 Apr 1835. Harriet Tarver: *GC*, 9 Apr 1836. Betty Rowland: *MAC*, 5 Dec 1835, 9 Jan 1836; *KM*, 16 Apr 1836.

Index

Alden or Aldin, Martha, 166
Alley, Peter, 3, 14, 16, 17, 50
Amos, Elizabeth, 154
Amphlett or Amplett, Betty, 169-70
Anatomy Act, xix, 90
Anatomy schools, 83, 84-5, 87, 89-90
Apprentices
  See Parish apprentices
Arnold, Ann, 172
Arsenic, x, 3, 34-5, 67-8, 80, 91-102, 159, 162, 170, 175, 176-7, 179, 183-5, 186-7, 188, 190, 195-6, 200-201, 203, 206-209
  detection of, 10-11, 18-9, 26-8, 67
  women and, 96, 99-100
  See also Fenning, Eliza; Miller, Elizabeth; Norfolk murders; Poisoning murders
Arson, x, xii, xix, 37, 107, 144-9, 151-2, 157, 167, 171, 173-4, 175, 203, 204
Attempted murder, x, 54, 92, 152, 175, 200
Aylesbury, Buckinghamshire (hanging at), 183

Bailey, Sarah, 132-3, 158
Baker, Ann, 161
Bamford, Ann, 39, 181, 204
Bank of England, xii, 103, 113, 126-8, 130-43, 156, 158, 159, 179, 180
  Policy towards forgery, 131
Bank Restriction Act, vi, xviii, 130-3, 142-3, 156

Plea bargaining, xii, 140, 142, 187
Barber, Ann, 188-9
Barber, Betty
  See Hulce, Betty
Barber, Elizabeth, 164
Barrington, Mary
  See Grimes, Mary
Bateman, Mary, 73-83, 91, 99, 168
Belly
  See Pleading the belly
Benson, Mary
  See Phipoe, Maria Theresa
Berwick upon Tweed, Northumberland (hanging at), 190
Bickle, Penelope, 92
Billing, Frances
  See Norfolk murders
Bissaker, Mary, 185
Blacklock, Sarah, 61
Bloody Code, x, 143, 150-2
Blundell, Rebecca, 168
Bobbett, Charlotte, 162
Bocking, Hannah, 34, 183-4
Bodmin, Cornwall (hangings at), 173, 186, 197
Boughton, Cheshire (hanging at), 159
Bradley, Rachael or Rachel, 192
Bristol (hangings at), 162, 206
Brockleby or Brokesby, Elizabeth, 153
Brown, Elizabeth, 156
Brownrigg, Elizabeth, 45, 171
Burdock, Mary Ann, xiv, 100, 102, 206-207

WOMEN AND THE GALLOWS 1797–1837

Burglary
  See Stealing
'Burking', 86-8, 90, 202
Bury St Edmunds, Suffolk (hanging at), 159

Caesar, Elizabeth, 163
Cain, Mary, 191-2
Canterbury, Kent (hanging at), 157
Carter, Elizabeth
  See Caesar, Elizabeth
Chandley or Chandler, Mary, 167
Chapman, Ann, 200
Chapple or Chapel, Martha, 162
Chester (hanging at), 172
Claridge, Sarah, 161
Clarke, Alice, 160
Clarke, Mary, 187-8
Clift, William, 89
Cock or Cook, Sarah, 176
Coining
  See Forgery
Commins, Elizabeth, 197
Cotton, The Rev Horace, 19-22, 24, 52, 88, 136-8
Cook, Mary, 174-5
Corn Law, 6, 30
Counterfeiting
  See Forgery
Coventry (hangings at), 185, 201
Cox, Jane, 170
Cruikshank, George, 142
Curran, Jane, 169

Daly or Daley, Elizabeth
  See Barber, Elizabeth
Davies or Davis, Diana or Elizabeth, 105, 154
Davies or Davis, Maria, 162
Davis, Ann, 164
Davis, Maria, 162

Derby (hangings at), 183, 190
Dissection (as postmortem punishment) xii, xiii, xix, 24, 42, 69, 73, 155, 168, 194, 199, 202
  demonstration at Leeds, 82-90
  at Royal College of Surgeons, 88-90
  end of, 85, 90
  postmortem relics, 74, 83, 196, 202
Dorchester, Dorset (hanging at), 174
Dowd, Margaret, 180
Dunn, Rebecca, 155
Durham (hanging at), 158

Eastwood, Hannah, 161
Edney, Sophia, 100-102, 209
Edwards, Rachael, 190
Eliot, George, 70
Ellenborough, Lord, xvii, 58-9, 61
Execution broadsides, xiv, 51, 153, 155, 184, 191, 200
Exeter, Devon (hangings at), 157, 164, 170, 184, 200, 202

Fauntleroy, Henry, 119-20, 150
Fenning, Eliza or Elizabeth, xv, 3-30, 92, 136, 142, 146, 175-6
Fletcher, Sarah, 172
Forgery and fraud
  coining, xix, 131, 143, 151, 155, 156, 165, 168, 185
  of signature on a financial instrument, 103, 119-29
  of bank notes, x, xii, 130-43, 181
  last person executed for, 143
  uttering, xv, 130-43, 156, 158, 159, 161, 162, 165, 169, 179, 180, 181, 187
Foster, Catherine, 171-2
Fountain, Azubah, 173
Frarey, Catherine
  See Norfolk murders

232

INDEX

Fraud
  See Forgery and fraud
Fricker, Elizabeth, 116-8, 178
Fry, Elizabeth,
  attitude to capital punishment, 114-5
  ministry to condemned women,
    116, 125, 135-8, 140-1, 180-1
  visit to Newgate, 13, 115-6

Garrow, William, 14, 37, 39, 50, 51
Gibbs, Mary, 174
Gloucester, Duke of, 141, 181
Gloucester (hangings at), 176, 181,
  186, 204, 207
Godfrey or Godfry, Elizabeth, 166
Gordon, Ann
  See Davis, Ann
Graham, Mary
  See Grimes, Mary
Graham, Robert, 68-9
Grant, Susan or Susannah, 168
Griffin, Grace, 190
Grimes, Mary, 126, 167-8
Grose, Nash, 107
Gurney, John, 14, 145, 147-8, 204

Herapath, Prof William, 102, 207
Halley, Hannah, 190
Hangings,
  botched, 118, 138, 158, 165, 166,
    192, 195, 196, 203, 208
  bread and water diet, xiii, xvii, 52
  horse and cart method, xvi, 183,
    199
  New Drop, xvi, 82, 124, 178, 183
Hardinge, George, 56-60, 70-2, 105,
  154, 164
Harris, Ann, 197-8
Harris, Mary
  See Bissaker, Mary
Hawlin Ann, 179

Haynes, Margaret
  See Hughes, Margaret
Hayricks
  See Arson
Haywood, Ann
  See Heywood, Ann
Hereford (hanging at), 166-7
Herring, Sarah, 165
Hertford (hangings at), 35, 159, 176
Hey, Dr William, 82
  See also Dissection (as postmortem
    punishment)
Heytrey, Ann, 31-43, 186
Heywood, Ann, 163-4
Hibner, Esther, xiv, 44-53, 199
Hibner, Esther (the younger), 44, 47-
  52
Higgins, Mary Ann, 201-202
Highway robbery, x, xi, 171
Hodges, Rebecca, 37-40
Holden, Mary, 204-205
Holroyd, Susannah, 176-7
Hone, William, 23-25, 28-9, 142
Horsemonger Lane Gaol, Surrey
  (hangings at), 165, 172
Horsham Common, Sussex (hangings
  at), 157, 164
Housebreaking, 174, 176
Howard, Rebecca, 154
Hughes, Margaret, 157
Hulce or Hulse, Betty, 164-5
Hunter, Mary, 147-8, 152, 203-204
Huntingford, Sarah, 182-3
Hurle, Ann, 120-5, 163
Hurst, Sarah, 183

Ilchester, Somerset (hangings at),
  174, 209
Infanticide 54-72
  conviction rates, 54, 59-60
  illegitimate babies, 154, 156-8, 160-3,

233

172, 174, 176-9, 181-2, 190, 192-4, 196-7, 202
  legitimate babies, 67-70, 162, 178
  hydrostatic test, 62, 202
  and insanity, 62-7
  legal defences of, 60-6
Ipswich, Suffolk (hangings at), 170, 172, 174, 175

Jackson, Mary, 165
James, Mary Ann, 124-5, 128-9, 135-6, 139, 179-80
Jamieson or Jameson, Jane, 198-9
Johnson, Elizabeth, 159
Jones, Mary Ann
  See James, Mary Ann
Jones, Sarah (1803), 163
Jones, Sarah (1827), xvi-xvii, 193-4
Jury of matrons, 80-1, 99, 123, 168
  See also Pleading the belly

Kellaway, Mary, 202
Kennington Common, Surrey (hanging at), 155

Lamb, Mary, 39-41
Lancaster Castle (hangings at), 161, 165, 167, 171, 176, 180, 192, 195, 204
Langham, Elizabeth, 163
Lappage or Lappidge, Mary, 162
Largham or Laughan, Elizabeth
  See Langham, Elizabeth
Laudanum, 9, 155, 173, 185, 196, 203
  See also Poisoning murders
Lavender, Elizabeth, 157
Leicester (hangings at), 188, 191, 203
Limpany, Betty, 157
Lincoln (hangings at), 153, 161, 173, 178, 179

Liverpool (hanging at), 208-209
Lloyd, Sarah, 105-111, 159
Lloyd, Mary, 159-60
Lofthouse, Ursula, 206
Long, Charlotte, 144-9, 152, 204

Manslaughter, xi, 1, 52, 60, 100
Mapson, Melinda, 111-4, 169
Martin, Mary Ann, 157
Mead, Ann, 34-5, 159
Miller, Elizabeth, 26-8
Mintor, Melinda
  See Mapson, Melinda
Monmouth (hanging at), 193
Morgan, Mary, 55-60, 70-2, 164
Morrey, Edith, 172-3
Mottershall or Mottershed, Susannah, 1, 161
Moulsham Gaol, Chelmsford, Essex (hanging at), 163
Murder, x, xviii, 154, 155, 157, 159, 160, 161, 166, 170, 172, 173
  See also Infanticide; Manslaughter; Petty treason; Poisoning murders
  accessory to, 50, 90, 96-7, 170, 172, 187, 188, 197
  of children, 44-53, 159, 161, 162, 166, 170-1, 172, 174, 175, 176, 179, 188, 196, 199
  of employers, xiii, 31-43, 153, 158, 186
  of husbands, xiii, xv, 31, 43, 85, 92-102, 153-4, 157, 164, 166, 172-3, 176-7, 182-3, 184, 186-7, 187-8, 188-9, 190-1, 194, 204-205, 205-206, 207-208
  of parents, 195-6, 198-9

Newcastle (hanging at), 198
Newgate, London
  See also Fry, Elizabeth

INDEX

condemned sermon, xiii, 21, 136-7
Ordinary of, 124, 165 *See also* Cotton, the Rev Horace
Recorder's Report, 18-19
women hanged at, 155, 156, 163, 165, 166, 167, 169, 171, 175, 177, 178, 179, 180, 187, 189, 191, 192, 194, 196, 199, 200, 202 *See also* Fenning, Eliza; Hibner, Esther; Ross, Eliza; Mapson, Melinda; Fricker, Elizabeth; Hurle, Ann; James, Mary Ann; Newman, Elizabeth; Kelton, Harriet
Newman, Charlotte, 125, 134-9, 180
Nicholson, Mary, 158
Norfolk murders, 91-9, 207
Northampton (hanging at), 187
Norris, Ann, 83, 189
Norwich (hangings at), 154, 166, 207
Nottingham (hanging at), 69, 161

Oakham, Rutland (hanging at), 161
Osborne, Elizabeth, 173-4
Owens, Sarah, 174

Page, Sarah
  See Herring, Sarah
Palmer, Hannah, 160
Pardons, 81, 133, 135, 159, 169
Parish apprentices, 44-53, 101, 166, 171, 186, 199
Parnell, Mary, 165
Peel, Robert, xviii, 45, 150-2
Penenden Heath, Kent (hangings at), 154, 156, 164,
Perjury
  See Fraud
Perry, Sarah, 63, 177
Petty treason, xiii, xviii, 31-7, 43, 153, 154, 157, 166, 172, 176-7,

182, 183, 184, 186, 188, 190, 191, 195
  Abolition of, 151
Phipoe, Maria Theresa, 1, 155
Pickpocketing, 104
Pleading the belly, 80-1, 160-1, 163, 168, 173
  See also Jury of matrons
Poisoning murders, 99-100, 153, 154, 157, 158, 173, 175, 176, 184-6, 188, 194, 196, 200-201, 203, 204, 206-209
  See also Arsenic; Laudanum
Polgreen or Polgrean, Sarah, 186
Pregnancy
  See Jury of matrons; Pleading the belly; Servants, pregnancy in
Presteigne, Radnorshire (hangings at), 60, 105, 154, 164
Price, Sarah, xv, xviii, 142, 187
Pugh, Sarah or Susannah, 166-7

Read, Hannah, 191
Riddiford, Dinah, 176
Riot, 171
Robbery
  See Stealing
Roberts, Amelia, 192
Rogers, Betty
  See Hulce, Betty
Rooke, Giles, 66
Ross, Eliza, 84-90, 202
Rowland, Betty, 208
Royal College of Surgeons, 89
  See also Clift, William
Ruthin, Denbighshire (hanging at), 160

Salisbury, Wiltshire (hanging at), 175
Scott, Jane, 195-6
Servants, 159

Lives of, 33-5
Criminal intent of, 9-10, 35, 37-41, 108-118
Pregnancy in, 54-9, 64
Sheep stealing and killing, x, xix, 103, 154, 161, 197, 198
Shoplifting, xix, 104, 118, 151
Shrewsbury, Shropshire (hangings at), 163, 197
Silvester, John, 14, 16, 18-19, 21, 25, 123
Skelton, Harriet, 139-41, 142, 180-1
Smith, Elizabeth, 170-1
Smith, Hannah, 171
Smith, Mary, 205-206
Smith, Sarah, 203
Southcott, Joanna, 73, 78, 82
Stealing, x-xi, xviii, xix, 19, 77, 104-118, 150-1, 154, 159, 161, 165, 167, 169, 171, 176, 178, 189, 192
Stafford (hangings at), 178, 205
Statham, Ann, 178-9

Tarver, Harriet, 207-208
Taylor, Peter
  See Norfolk murders
Theft
  See Stealing
Thompson, Frances, 169
Thorpe, Mary, 66-7, 158
Tigh, Ann
  See Tye, Ann
Transportation, x, xii, xix, 99, 105, 131, 134, 142, 151

Tyburn, London, xv, 45
Tye, Ann, 181-2

Uttering,
  See Forgery and fraud

Voce, Mary, 67-70, 161-2

Waltham Black Act, xi, 151
Warner, Ann, 156
Warriner, Elizabeth, 179
Warwick (hangings at), 160, 161, 162, 168, 179, 181, 185
Waters, Esther, 188
Welch, Catherine, 64, 88-9, 196-7
Westcombe, Kezia, xiv, 85, 200-201
White, Sarah, 175
Whiting, Elizabeth, 178
Williams, Sarah, 156
Winchester, Hampshire (hangings at), 163, 168, 169, 182
Wittenback, Mary, 194-5
Wollerton, Elizabeth, 175
Woodman, Mary, 184-5
Woodward, Sarah, 175
Worlock, Rebecca, 186-7
Wright, Mary
  See Norfolk murders

York (hangings at), 158, 159, 162, 163, 168, 169, 188, 203, 206
'Yorkshire Witch'
  See Bateman, Mary